Teaching Secondary Scienc

'This is one of the ....ung their secondary school science .... or Michael Reiss, *TES*

'Every Science department should have a copy of this book available for the teachers and
trainee teachers working there...'

British Journal of Educational Technology

Now fully updated in its third edition, *Teaching Secondary Science* is a comprehensive
guide to all aspects of science teaching, providing a wealth of information and ideas
about different approaches. With guidance on how children understand scientific
ideas and the implications this has for teaching, teachers are encouraged to construct
their own meanings and become reflective in their practice. Relating science to
government agendas, such as the National Strategies, Assessment for Learning and Every
Child Matters, this new edition reflects on and maps changes to national standards.

Key features include:

- Illustrative examples for use in the classroom
- Theoretical grounding linked to practical application
- The pros and cons of different approaches
- M level support materials
- Additional section on Earth, atmosphere and space
- Advice on teaching 'difficult ideas'
- Education for sustainable development
- Managing the science classroom and health and safety
- Support for talk for learning, and advice on numeracy in science.

Presenting an environmentally sustainable, global approach to science teaching, this
book emphasises the need to build on and challenge children's existing ideas so they
better understand the world in which they live. Essential reading for all students and
practising teachers, this invaluable book will support those undertaking secondary
science PGCEs and provide material suitable for those studying at M level.

Keith Ross is a former teaching fellow in Science Education at the University of
Gloucestershire, and now, partly retired, helps to run the www.scitutors.org.uk
website.

Liz Lakin is Senior Lecturer in Science Education at the University of Cumbria,
Lancaster.

Janet McKechnie is Secondary Science Leader for the Secondary Science PGCE at
GITEP at the University of Gloucestershire. She also teaches physics as an AST at
Pate's Grammar School, Gloucestershire.

Teaching Secondary Science

Constructing meaning and developing understanding

Third Edition

Keith Ross, Liz Lakin and
Janet McKechnie

Routledge
Taylor & Francis Group

LONDON AND NEW YORK

First edition published 2000 by David Fulton Publishers
Second edition published 2004 by David Fulton Publishers
This third edition published 2010
by Routledge
2 Park Square, Milton Park, Abingdon, Oxon OX14 4RN

Simultaneously published in the USA and Canada
by Routledge
270 Madison Ave, New York, NY 10016

Routledge is an imprint of the Taylor & Francis Group, an informa business

© 2010 Keith Ross, Liz Lakin and Janet McKechnie

Typeset in Bembo by Wearset Ltd, Boldon, Tyne and Wear
Printed and bound in Great Britain by TJ International Ltd, Padstow, Cornwall

Every effort has been made to contact copyright-holders. Please advise the publisher of
any errors or omissions, and these will be corrected in subsequent editions.

British Library Cataloguing in Publication Data
A catalogue record for this book is available from the British Library

Library of Congress Cataloging-in-Publication Data
Ross, Keith, 1944–
Teaching secondary science : constructing meaning and developing understanding /
Keith Ross, Liz Lakin and Janet McKechnie. – 3rd ed.
p. cm.
Includes bibliographical references and index.
1. Science–Study and teaching (Secondary) I. Lakin, Liz. II. McKechnie, Janet. III. Title.
Q181.R667 2010
510.71'2–dc22

2009034169

ISBN10: 0-415-56804-8 (hbk)
ISBN10: 0-415-46886-8 (pbk)
ISBN10: 0-203-85751-8 (ebk)

ISBN13: 978-0-415-56804-3 (hbk)
ISBN13: 978-0-415-46886-2 (pbk)
ISBN13: 978-0-203-85751-9 (ebk)

Contents

Illustrations

Figures

Tables

Boxes

Preface

Our approach to teaching secondary science is based on a concern that future generations take better care of the planet than at present. We take an approach to learning where we expose children's existing ideas, so they can be challenged or built on to enable them to understand their environment and build a sustainable future, encapsulated in the idea of Education for Sustainable Development. The book takes account of the following:

- The TDA document Professional Standards for Teachers (TDA 2009):
  Professional Attributes (Q1–9)
  Professional Knowledge and Understanding (Q10–21)
  Professional Skills (Q22–33)

- National Curriculum for England (QCDA 2007)

- The National Strategy for Science (2009)

- The QCDA Schemes of Work for science at Key Stage 3 and citizenship at Key Stages 3 and 4.

The five parts of this book are linked to the three standards above for gaining Qualified Teacher Status:

- *Professional Attributes.* We need to know what science is all about, to justify its place in the curriculum and to recognise the qualities of a professional science teacher (Parts I and V of this book).

- *Professional Knowledge and Understanding.* We need to understand what ideas pupils bring with them, and how best to introduce new (and sometimes strange) scientific ideas to them (Parts II and III and aspects of Parts IV and V).

- *Professional Skills: planning, teaching, assessing, monitoring and giving feedback, reviewing teaching and learning, the learning environment and team working and collaboration.* Our planning must take account of individual needs, our teaching must allow time for pupils to make sense of the new ideas and experiences we offer, and our management needs to be sensitive and effective (Parts I, IV and V).

The Scitutors website, in association with the Association for Science Education (ASE), now has downloadable support material for tutors in science education, including many links to other useful websites (visit www.scitutors.org.uk).

There is a CD-ROM that is linked with this book, *Science Issues and the National Curriculum* (Ross *et al.* 2002), which covers most of the topics in the Science National Curriculum. It uses a constructivist approach to developing an understanding in science, and sets the science in everyday or environmental contexts, an approach that we put forward in this book (details at www.scienceissues.org.uk).

Throughout this book we make reference to this CD-ROM, indicating in which of the 10 topics the link will be found (e.g. Ross *et al.* 2002: CD – Energy). *Italic gives an example of one of the animations from each section.*

Matter. Solid waste management and recycling. Atoms of the periodic table. *Atoms animated during boiling and burning.*

Genetics. Cell function and genetic engineering. *Protein synthesis transcription from messenger RNA.*

Atmosphere. Ozone depletion, the greenhouse effect and acid rain. *Animation of cycling of sulphur atoms used by life and acid rain.*

Biodiversity. Evolution and chaos theory. *Predator–prey model and effect of camouflage on evolution.*

Energy. Its distinction from matter and its degradation over time. *Using milk delivery in milk bottles to explain electric circuits.*

Radioactivity. Its uses and safety issues. *Animation of how carbon-14 dating works.*

Agriculture. Plants, animals and the soil. *Step-by-step explanation of the cloning of Dolly.*

Health. How our body works. *Animation of the path of food from mouth to cells.*

Home. How materials and energy are used in our homes. *Interactive model of materials that enter and leave our homes.*

Transport. Forces, energy and navigation. *Balanced forces on a car travelling at speed.*

Note on major changes in the third edition:

The book opens (Chapter 1) with an example of a 'good' science lesson to exemplify the sections that follow. Chapter 15 (Earth and space) is new. Part IV on Planning, Assessment, Teaching and Class Management has been completely updated. The contents of the information and communication technology (ICT) chapter are now spread throughout the book, providing examples as and where appropriate. Finally, we have strengthened the important message about sustainability and the role science education must play in educating a public who can better understand the pressures humanity is placing on the planet.

Acknowledgements

We thank David Brookes, Clive Sutton, George Burch, Keith Brooke, Craig Pepperell, Dick Hanson and our trainee teachers and colleagues in the Gloucestershire Initial Teacher Education Partnership (GITEP). We also thank Pete Callaghan for his contribution to the first two editions of this book, which was published by

David Fulton Publishers Ltd

Ormond House, 26–27 Boswell Street, London WC1N 3JZ

www.fultonpublishers.co.uk

Abbreviations

AF	The five Assessment Focuses of each National Curriculum level
AfL	Assessment for Learning
APP	Assessing Pupil Progress
APU	Assessment of Performance Unit
AQA	Assessment and Qualifications Alliance
ASE	Association for Science Education
ATP–ADP	Adenosine triphosphate and adenosine diphosphate
BSE	Bovine spongiform encephalopathy, or 'mad cow disease'
CFCs	Chlorofluorocarbons
CLEAPSS	Consortium of Local Education Authorities for the Provision of Science Services
CLIS	Children's Learning in Science (project at Leeds University)
COSHH	Control of Substances Hazardous to Health
CPD	Continuing professional development
DCSF	Department for Children, Schools and Families
DfEE	Department for Education and Employment; now DCSF
DfES	Department for Education and Skills; now DCSF
DNA	Deoxyribonucleic acid
DTI	Department of Trade and Industry
EAL	English as an Additional Language
ECM	Every Child Matters
GCSE	General Certificate of Secondary Education
GRA	General risk assessment
HASAWA	Health and Safety at Work Act
ICT	Information and communication technology
INSET	In-service education and training
ISA	Investigative skills assignments
KS	Key Stages (The four stages of the English National Curriculum)
Key Stages 1/2/3/4	Key Stage 1 (5–7 years), Key Stage 2 (7–11 years), Key Stage 3 (11–14 years), Key Stage 4 (14–16 years)
L(E)A	Local (education) authority
LAT	Level-assessed task
LOtC	Learning Outside the Classroom
NACE	National Association for Able Children in Education
NQT	Newly Qualified Teacher

PGCE	Post-Graduate Certificate of Education
PSA	Practical skills assessment
PSHE	Personal, social and health education
QCDA	Qualifications and Curriculum Development Authority
QTS	Qualified Teacher Status
SATs	Standard Attainment Tests
SATIS	Science and Technology in Society
SEN	Special Educational Needs
SENCO	Special Educational Needs Co-ordinator
SI	Système International (for units)
SMOG	Simplified Measure Of Gobbledygook – simple measure of readability of a text (see Box 9.1)
SSERC	Scottish Schools Equipment Research Centre
STEM	Science, Technology, Engineering and Mathematics network
TDA	Training and Development Agency
Year 1	Ages 4–5 in England and Wales
Year 2, etc.	Ages 5–6, etc.
Year 11	Ages 14–15

Science and Why We Teach It

Introduction

Science deals with ideas about our environment. These scientific ideas must be tested against our sense experiences. Progress in science happens when our existing ideas are challenged and we have to invent new theories that deal with the anomalies better. Thus germ theory deals with transmission of diseases better than traditional beliefs, yet BSE in cows seems to be transmitted by a prion vector whose mechanism is not yet accepted. Newton's ideas about gravity have been superseded by Einstein's theory of relativity, but there are still inconsistencies between relativity and quantum mechanics. Scientific ideas are never complete or absolutely true.

In the same way, children build up pictures of the world in their minds. Simple pictures that help them make sense of the data they receive from their senses. Babies soon recognise 'down-ness' as they look for their dropped rattle on the floor – they don't look for it on the ceiling! But these naïve ideas get replaced as children need to make their mental models more widely applicable, as 'down-ness' transforms to notions of 'gravity'.

As science teachers we must understand some of these naïve ideas and help children develop alternative, more powerful, scientific ways of interpreting their environment that can go alongside their 'everyday' beliefs. Children need time to reconstruct their ideas to take account of the scientific theories that we presently hold, and to appreciate that they will change over time. They also need to appreciate that the process by which the ideas came into being, the very process of being scientific, forms an important part of their scientific education, encapsulated in the National Curriculum Orders for England (DfES 2006a): *How science works.*

However, in order to help children understand their world in this scientific way the children must be in a safe learning environment. A single teacher deals with approximately 30 pupils, many of whom need to be convinced that their time in school is worthwhile. As science teachers we must also understand how to create a pleasant working atmosphere in our classes, where children feel safe, where the science they are studying is relevant and useful to them and where we can expect them to do their best.

These two facets – *teaching science* and *teaching pupils* – are at the heart of being a successful science teacher as a result of which the pupils in our charge can come to enjoy, understand, and use the scientific way of viewing their world.

The aim of the first part of this book (Chapters 1–3) is to look at the way scientific ideas have developed over time and to compare this with the task our pupils have in coming to understand those ideas themselves. We cannot expect pupils to do this unaided, but we do need to start with their existing ideas, and we need to give them time to test out, practically and verbally, these new and often strange ideas that are part of our present-day scientific understanding. In Chapter 1 we start by looking at how a good science teacher might achieve this. In Chapter 2 we explore the way science works, and in Chapter 3 we visit the real world of our pupils: their environment and their future. As science teachers we need to provide an understanding of the need to make this a *sustainable* future.

What Makes a Good Science Teacher?

Chapter overview

Good teaching involves many different aspects: planning lessons so that pupils are motivated to learn; evaluating and reviewing; taking risks to experiment with new ideas; developing a positive classroom climate; fostering a rapport with the pupils that rewards their *effort* rather than their *attainment*. The additional demands on a science teacher include developing expertise in a subject they may not have studied since GCSE level, planning for the scientific misconceptions held by pupils, and supporting pupils as they develop their understanding of very challenging concepts.

Rewards of teaching

The rewards of teaching science are many: the enthusiasm of pupils learning how their world works (especially important as we work towards developing a sustainable future for the planet); the fun of problem-solving; the satisfaction of hearing pupils argue enthusiastically about different theories; the pupils' fascination with hearing the stories of scientific discoveries; their enjoyment of a wide variety of practical and project work; and above all the stimulation of guiding and supporting pupils as they develop their ability to reason, explain and argue.

Personal statements on application forms show that many prospective science trainee teachers believe teaching consists largely of 'passing on' information and understanding about scientific ideas. Of course, when they start training they quickly realise that this is very far from the truth. Traditional 'explaining' is an important, but relatively small, constituent in the complex and varied diet demanded by today's pupils, and required by the National Curriculum, the National Strategy and the exam specifications. This complex and varied diet, which we develop in the chapters that follow, is based on the outcomes of research into how children learn.

To be successful, teachers of all subjects have many aspects of teaching to consider – just study the list in Box 1.1 for a few moments. Just managing all of these requires detailed planning, constant checking and honest evaluation. The effective teacher needs a toolbox of imaginative and effective strategies, needs to take risks and be prepared to fail, and must be prepared to change (see Chapter 16, *Planning for Progression*). Only complacent teachers expect the same thing to work the same way on successive occasions; every class responds differently and this necessitates changing the structure and focus of the lesson, even if some of the resources can be reused.

Box 1.1 Some of the many aspects of teaching and learning for all teachers

Every Child Matters	National Curriculum	National Strategy
Exam board specifications	Assessment for Learning	Behaviour for Learning
Personal, learning and thinking skills (PLTs)	Classroom climate	Differentiation
	Higher-order thinking	Numeracy
Learning styles	Health and safety	Questioning
Literacy	Misconceptions	Independent learning
Active learning	Learning skills	Pedagogy
Building Learning Power		
…and many more		

Demands made on science teachers

In addition to the generic demands of teaching, *science teachers* have additional pressures and issues.

- *First*, take the issue of the range of subjects. Science teachers are most likely to have a degree-level qualification in one science (often biology-based, chemistry-based or physics/engineering-based). In most schools, they are expected to teach all three curriculum sciences at Key Stage 3 and sometimes also at Key Stage 4 – there is plenty of overlap of skills, strategies and language but less overlap of subject knowledge and understanding. Compare this with a language teacher – a specialist in German, for example, is unlikely to be expected to teach Mandarin.

- *Second*, consider the issue of pupils' prior knowledge and understanding. From a very early age, children have been making sense of their world using their common sense and ideas from parents and teachers. When they enter secondary school, they have already reconciled thoughts and observations in their own way – this prior knowledge often contains misconceptions (see Chapter 5, *Elicitation*) and science teachers must acknowledge these in their teaching or risk having the more scientific models and theories rejected in favour of the more familiar ideas. Compare again with the teacher of German: most pupils start learning from a completely empty baseline and do not need to reconcile new ideas with their naïve, everyday ideas (though obviously there will be linguistic links).

- *Third*, many scientific ideas, theories and models are complex and require the pupils to sustain their concentration at a high level for prolonged periods; they must invest much and be prepared to be patient for the delayed gratification of that 'ah ha' moment of deep understanding.

So how does a science teacher incorporate all of these considerations and teach good lessons? And if they manage it, how do they know it is a good lesson? The answer is simple: focus on the *pupils*. Are they interested, excited, focused, engaged, stimulated to ask questions – or are they bored, passive, accepting or, even worse, disruptive? Of course, this is also dependent on the nature of the pupils in the class, but if you plan lessons to engage and stimulate at the appropriate level as well as allowing pupils to take *ownership* of their learning (see Chapters 6–10), then at least you know that the few pupils who do refuse to engage are doing so because they have personal issues that cannot be solved by one teacher alone (see Chapter 19 for discussion of management of pupils in science lessons).

The 'eureka' moment

To illustrate, here are three different versions of the same Key Stage 3 lesson. As you read them, reflect on how you want your own lessons to be received by the pupils.

To set the scene: the pupils have already learnt about density; they know that 1 cm^3 of different materials have different masses (as weighed on a top-pan balance); they can calculate density of rectangular blocks of different material. They have discussed the answers to questions such as 'Which is heavier, wood or paper?' and 'Which is heavier, a ton of feathers or a ton of lead?' (see Chapter 4, p. 38, *Grains of truth*).

Lesson 1: 'How to measure density'

TEACHER ACTIVITY	PUPIL ACTIVITY	COMMENTARY
■ Teacher introduces lesson objective: 'to learn how to measure the density of an irregular object'.	■ Pupils copy down objective.	■ Copying requires no processing or thinking. Slower writers will find this challenging.
■ Teacher asks questions to elicit pupils' understanding of density from previous lesson.	■ Pupils answer questions when asked.	■ Initially many hands go up but the number reduces as pupils get bored of playing the game.
■ Teacher explains how to measure density of irregular object and issues worksheet with instructions for practical (measuring volume using displacement method).	■ Pupils carry out practical to measure density of objects such as rubber bungs, glass stoppers, etc. and complete prepared table on worksheet.	■ Pupils enjoy the practical and learn the displacement method for measuring volume.
■ Teacher asks pupils to clear away the experiment and issues a set of questions to practise the new method.	■ Pupils clear away and complete the set questions.	■ Pupils take ages to clear away because they don't want to start the questions.
■ Teacher goes through the answers to the questions to check understanding.	■ Pupils mark their answers.	■ Many pupils will lose concentration at this stage and will not mark their work.
■ Teacher sets homework to find out about Archimedes and the King's crown.	■ Pupils research on the internet and discover the story of Archimedes.	■ Some pupils will copy other pupils' work.

Lesson 2: 'Density and Archimedes'

TEACHER ACTIVITY	PUPIL ACTIVITY	COMMENTARY
▪ Teacher issues word search made up of key words from last lesson.	▪ Pupils complete word search as soon as they enter the lab.	▪ Pupils settle to work quickly even though they arrive at different times.
▪ Teacher introduces lesson objective: 'to learn how to measure the density of an irregular object'.	▪ Pupils do not copy objective but listen.	▪ If the objective is on the board, teacher and pupils can check it throughout the lesson.
▪ Teacher tells the story of Archimedes using projected pictures.	▪ Pupils listen to the story.	▪ Pupils enjoy the story.
▪ Teacher hands out instructions for practical to measure density of irregular objects.	▪ Pupils carry out practical to measure density of objects such as rubber bungs, glass stoppers, etc. and complete prepared table on worksheet.	▪ Pupils enjoy the practical and learn the displacement method for measuring volume.
▪ Teacher hands out worksheet containing a mixture of activities: calculations, quiz questions about Archimedes, sorting 'muddled method' sentences for the experiment, etc.	▪ Pupils answer the questions and use the internet to research about Archimedes.	▪ Pupils enjoy the variety of activities and freedom to use computers, etc. Several 'forget' to clear away their experiment.
▪ Teacher hands out plenary crossword made up of words from the lesson to check learning.	▪ Pupils complete the crossword and discuss with partner.	▪ Pupils settle quickly to this task and show satisfaction at completing it.
▪ Teacher issues homework to tell the story of Archimedes and the King's crown in words or pictures.	▪ Pupils write or draw the story.	▪ Pupils complete homework task as it offers a choice but the accounts are mainly descriptive and reveal little understanding of the science.

Lesson 3: 'The gold standard'

TEACHER ACTIVITY	PUPIL ACTIVITY	COMMENTARY
▪ Teacher enters the lab dripping with 'gold' chains and other jewellery.	▪ Pupils shout 'Is that real gold?' 'Why are you wearing all that?'	▪ Pupils are immediately hooked and become lively.
▪ Teacher tells pupils that it is all real gold.	▪ Pupils challenge teacher: 'We don't believe you', 'Prove it'.	▪ Pupils are loud and challenging.

TEACHER ACTIVITY	PUPIL ACTIVITY	COMMENTARY
■ Teacher asks pupils to settle and tells them the story of Archimedes using projected pictures.	■ Pupils listen to story and ask lots of questions.	■ Pupils settle quickly because they want to know more.
■ Teacher explains the objective of the lesson: to work out how to find out if the metal is gold.	■ Pupils immediately start discussing in small groups how to find out if the jewellery is real gold.	■ Pupils are engaged even though they know that it can't be real gold!
■ After 5 minutes, teacher calls for silence, asks some named pupils for their ideas. She skilfully leads the discussion to include a revision of density and outlines the resources available (apparatus, sheet of density values).	■ Pupils explain their ideas when asked and contribute to the discussion with other pupils. They revise their understanding of density. Most realise that they need to measure the volume of the jewellery and begin to devise a way to do this.	■ Pupils answer with confidence because they have already explained to their peers.
■ Teacher asks pupils to sketch what they are going to do and circulates the room to assess progress and assist weaker pupils.	■ Pairs of pupils draw the stages of the experiment and are helped by the teacher if necessary.	■ Pupils are doing all of the thinking and planning for themselves. They work fast as they want to start the experiment.
■ Teacher allows pupils to start experiment when they have a sensible plan.	■ Pupils start experiments using individual pieces of the jewellery of different sizes. They make decisions about which is the most suitable apparatus for their piece of jewellery.	■ The staggered start minimises disruption around the apparatus. The experiment has a purpose as it is the actual jewellery worn by the teacher and the different pieces ensure that each experiment is different.
■ As pupils finish the experiment, the teacher asks them to draft a letter from Archimedes to the King explaining what he has found out about the crown. Key words are written on the board. Help sheets are provided for slower writers.	■ Pupils are keen to tell the teacher that they have proved that it isn't gold. They draft the letter in pairs using all of the key words.	■ Pupils are keen to write as they understand what they have done. They enjoy the opportunity to be scientific experts.
■ For homework, the teacher asks the pupils to produce the final version of the letter by editing their draft, illustrating it and referring to the level ladder provided.	■ Pupils complete the homework to the highest possible standard using the level ladder as a guide.	■ Most pupils complete the homework as they have already drafted the letter with a peer and have clear guidelines for improving it.

Commentary on the three lessons

'How to measure density'

This is a very traditional, teacher-directed lesson with lots of explaining and instructions; the practical work is guided by use of a recipe. Pupils will learn but won't feel any sense of their own control or independence. Disruptive pupils will find other ways of taking control!

'Density and Archimedes'

This is a more stimulating teacher-planned lesson with lots of activities but insufficient explaining so pupils don't end up with clear understanding. Pupils will become more engaged by the variety of activities and enjoy the fun ones. They may leave having enjoyed the lesson but not having a deep understanding of the scientific issues due to lack of appropriate intervention.

'The gold standard'

This is a teacher-facilitated lesson with lots of drama and stimulating episodes, a sophisticated range of discussion, pupil problem-solving and purposeful practical activities, plenty of time to think and discuss with adequate intervention from the teacher and other thoughtful resources. Pupils have driven their own learning in this lesson – they really wanted to find out for themselves. They will remember the lesson, look forward to the next one – and have a deep understanding of the concept of density.

In essence, these three lessons cover the same learning objectives and incorporate the same activities. By changing the order of events, an effective but traditional lesson can become a perfect opportunity for pupils to direct their own learning, but still under careful guidance and planning by the teacher, thereby maximising their motivation, enjoyment and learning.

A safe learning environment

Finally, we need to consider other facets of successful teaching: the atmosphere in the classroom, often referred to as classroom climate, and pupils' attitude to learning. Nine facets of classroom climate identified by Hay McBer (2000) are *clarity*, *order*, *standards*, *fairness*, *participation*, *support*, *safety*, *interest* and *environment*. Consider, for now, only the seventh element, *safety*: this does not simply refer to making adequate risk assessments during practical work (see Chapter 20 for this). Pupils can only learn when they feel safe – in a classroom where they can ask and answer questions or think out loud with no fear of ridicule from the teacher *or their peers*. They know that their efforts will be supported, respected and responded to in a positive manner.

Pupils will only be open to learning new ideas if they appreciate that their intelligence is not fixed, but their brains continue developing throughout life if they receive the correct stimulation. Without this understanding, the more able may become lazy as they believe that they will 'do all right' because they have always done well and don't need to work hard, but the less able will feel that there is no point as they always do badly in tests, and so on. Research carried out in the USA (Blackwell *et al.* 2007) found that pupils' attitude and progress improved dramatically when they received intervention explaining how their brains have 'plasticity' and that they can be worked to improve performance just like a muscle (it is of course important to explain to pupils that the brain is not a muscle!). Research is currently being conducted (by the Institute for the Future of the Mind at Oxford University – www.futuremind.ox.ac.uk) to measure the effect of similar intervention in the UK. Teachers can encourage this attitude in pupils by praising their effort and improvement rather than their attainment.

Summary

Imagine eavesdropping on an imaginary exemplary lesson: the teacher and pupils are working together to solve problems; the ideas and opinions of all occupants of the room are heard and respected; the teacher is regarded as a guide and supporter of learning. The common pattern 'of teacher asking questions and pupils answering' frequently transforms into a more even spread in which pupils answer each other's questions and ask questions of the teacher. In this way a genuine discussion develops with the teacher playing a skilful supportive role. The pupils have confidence in their safety, their ability to learn and the expertise of the teacher. You can see how all this can be achieved as you work through this book, and you gain experience working with your own pupils.

2

How Science Works

Chapter overview

As science teachers we need to think about what science is and what it does. In this chapter we develop a model of how science works, and later on use this to show the enormous task science teachers have to achieve, because where humanity has taken centuries to develop an understanding of how our world works, our pupils must do the same in only a few years. It is also important for our pupils to understand that the scientific ideas we have of how the world works must be validated by experiment or observation of the world and universe so in this chapter we discuss the important role of practical work.

How science works

How science works is more than just scientific enquiry. It provides a wonderful opportunity for pupils to develop as critical and creative thinkers and to become flexible problem-solvers. This strand has been split into two significant areas of skills development: Explanations, argument and decisions, [and] Practical and enquiry skills.

(National Strategy for KS 3 –
www.standards.dcsf.gov.uk/secondary/framework/science/fwg/hsw)

This chapter examines three issues which relate to *How science works*:

- developing a mental model of how science works

- carrying out scientific investigations in school

- examining the purposes of practical work in school science.

As science teachers we need to reflect on what people think science to be. Consider these two questions:

1. What do scientists do?
2. What does it mean to be scientific?

To help you, try sorting these words into a concept map or flow diagram to show how they are linked – add extra words or omit some as needed. A discussion follows below.

experiment	communicate	notice things
predict	discover	hypothesise
observe	search for the truth	have ideas
make theories	test ideas	investigate
evidence	collecting data	validate ideas

Science is not the same as technology, but the two are intimately linked. Now try answering these two questions (see below for a discussion of these):

3.   What is the product of science and what is its purpose?
4.   What is the product of technology and what is its purpose?

How science works: discussion of questions 1 and 2

Until the middle of the twentieth century philosophers of science thought that science was the quest for absolute truth, and that the 'laws of nature' could be induced from the observations we made. Karl Popper (1959) and Thomas Kuhn (1970) and philosophers since then have shown that scientific ideas are simply that – ideas – created in our minds to try to explain what we perceive. To be scientific an idea must be able to be *tested* using our senses (often involving measurement) in experiments and observations. A fuller picture is developed in Chapter 24.

A simple picture of how 'being scientific' begins may look like that shown in Figure 2.1a: Start with '1. Notice something' and follow the arrows round at the top of the diagram. You should compare this with your own version from answering question 2 above.

(a)

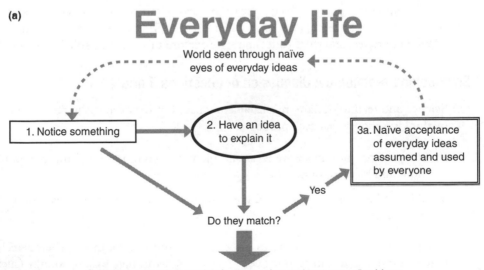

FIGURE 2.1a A simplified picture of how we develop our everyday ideas

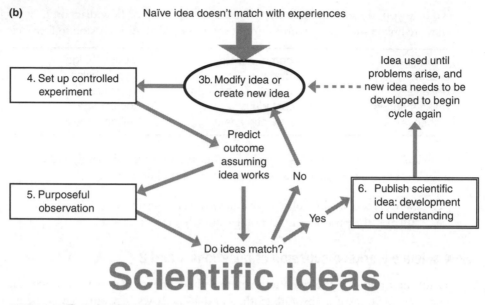

FIGURE 2.1b The scientific method – ideas are generated and tested

Figure 2.1a shows how we all try to make sense of our everyday world – our ideas are expressed as the words of our everyday conversations. Scientists question these everyday ideas that we take for granted. They realise that our naïve ideas do not tell the whole story, so they modify the ideas or create new ones (see oval 3b. in Figure 2.1b, at the top of the diagram). These new ideas must be tested against our experiences, through controlled experiments or observations (4. and 5. in Figure 2.1b). When the scientists are happy that the ideas and experiences seem to match they will publish their findings (6. in Figure 2.1b). We cannot expect pupils to make this scientific leap of imagination from their naïve ideas without help (though some may do so!), so our job as teachers is to share these scientific insights with our pupils and allow them to test and try the ideas out. We explore this teaching role in Chapter 6.

Science and technology: discussion of questions 3 and 4

Science and technology are intimately entwined, but they can easily be distinguished by thinking about what each produces:

- the products of science are ideas and theories – communicated through publications and by word of mouth

- the products of technology, in contrast, are artefacts and processes – things and procedures we want or need.

The purpose of science is to try to make sense of our environment, whereas technology's purpose is to satisfy our needs (and wants) through making things (such as sliced bread) or developing processes (such as keyhole surgery). Nowadays they are so interdependent that it is not easy to see this essential difference.

The scientific investigation in school

Investigations are needed after you have noticed something interesting, and have had an idea of what might be going on. Ideas come from the creative side of science (guesswork), but they must be investigated carefully, which is part of the logical (checkwork) side (Medawar 1969). It is this checkwork that people usually think of as 'the scientific method', and they forget about the ovals in Figure 2.1 – the creative side to science (see also Chapter 24). Note that theories can be useful but they can only ever be an approximation to the truth. They are *created* in our minds, but they must be *tested* against reality – this provides a clear distinction between the creativity of Dalton (*Atomic theory*) and of Shakespeare (*Macbeth*).

To illustrate this, here is an investigation you might do with a Key Stage 3 class.

Electricity from metals in a lemon

You notice that when a copper and a zinc strip are pushed into a lemon, a voltage is generated between the two metal plates. What is going on? (See Figure 2.2.)

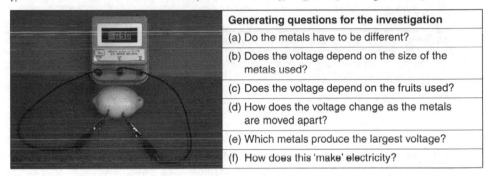

Generating questions for the investigation
(a) Do the metals have to be different?
(b) Does the voltage depend on the size of the metals used?
(c) Does the voltage depend on the fruits used?
(d) How does the voltage change as the metals are moved apart?
(e) Which metals produce the largest voltage?
(f) How does this 'make' electricity?

FIGURE 2.2 Investigating the voltage from a lemon

In order to get a satisfactory answer, we need to work through a number of stages, as illustrated in the planning boards shown in Figure 2.3. Planning boards are a simple system for helping pupils keep a careful and separate track of input (or independent) and output (or dependent) variables, and are based on the work of Goldsworthy and Feasey (1999).

Planning

We are investigating ... Pupils think up possible input (independent) variables – things they could change that might affect the voltage (e.g. type of metals, size of plates, distance apart, type of fruit...) and write them on separate Post-it notes. We have already identified the output (dependent) variable as the voltage. Although we have decided to measure the voltage, we could look for other outcomes; for example are there signs of chemical reaction? or how long does the voltage stay steady? (see left-hand picture in Figure 2.3).

Our question is ... Here we identify which variable we will actually change. All the others must therefore be kept constant (controlled variables) – a process which we

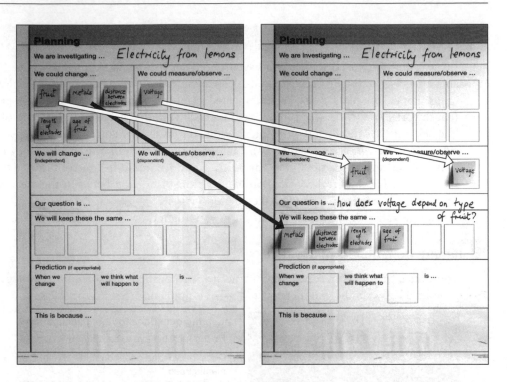

FIGURE 2.3 Planning boards in action. Black arrow shows that things we could change must be kept constant, except the one we choose (in this example, the fruit)

call *fair testing*. We also need to identify those which we will measure or observe as a result of the change we make (our output or dependent variable). We may have to do preliminary work to help set controlled variables at a sensible value (e.g. if we decide to change the metals, we need first of all to see if the size and distance apart might affect the voltage, so we can set these at a suitable constant value). Framing the question turns ideas into a form you can actually investigate and is the key to a good investigation.

Prediction ... Here we make a prediction of what we think might happen, with a justification if possible. 'This is because as the metals become increasingly different in their reactivity I expect a more vigorous reaction, and so a higher voltage.' All the time our Post-it notes have moved down our planning boards.

Obtaining evidence

Now we can set up a table to record our results and record/measure the dependent variable (voltage) as we make the changes to our input variable.

Presenting the results

We can use the Post-it notes to label the axes of a graph if appropriate (see Chapter 11 for more comment on the use of graphs in science).

Considering evidence and evaluating

Do our results agree with our idea – what have we learnt? Reliability will come (or not!) from repeated tests (note that this does not make the test 'fair' as many pupils think). Validity attempts to assess whether the experiment really does what it is supposed to do. Preliminary or trial runs allow us to take decisions about what value we will fix for the variables we keep constant (controlled). Trial runs also give us an idea of the limits of accuracy that we can hope to work within. In school, to save time, we usually do these in advance for our pupils to ensure that the experiment 'works', thus missing out an important part of an investigation.

Types of variable and their names

Figure 2.4 is a 'directed activity related to text' (a DART – see Chapter 9) to help sort out types of variable.

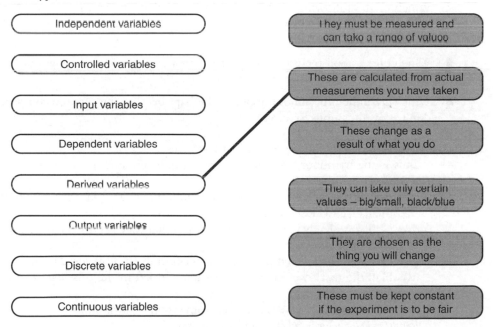

FIGURE 2.4 Types of variable

Investigations become more complex as discrete variables (type of fruit) become continuous (distance apart in centimetres), and as you attempt to investigate more than one input variable at a time. For example, at Level 4 pupils might have asked whether the voltage changes when we push the metals in *deep*, compared with *shallow*, whereas at Level 7 pupils could investigate changing two or more variables, for instance separation distance and depth of metals, both measured in millimetres.

We return to investigations in Chapter 18, particularly how they are assessed as coursework for GCSE. Investigations represent the main focus for practical work by practising scientists but practical work in school has a number of other purposes, which we discuss next.

The purposes of practical work in school

In recent years in the UK teachers have been scared to spend too much time doing practical work, partly because of safety worries but also because they have been told too many times that practical work must add value over any alternative method, for example computer simulation, demonstration, and so on. Whilst this may be true, especially when pupils simply 'follow a recipe', we must not underestimate the value of hands-on practical experiences.

Eight activities are described below involving the process of rusting. They are designed to help us focus on the role played by practical work in science lessons, but note that not all of them are practical work in the strict sense. Although described as activities for Key Stage 3 pupils these activities, when undertaken together, are also useful as a workshop for science teachers to stimulate discussion of the purpose of practical activities in school.

- Which of the following are best in helping pupils to understand what happens during rusting? (They may, for example, think the iron 'rots' like wood – an idea we need to challenge.)

- Which give a good picture of how science works (following the stages in Figure 2.1)?

- Which are unhelpful in both respects? (Perhaps because they are too complex, or don't allow the pupils to think.)

1. **'Nail tubes'** – Iron nails left in four test tubes
   This is the traditional experiment where pupils place clean iron nails in four test tubes:
   (a) Anhydrous calcium chloride at the bottom, covered by cotton wool then the nail, and closed with a bung.
   (b) Nail completely covered with freshly boiled water. This is covered with a layer of oil.
   (c) Half the nail covered with water and left in the tube exposed to the air.
   (d) Half the nail covered with salty water and left in the tube exposed to the air.
   Leave the four tubes for a week and comment on your findings.
   Result: only the nails in tubes (c) and (d) have rusted.

2. **'Water and air'** – Are water and air both needed for rusting?
   Begin the lesson by acknowledging that most people agree that water is needed for iron to rust. Talk about the way some iron objects have been preserved in boggy or muddy conditions (Roman nails, cannon recovered from wrecks) where the air cannot reach. We might conclude that air and water are *both* needed for rusting.

   - When the discussion is over ask each group of pupils to design an experiment to test the idea that air and water are *both* needed for rusting.

   - Make sure they say (predict) what they think might happen before carrying out the experiment.

3. **'Damp fibre'** – Damp iron 'wool' [better called 'fibre'] left in a tube over water
    This is another experiment often performed in school.

    ■   Place some damp iron fibre at the bottom of a boiling tube.

    ■   Invert the tube, with the damp iron and air in it, over a beaker of water, and clamp it so most of the tube is above the water line.

    ■   Leave it for 2 hours and then look at the water level inside the tube, and observe the iron for rust.

    Can you explain why the water has risen up into the tube and the iron has gone rusty?

4. **'Air is used'** – Someone suggested that air is used up when iron rusts
    Start with a similar discussion to 2. above. If air is involved perhaps it is actually used up when iron rusts? Get pupils to design a way to test this idea.

    ■   'Say what you think will happen if air really is used up when iron rusts.'

    ■   'Say what you think will happen if rusting does not use up air.'

    ■   'Finally record what actually happened, and comment on the results.'

5. **'Weight'** – Weight changes on rusting
    Tell this story to your pupils:

    Two iron nails, both weighing the same, were left to go completely rusty – no iron metal was left, there was simply a pile of rust. If you could collect all the rust up from one of the nails and weigh it, would the pile of rust weigh much more, about the same or much less than the original nail? If you weighed the rust from the second nail, would the result be about the same as the first, or could it be completely different?

    This question addresses many misconceptions people have about rusting:
    ■   some think it has been eaten away, so gets lighter
    ■   some think a mould has grown on it, so it may get heavier, but the two nails would not behave exactly the same way.

    When they have recorded their answer say: 'Each nail had a mass of 10 g. The pile of rust from each nail had a mass of nearly 15 g. So, on weighing, we found both the iron nails got heavier.'
        The pupils can now discuss this result in their groups. If necessary they need to change the reason they gave originally. They could think up another experiment they could do to see if their (new) idea was right.

6. **'Protecting'** – Protecting iron from rusting
Get your pupils to think of all the ways we protect iron from going rusty (bikes, buses, bridges, boats...). For each method see if they can think how it works. You could provide reference books for them.

7. **'Other metals'** – Do all metals rust?
Get your pupils to put small samples of a range of metals on damp cotton wool. They can predict which will 'rust'.
Result: only the iron will rust (go rust coloured) but many of the others will corrode, usually forming whitish coatings.

8. **'At home'** – Nails left at home
Ask your pupils to take two clean (i.e. degreased) bright nails home and leave one in a place that they think will make it go rusty, and the other in a place where they think it will stay shiny. They bring them in a week later, mounted on card to say where they were placed and whether they thought they would rust or not. Arrange them along a bench or wall display from most to least rusty (Driver *et al.* 1994, pp. 11 and 12). We will undoubtedly find that many nails, left in very wet places, have not rusted as much as the pupils thought. Those kept dry will have remained shiny. The lesson can now explore the ideas children have about rusting, and could lead to investigations (such as 2. and 4. above) to test out new ideas to explain why rusting did not happen as much as they thought.

Discussion of the rusting exercises

In this discussion of the eight activities above, they are referred to, in bold typeface, by their number and short name.

Recipe-following

Unless we are very careful about setting them up, **1. 'Nail tubes'** and **3. 'Damp fibre'** are in danger of being undertaken as a recipe with no purpose and from which pupils will learn little. This can be especially true of the traditional approach of **1. 'Nail tubes'** – particularly if the expressions *anhydrous calcium chloride*, and *freshly boiled water*, are not fully explored. Until pupils understand what function these strangely named materials have they will follow the instructions but without meaning. 'Stuff to make the air dry' and 'water which has had all the dissolved air removed' would be better terms to use at Key Stage 3. Both of these assume that pupils realise that air can contain water (vapour) and water can contain (dissolved) air. Both are important ideas which need to be explored before undertaking this rusting investigation; they can be linked to the formation of dew and clouds (damp air) and the fact that water-dwelling animals, such as fish and water fleas, use dissolved air for respiration. These same two investigations could arise from the discussions in **2. 'Water and air'** and **4. 'Air is used'**, but this time pupils would have had a far greater sense of ownership of the investigation, and would have predicted possible outcomes.

The role of air in rusting

Pupils will not normally think about the role of air, which is shown by the first four investigations. However, by getting the pupils to participate in the design of the investigation, we immediately allow them to see its purpose. The discussion arising from **8. 'At home'**, where they bring their own nails in, illustrates an ideal situation which mirrors the process of scientific method from Figure 2.1: we notice water causes rusting, so we test this idea – but our nails don't rust much. Perhaps air is needed as well?

This would lead children to plan an investigation, **4. 'Air is used'**. They will see that the water level does rise so they will begin to believe that air (or a part of it) has joined the iron. This may lead them to predict that it will increase in weight. **5. 'Weight'** is a very slow experiment to do. The faster process of igniting and blowing on 10 g of iron fibre while it is resting on ceramic paper on a top-pan balance (*safety*: wear eye protection) involves combustion rather than rusting and may not be seen by pupils as analogous, though the gain in weight is surprising to many pupils! However, we can give results to pupils – a case where we can still learn from the experiment without actually performing it. **6. 'Protecting'** is an extension of this approach practical experiments are not the only, nor necessarily the best, way for pupils to understand scientific ideas! **7. 'Other metals'** is an important investigation for pupils to do practically, not so much to learn about ways of investigating, though we need to keep all the metals in similar conditions; in this case the practical work gives experiences that pupils will not normally get from their everyday lives.

Between them, these eight activities introduce pupils to ideas about rusting and the process of being scientific. Some focus more on the process (**2. 'Water and air'** and **4. 'Air is used'**) and others more on ideas about rusting (**5.–8.**). A couple, **1. 'Nail tubes'** and **3. 'Damp fibre'**, are recipes and need to be given purpose – our aim for all practical work.

Giving practical work a purpose

Sutton (1992, p. 2) makes a strong case for giving pupils time each side of any practical work to enable them to think:

> [T]he national curriculum specifies an entitlement to be involved in planning as well as doing investigations. This goes some way towards ensuring that the practical activities will be adequately embedded in a process of grappling with scientific ideas, but more generally there remains a problem of connecting practical work with the discussion and appreciation of ideas [approached through] WORD WORK as the core of a science lesson.

Time for *word work* has now been recognised by the National Strategy (Standards 2009) in the importance it places on plenaries in lessons where your pupils can *reflect* on what the lesson is all about.

Practical work has many uses in science. To finish this chapter here are some possible reasons why we provide practical activities for learners in science:

Gaining experiences

Before children can begin to think about why something happens they must have experienced it. For example:

- **7. 'Other metals'** where pupils see corrosion of other metals

- an opportunity to experience (safely!) the 50 cycles a second of AC mains electricity (see Box 2.1)

- experiencing the repulsion between two strong magnets

- watching beans germinate then grow on as plants

- examining rocks and living things with a hand lens or under a microscope.

All these can be the starting point for investigations, questions, predictions, hypotheses.

Box 2.1 Experiencing 50 Hz mains

Hold a very strong small magnet in your clenched fist, and hold it near a transformer working off the mains (e.g. a lab pack). When you switch the transformer on you feel the 50 cycles a second vibration because the cycling magnetic field from the mains drags the magnet to and fro.

Illustrating ideas

When you have challenged children's ideas about why something happens you may want them to test out the new, scientific, idea you are giving them in a controlled environment. For example:

- **1. 'Nail tubes'** and **3. 'Damp fibre'** as long as the pupils predict the possible outcomes

- asking them to feel their heartbeat/pulse rate after exercise to suggest a link between blood flow and supplying food and air to the muscles

- swapping a bright and a dim bulb in a series circuit to show that it is the bulb itself that is dim, not that it is dim because of its place in the circuit.

Making observations

Observations cannot be naïve. What we observe (i.e. take notice of) is always a combination of the ideas stored in our brains and the sensory data we receive. Each child will observe only what they are able to make sense of. Asking children to 'observe' carefully is a good way of finding out what ideas they do have in their minds. For example:

- **2. 'Water and air', 4. 'Air is used'** and **8. 'At home'.** Few children will arrive at the rusting lesson thinking that rust is an oxide. What they say they will observe will give you an idea of what they are thinking.

- Let them observe a range of (pictures of) birds' beaks. Those that realise that their shapes relate to the food they eat will observe far more than the others.

- Let them gently heat some cold water until it boils. Those that observe the tiny bubbles of air that first rise to the top increasing in size, followed later by the bubbles of steam that get smaller as they rise, are those that already have the idea that air is dissolved in the water. The others are unlikely to notice the difference (unless it is pointed out to them).

Basic skills

Sometimes it is important to teach children how to use a particular technique or piece of equipment. It is much better to embed such introductions into an investigation, but the newness of the task means that you want the investigation to be simple. For example:

- learning how to 'catch gases' in **3. 'Damp fibre'**

- learning to use a microscope by examining bits and pieces they find around the room

- learning how to read the scales on analogue equipment such as thermometers.

Motivation

Practical work is said to motivate children, and we sometimes threaten withdrawal of practical work as a way of encouraging good behaviour, in the knowledge that pupils usually enjoy *doing*. However, practical work that lacks purpose and focus cannot provide that motivation – it will be just another recipe for the pupils to work through. For example:

- **8. 'At home'** where pupils bring in their own rusted nails should be far more motivating than following the recipe in **1. 'Nail tubes'.**

Investigations

This could be described as the ultimate aim of practical work in school. **2. 'Water and air', 4. 'Air is used', 7. 'Other metals'** and **8. 'At home'** are whole investigations, but **5. 'Weight'** is very much an investigation too, though pupils only do the thinking part of it. The investigation of the voltage from metals in a lemon is another example. Investigations arise from observations and discussions and require ideas that need testing. They encourage pupils to think, plan, carry out and interpret. (See Chapter 18 for further discussion of investigations at GCSE.)

We need to re-examine all the practical activities we ask pupils to do in school. We shouldn't ask the class to do 'the practical' simply 'because this experiment has always been done this way'. If we ensure that all practical work has purpose it will regain its rightful place in school as an important learning activity for pupils.

Summary

In this chapter we explored the nature of science (how science works), and the need to give purpose to our practical work in schools. This was emphasised in Chapter 1 when we looked at the attributes of a good science teacher. In Part II (Chapters 4–11) we examine this scientific process from the starting point of the pupils rather than scientists themselves. The pupils come with ideas about their world that we, as teachers, need to become aware of. Only then can we help them see the wonder and power of scientific explanations that have been developed over the ages. We have only a few years to do what has taken humanity centuries, but we must be successful in this if they are to leave school with an understanding of how their planet works; an understanding that should help them to look after it – a clear message from the next chapter.

CHAPTER

3

Science Education and Sustainability

Chapter overview

For many years science has been recognised as an effective vehicle through which environmental education can be taught. The term is now subsumed within 'Sustainable futures and the global dimension' of the Secondary National Strategy. Yet the role of science is as important as ever. How can we begin to understand the world we live in and recognise the impact we have on it without a grounding in the science that explains and supports it? How can we begin to act as responsible stewards of the planet without appreciating how it works? This chapter explores such questions and brings together ideas and examples of how science, sustainability and effective citizenship come together – orchestrated, of course, by quality teaching and learning.

Why the links with environmental education and citizenship?

It is generally accepted by government and society that education about, for and through the environment is an essential requirement for the survival of humanity. We don't have to look far to hear the call for a more environmentally literate workforce and a more environmentally aware public. Yet over the past two decades environmental education has been progressively marginalised from the school curriculum – perhaps even more so during the evolution of the National Curriculum. With the advent of personal, social and health education (PSHE) and citizenship within the National Curriculum, environmental education seems to have found its niche under the term 'Sustainable futures and the global dimension'. This emphasises the important relationship between environmental concerns and global issues. The Qualifications and Curriculum Development Authority (QCDA) recognises *sustainability* as a whole-school curriculum and management approach, not a new subject, and recognises that its roots are in environmental and (world) development education. However, being able to translate the rhetoric of 'sustainable futures' into practice with a view to altering attitudes and behaviour requires more than exposure: it requires relevance and understanding. To achieve this it is necessary for pupils to look at the underlying principles, which are often rooted in science (see Box 3.1).

Box 3.1 Misconceptions about climate change

Climate change and global warming are key environmental topics that contain their own collection of misconceptions. Try answering these questions:

- Is the greenhouse effect a natural or human-induced phenomenon (or both)?
- What is the difference between carbon dioxide emissions from burning fossil fuels and those from burning biomass?
- Does the hole in the ozone layer let heat in to cause global warming?

(See Box 3.3 at the end of the chapter (p. 28) for comments on these questions.)

The science of environmental issues

In order to develop a clear understanding of human impact on the environment, it is essential to understand how the environment works – the diversity and interactions both of the organisms that exist around us and of the particles that they are made of and which make up the environment they live in. We need to consider, especially, the atmosphere – its composition both now and in the past, and the effect of solar radiations on it. These insights are fundamental if we want to understand issues such as global warming and the possible long-term effects it will have on the planet.

Gaining an understanding of the science behind environmental issues forms the underpinning philosophy supporting this book. References are made throughout to the CD-ROM *Science Issues and the National Curriculum* (Ross *et al.* 2002 – see Preface, p. xii, for details) which explores key environmental issues and the science behind them. Without this understanding science exists in a vacuum and science education becomes meaningless to most pupils; learning in science needs to relate to everyday life.

Becoming a good citizen

Having knowledge is one thing, but knowing what to do with it is another. A key aspect of becoming a good citizen is knowing how to behave responsibly towards yourself, others and the environment in which you live. Research indicates that there are various dimensions to becoming a good citizen (Kerr *et al.* 2001):

- engagement (in something)

- knowledge (of something)

- skills (such as problem-solving)

- concepts (understanding the science behind the issues)

- attitudes (the development of positive attitudes)

- participation (taking an active role in society).

Promoting, enhancing and developing these dimensions underpin what education is all about. Towards this end the Secondary National Strategy advocates the use of constructivist and social constructivist approaches to teaching and learning – active learning and participation (where children are encouraged to assess evidence, negotiate, make decisions, solve problems, work independently and in groups, and learn from each other – as we saw in the third lesson in Chapter 1). All are central to the learning process put forward. We discuss these approaches to learning in Part II of this book. We also emphasise that, during teaching, opportunities should be made available for pupils to:

- take some responsibility for their own learning
- explore and discuss topical issues
- participate in groups of different sizes and composition
- find information and advice
- work with adults other than teachers
- work outside the classroom
- take time to reflect.

The issues associated with citizenship education can be highly controversial and provide opportunities to explore an array of teaching and learning methods, especially debating. As with any discussion-led activity, its success in terms of teaching and learning is largely governed by the experience and expertise of the teacher and a need for the pupils to have a firm grasp of the underlying principles. Pupils need to see the big picture, make connections and have the conceptual tools to construct their own understanding. This is where science comes in. The 'hot potatoes' of the world of debate include climate change, global warming, genetically modified organisms, conservation, biodiversity and the use of drugs – all of which require good scientific understanding before the pupil can take ownership of the concept and play an active role in debate.

Activities to support teaching

Pupils need to be fully equipped to play this active role and this requires the development of certain critical thinking skills that are fundamental to our decision-making process. These skills include:

- enquiry
- information-processing
- problem-solving
- creative thinking
- reasoning or critical thinking
- evaluation skills
- metacognition (thinking about thinking).

These skills don't develop overnight; they need to be honed and nurtured, and opportunities should be offered whereby they can be practised and perfected. One activity that goes some way to support this is the process of 'diamond ranking' (see Box 3.2).

Box 3.2 Diamond ranking

> Pupils are given a set of 13 prepared statements relating to the topic for debate. Working in groups, they have to arrange the statements in a diamond shape: the most and least agreeable statements at the top and bottom, with the others arranged in the middle forming the shape of a diamond – rows of 1, 3, 5, 3 and 1.

This approach allows the pupils to externalise their own ideas and to listen to and discuss each other's. To establish the situation where this activity works effectively, the pupils have to feel unthreatened and be free to talk. This is easier to achieve in a group situation than in a whole-class debate. The pupils can then begin to respect their own and each other's thoughts and ideas. This activity can eventually progress to semi-structured and then open debate without the scaffolding of the prepared statements. For further discussion on pupil talk see Chapter 8.

Sometimes it is desirable to move away from teacher-initiated activities to draw on examples from around the world, as we see in the next section.

Global citizenship

We are urged to think globally but act locally. A group of trainee students working with the Global-ITE (Initial Teacher Education) project visited a primary school in rural India, where water was so scarce that pupils were urged to use only a drop at a time to clean their slates (mini-whiteboards are a Western equivalent). In Mumbai the students stayed in high-class hotel accommodation with flush toilets and showers, and visited schools with networked television in every classroom. You don't have to travel to become aware of contrasts in the conditions under which humanity lives, but in the affluent West we are shielded from such contrasts, and tend to take what we have and our lifestyles for granted. If we are to have a sustainable future the resources of the world, which are not limitless, need to be shared more evenly. By bringing global images to the UK classroom in a sensitive way, we can begin to ask UK pupils to examine their lifestyles and to question the way we treat resources as if they are limitless.

Acting locally

The pressures we place on the planet from our energy and food demand and waste disposal are reflected in all aspects of the natural environment:

- water supply, distribution and quality
- soil quality and availability

- species biodiversity

- atmospheric composition and the unpredictable nature of climate change.

Government and inter-governmental level summits have come and gone and the environmental debate is never far from the media focus. Initiatives and policies have been introduced and they can work, but usually at a superficial level only. In the classroom awareness and appreciation of our own impact on the environment must be fundamental to teaching and learning. We need to encourage our pupils to think about their impact and take responsibility for their own actions, such as:

- 'Switching it off!' when the lights are not required. Encourage the pupils to think environmentally outside of school. Most children have access to a television and computer of their own. How many leave these and other electronic equipment on 'standby'? This uses electricity, wasting in total the equivalent of a quarter of a large power station's capacity. This has financial implications as well as depleting non-renewable natural resources and adding to the carbon footprint of the UK. These reasons for 'switching it off!' may not mean much initially, but if you explain that the majority of household fires are caused by equipment left on 'standby', the message soon gets home.

- Thinking about waste generally and the impact of packaging on the environment – for example, ensuring paper is reused and overall usage is reduced.

- Thinking about water use and abuse – the importance of water and other natural resources can form the basis of several science and environmental sessions.

- Encouraging the pupils to learn more about their local environment and the influences on it (see Chapter 23 on learning outside the classroom). This introduces not only the physical but also the biological environment, developing a sense of caring and ownership. Ideas leading to conservation and sustainability can be developed from this.

It is by no means clear how our global future may unfold, but as humans we have the ability to model a range of possible scenarios, tested against the facts available now. It is up to us as teachers to ensure our pupils understand the mechanisms of this finite environment and our impact on it so that we can collectively do something about it.

Summary

We have emphasised the need to relate learning in science to everyday life and to the issues and concerns that go with it. Pupils will develop their own viewpoints on issues of sustainability and citizenship, but they will need help, guidance and support along the way. This is an exciting yet challenging aspect of the curriculum, which is essential for the next generation to move towards a more sustainable future. Good-quality teaching and informed learning go a long way to ensuring this is achieved.

Box 3.3 Responses to the questions in Box 3.1 (p. 24)

The *natural* greenhouse effect is a natural phenomenon due to the existence of carbon dioxide and water molecules present in the atmosphere. Without it the temperature on Earth would be too low to support life.

The *enhanced* greenhouse effect is another matter. Through human activities we have increased the amounts of carbon dioxide and other greenhouse gases in the atmosphere, causing an increase in the surface temperature of the Earth, and resulting in global warming.

By burning fossil fuels we are adding significantly to atmospheric carbon emissions because that carbon had been locked away in the form of oil, coal and natural gas for hundreds of millions of years. By burning biomass (e.g. fuelwood, agricultural waste), which captured its carbon very recently, the carbon released will be part of that natural cycle, and does not add to it.

Carbon dioxide, methane, water vapour, ozone and nitrogen dioxide in the lower atmosphere (troposphere) are all examples of greenhouse gases which prevent some infra-red radiation from leaving the Earth. Ozone (O_3) is manufactured naturally in the upper atmosphere (stratosphere) by the action of ultraviolet (UV) light from the sun, and then stops much of the UV from reaching the Earth's surface. Its formation is inhibited by the presence of ozone-destroying pollutants such as CFCs. This has nothing to do with the greenhouse effect.

II

How Children Make Sense of Their World

Introduction

The importance of *context* when we learn new ideas has been recognised in the new Secondary National Curriculum in England, which began in September 2008. Science concepts may form an interdependent array of ideas, but until they are linked to everyday happenings they remain obscure and irrelevant to most children (and adults). For example, to understand climate change many scientific concepts need to be addressed, such as solar energy, atmospheric gases and so on. To understand why a diet high in red meat can be unhealthy and bad for the planet, we need ideas such as food chains, liver function and the structure of proteins. If these topics are studied as isolated and unrelated concepts in a science curriculum they may provide little interest for most children, but package them within an interesting topic, which possibly spreads across many curriculum areas, and the whole study comes alive and has purpose.

But starting with everyday ideas has its own problems. Our understanding is acquired through everyday experiences, and may often conflict with the scientific view. So we begin, in Chapters 4 and 5, by examining the way children use the words (and ideas) of their everyday lives – this forms the part of the lesson where we *elicit* their ideas. Only then can we begin to help them develop and, where necessary, revolutionise these ideas into a growing scientific understanding (Chapters 6–11). We must compress into just a few years of schooling an understanding which took humanity many centuries to develop. We cannot expect many children to come up with these scientific ideas by themselves, so our job as teachers is to present the ideas to the pupils (the *intervention* phase of a lesson). Scientists take time to take on new ideas; often members of the 'old school' had to die off before the new ways of thinking became part of the establishment. As teachers we have to take children through similar revolutions in thought (the *reformulation* phase of a lesson) in order that they can share the powerful scientific ways of thinking which have enabled us to begin to understand our environment. This *constructivist* approach to teaching and learning (Chapter 6) needs to be set into realistic, useful and meaningful contexts for the pupils.

So we move away from last-minute revision guides, full of *markobine gandos* (Chapter 4) which children learn by heart, to put in their short-term memory and pass an exam. The purpose of teaching science is to help young people come to understand the way the world works, and enable them to look after it (and themselves). If they *understand and use* these scientific ideas, then they *truly* know. The ideas they have met in school need to become a part of their make-up and way of life. With this deeper understanding pupils can pass an exam now, next week or next year – revision becomes a daily activity as pupils *use* their scientific ideas. Anything that has to be revised last minute has clearly not been useful to the learner, and after the examination will probably be forgotten. In contrast, ideas that are *used* become embedded in our minds. This approach to learning is developed in Chapter 6 where we draw a parallel with the way science itself advances.

Chapters 7–11 explore in some detail how we can give pupils the time to take on board (*reformulate*) the new ideas and experiences we have given them through our *intervention*. We have called these 'active learning' techniques.

Learning through Language and Observation

Chapter overview

This chapter examines the way we observe the everyday world and begin to describe it using words and ideas. We contrast this with the words and ideas used by scientists and look for ways to enable our pupils also to come to an understanding of these scientific concepts. Single definitions of words need to be replaced by a real feeling for the ways the words are used and connections have to be made to ideas the pupils already understand.

We only see what our brains allow us to see

Ask a fashion designer, a doctor, an architect, a parent and a motor mechanic to walk along the high street and then ask them to describe what they saw – all will give a different picture. Ask them to walk through the rain forest of an Amazonian Amerindian and they will see none of the complex detail that the tribal people take for granted. In your home town you feel at ease, you know where everything is and what each noise means; but a stranger, receiving exactly the same sensory data, can become bewildered and lost.

Naïve observation is not possible. The myth of 'an objective scientist', able to collect data without putting any of his or her own ideas into what is collected, has long been put to rest.

'How science works' could be summarised by the words 'purposeful observation'. Observation is a product of the interaction of sensory data with the concepts and ideas which are already stored in our memories. These mental concepts influence what we look for, and thus what we perceive. Those who are blind from birth and have their sight restored take weeks or months to learn what the light inputs to their eyes mean. Those setting foot in a land whose language they do not understand receive the same sounds as the natives but make no sense of them. Only later do they begin to make sense of what they hear.

To most people the green blobs in the centre of clear circles on Alexander Fleming's bacterial cultures on agar plates meant nothing – but Fleming, a microbiologist, saw moulds (the green blobs) killing bacteria and penicillin was discovered. Darwin had seen selective breeding among pigeons at home, and saw the same sort of thing with Galapagos finches. Many others would have taken no notice. Mendel, a trained mathematician and the 'father' of modern genetics, saw huge significance in his 3:1 ratio of tall to short peas, but his results failed to impress his peers until many years after his death.

You may feel uncomfortable that we are saying scientists are biased in their observations – aren't they supposed to be *objective*? The answer is that objective observation is meaningless, it cannot be done. When we observe, our minds are trying to make sense by comparing our existing ideas with the incoming sensory data. Consider this scenario, acted out in a GCSE science lesson on photosynthesis where leaves (some left in the dark and some in the light) are tested for starch:

Lesson on photosynthesis – testing leaves for starch

As teachers we make sense of the scientific words written on the worksheet and of the iodine going black on one leaf but not on the other which was kept in the dark. We connect this all together with our picture of the process we call *photosynthesis*.

Many pupils, however, see strange words on bottles, go through a complex series of processes with a couple of leaves, one of which goes black. They dutifully write: 'This shows that photosynthesis requires light'. Without the complex set of ideas held by the teacher, pupils may make little sense of this wonderful 'experiment'.

When scientists do want to avoid bias in their observations, for example during the trialling of new drugs, they have to undertake experiments under what is called *double-blind* conditions: half the patients get a dummy drug (the *placebo*), but neither the doctors nor the patients know who has the real drug and who has the dummy. In this way neither can the patients 'think' themselves better, nor can the doctors 'see' improvements that are not really there. (The *placebo effect* means that all the patients are likely to improve but hopefully those with the real drug will do even better!)

The role of language in learning and the value of finding the roots of meaning

Words and ideas are useful but there can never be one correct meaning or definition of each one. Despite the best efforts of scientists to keep meanings fixed and precise, the meaning of what is written and said in science (as in any aspect of human life) changes over time – public meanings change over historical time, and private understandings change over the lifetime of an individual. It is therefore important to uncover how children use words. We may accuse them of muddled thinking, when it is simply that they are using words differently from us. As teachers, we need to listen carefully to children as they use words, and watch out, especially from the context of what they say, for understanding conveyed through an underdeveloped and possibly inadequate vocabulary. There are *grains of truth* in what children say, as we see towards the end of this chapter. But first we look at the place of language in learning.

Language plays a pivotal role in learning. Imagine going into a classroom where all the scientific words have been substituted by made-up words like *giky martible* (Sutton 1992) and *markobine gando* (Ross 1998). You would read or hear things like:

> When an orbal of quant undual to the markobine bosal passes through a dovern mern it is deranted so as to cosat to a bart on the bosal called the markobine gando.

Nonsense, you may say, but you can still answer questions such as:

> What happens to the deranted orbal when it passes through a dovern mern?
> (See Box 4.3 at the end of the chapter (p. 38) for an acceptable answer.)

We need to ensure that our science lessons and texts are not perceived this way by our pupils, leaving them to learn things by heart in order to pass examinations.

Private understandings and public knowledge

When children use one word for two separate ideas it is time to teach them a new word. For example, the words *shadow* and *reflection* are often muddled up by children in primary school. By teaching the word *shade*, and showing it is the same as *shadow*, children can associate it with places where light has been blocked out. Less useful is the link with *flexible* meaning bendable where children might connect the word *reflection* with light bouncing off a surface.

Some materials let light through without much distortion – they are *transparent*. Primary school teachers often describe such materials as 'see-through'. There are other materials which light passes through, but you cannot see through them; they are *translucent*. This is less easy to translate into English; 'lets-light-through-but-you-can't-see-through' is cumbersome. Telling children that the scientific word for see-through is *transparent*, and the other is *translucent*, can be like using the words *markobine gando*. They have no meaning, so just have to be learnt. But children know many words with the Latin word 'trans' (meaning *through*) in them: transport, transfer, trans-Atlantic, Ford Transit van. In each case they can see that something is moving, either 'through' or 'across'. Less easy, but worth exploring, is the difference between -*parent* and -*lucent* (meaning 'see' and 'light'). What other words do they know containing these roots? Ap*parent*, ap*pear*, '…to *peer* into the gloom' are all linked with seeing; and *luc*id, *Luc*ifer link with clear and light. By contrast the Greek word for light is *photos* which gives us words such as photo-graph and photo-synthesis.

Many scientific words have a classical origin, and most teachers point this out for their pupils. Box 4.1 lists a few of them.

Box 4.1 Some classical roots of scientific words

Words in Greek and Latin:

micro = small, *scope* = look at, *tele* = far, *vision* = see, *graph* = draw, *lysis* = to break, *phone* = hear, *hydro* = water, *electron* = amber (when rubbed it becomes electrically charged) give us these scientific words: microscope, telescope, television, telegraph, telephone, hydrophone, hydrolysis, electrolysis, etc.

(Thus *hydro*-gen is the water generator or the *element which generates water* – when hydrogen burns it forms water, H_2O.)

Words for Greek and Latin numbers help us understand words like:

*bi*cycle, *bi*nocular, *di*oxide (2); *quad*ruped, *quad*rant (4); *hexa*gon, *hexa*ne (6); *octo*pus, *Octo*ber (8); *deci*mal, *deca*ne (10); and *cent*ury, *centi*pede (100).

(Note here the *-pus*, *-ped*, *-pede* all mean foot [as in pedestal, pedal, pedestrian], though centipedes don't actually have 100 feet, just as millipedes don't have 1000.)

Origins of words

Let us consider the origin of more of the words used in science, but whose origin (etymology) is perhaps less obvious.

For each word in the list that follows, see how far you are able to uncover the root meaning:

circuit	ovary	electricity	evaporate	igneous
insulate	mammal	month	vaccination	volatile

- Think of how the word came to be used in science.

- Look for other words with similar roots (perhaps in other languages such as French) which might help children come to understand how they are used.

Box 4.4 at the end of the chapter shows the etymology of each word, and indicates other words that might help children uncover the meaning.

By revealing to children how words got their meaning and comparing them with other familiar but similarly derived words we can help children understand the accepted literal meaning of new words used in science. It helps them move away from learning *markobine gandos* by rote, towards building the word into their real understanding. Sutton (1992, esp. chapters 3, 5 and 8) shows the value of knowing where words came from and how they get used.

How did new scientific words come into being?

Think of the time when no word yet existed for the idea scientists wanted to talk about – how did they go about inventing a new word? We still have the same problem today as scientific ideas develop, and new words are needed.

TABLE 4.1 Words associated with the use of fuels (Ross 1989)

English	smoke	steam	heat
Mandinka	sisiyo	fingjalo	
Wolof	sahar		tangor

Consider the words in Table 4.1 associated with the use of fuels from two West African languages.

In Mandinka one word covers steam and heat. This means that the material nature of steam, as a mixture of water vapour and condensation, could be confused with heat energy in the form of infra-red radiation – the glow you feel round a fire. In Wolof, where one word covers smoke and steam, the confusion between the solid particulates associated with smoke and the water droplets associated with visible steam cannot be as easily sorted, as it could be in Mandinka and English. English-speaking children frequently use the words steam and smoke synonymously, but at least we have the words available to separate out the two ideas. Having the word in your brain helps you *observe* the differences between smoke, steam and heat.

New words for scientists

Children will hear new words being used by their teachers long before they will be confident enough to use them themselves. Children should begin to use scientific vocabulary when everyday words become inadequate and further delay would cause confusion. In a similar way scientists will increasingly feel the need for new words to represent the new ideas that they are working on. When a new word was needed, scientists did not always invent a new word – sometimes they took an existing word and used it a special way. While new words suffer the problem of strangeness, and lack all meaning at first, familiar words come with a whole baggage of meaning that can be equally confusing. Both processes of word acquisition have their problems.

Consider the common words in Table 4.2 that have been used for a special meaning in science – tick the box to show if their scientific meaning is extended, restricted or just different, compared with their everyday use. You will find a commentary on these words in Box 4.5 at the end of the chapter which you can use with your pupils.

Scientific words – should we use existing words or invent new ones?

There are going to be problems whether scientists invent or borrow words for their new ideas. As science teachers we need to be acutely aware of conflicts in meanings of *borrowed* words, and give as much help as possible for *invented* words. We need to be aware that children may not be using a word the way we might wish them to. It may be that they understand the science very well, but are using the wrong word. Equally they may appear to be using the right words but have no real idea of what they are saying.

To end this section on words and ideas we invite you to consider the *grains of truth* in the following statements made by children and adults which appear to contain *misconceptions*. We discuss the issue of misconceptions more fully in Chapter 5.

TABLE 4.2 Common words with a special meaning in science

	SCIENTIFIC WORD, COMPARED WITH ITS EVERYDAY MEANING, IS:		
	EXTENDED	RESTRICTED	DIFFERENT
Animal			
Current (electricity)			
Energy			
Force			
Fruit			
Growth (of living things)			
Plant (life)			
Power			
Table (of results)			

Grains of truth

When children use words they often mean something rather different from the accepted scientific meaning. In the ideas given in Box 4.2 there is a 'grain of truth' in what the children (and adults!) are saying, but they all represent an inappropriate use of words from the scientific point of view. Many are phrases we all have come to use in our everyday language, which set up barriers against a scientific understanding.

Box 4.2 Grains of truth

In the following 'grains of truth':

- explain in what way the accepted *scientific* view is contradicted by these statements
- spot the grains of truth in them (some are very big grains)
- consider the implications for teaching.

(The italicised statements below are discussed in this chapter. For a discussion of the others see Chapters 5 and 12–15 which deal with misconceptions.)

Chemistry (Chapter 12)
When things burn they are destroyed
Petrol is turned into energy to make the car go
Wax is fireproof
Water in a puddle disappears

Physics (Chapter 13)
Things sink because they are heavy
A ton of lead is heavier than a ton of feathers
Heavy objects fall faster than light ones
Hot air rises
Gravity operates downward
There is no gravity in space/on the moon
Moving objects need a force on them to keep them going
Energy is used up
Electric current is used up
We see when our eyes look at objects
Blankets make things warm
Wood is warmer than metal

Biology (Chapter 14)
Plant roots breathe
Food is turned into energy in our body (during digestion)
Plants feed on soil through their roots
Air keeps us alive
Animals are furry and have four legs

'When things burn they are destroyed'

This is a case where the West African languages, Mandinka and Wolof, come out better than English. Wolof has two words for the English word *burn*: *laka* is similar to our char, and is used (normally) for the decomposition reaction when organic matter is heated, forming inflammable smoke and char. This has been called char-burning (Ross 1991). *Taka* is used for the combination of air and fuel when flames are seen (flame-burning) (see Table 4.3).

Burning certainly destroys the *object*, whether energy has caused it to decompose (char-burn), or whether oxides have built up releasing thermal energy (flame-burn). That is the very big grain of truth. But at an *atomic* level there is no destruction.

The implications for teaching are clear – at junior level we need to be careful to distinguish between the two types of burning (*laka* and *taka* – char and flame), both in the words we use and in getting children to observe the contrasts. A log of wood put on the fire takes heat from the fire until it is hot and begins to give off the flammable smoke – only then does it burst into flames and begin transferring energy. Later on the molecular explanations can be given – and flame-burning can be seen as a constructive process, where fuel and oxygen combine.

TABLE 4.3 Meanings of the word burn (Ross 1989)

ENGLISH	BURN	
	flame-burn (combust)	char-burn (scorch, char)
Mandinka	maala	jani
Wolof	taka	laka

There is an exact parallel with the way we deal with food. The *digestion* process is equivalent to *char-burning* (breaking the fuel up into small bits for entry into the blood) and *respiration* is equivalent to *flame-burning* (combination of these broken bits with oxygen to build up oxides). (See Figure 4.1 representing an everyday view.)

'Things sink because they are heavy'

There is a grain of truth in this if children use the word *heavy* to mean *dense* – as we all do. 'Wood is lighter than stone.' 'Metal is a heavy substance.' 'A ton of lead is heavier than a ton of feathers.' What we need to do is to show children that the word *heavy*, in its strict scientific sense, is a measurement of the force of gravity acting on the mass of body – a measure of its weight. So you can have a light piece of lead, and a heavy bag of feathers, but the density of the lead is still high, so it will still sink.

When children say a ton of lead is heavier than a ton of feathers, or that heavy objects sink and light ones float, they probably understand the science well enough but it is their use of the words *light* and *heavy* that we must sort out. They know that certain materials are much 'heavier' than others, meaning (in adult, scientific use of words) that the material is more dense than others. The children use the same word 'heavy' for two different ideas: absolutely heavy (this is a heavy book, you are too heavy to lift) and high density (lead is a heavy material, so it sinks). When the same word is used for two different ideas, there is bound to be some degree of confusion (refer again to Tables 4.1 and 4.3 with the meanings of 'smoke', 'burn', etc.).

Summary

This chapter began by showing that naïve observation is not possible. There are no such people as objective scientists, able to collect data without using any of their own ideas. The scientific method may start when we notice something, but even this process depends unconsciously on the ideas that are already in our minds. These ideas or concepts are often labelled by single words, so it is important to find out what each person, whether learner or learned, understands by these words.

Figure 4.1 makes a useful summary for this chapter. It is a profile of the way the Mandinka language handles the concepts associated with fuels and burning (Ross 1989). As you read the Mandinka words on their own they have no meaning (assuming you do not speak the language). They are like the scientific words we present to children. As we explore the range of meanings and the origins of words with our children, they gradually build them into their own world. We also see here the way concepts are embedded into everyday language – our naïve ideas about how things work.

Our task, as science teachers, is to become aware of these in-built but naïve ways of thinking – and that is the focus of Chapter 5 which follows. Subsequent chapters in Part II will explore the ways we can build on or challenge these everyday ideas in our teaching.

Box 4.3 An acceptable answer to the question on p. 33

'It cosats to a bart on the bosal called the markobine gando.'

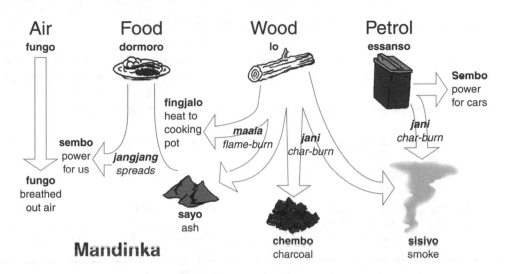

FIGURE 4.1 A concept profile of the way the Mandinka language handles the concepts associated with fuels and burning (from Hoss 1989)

Box 4.4 Origins of words used in science (see p. 34)

Circuit. Circle, bicycle, circus, all suggest going round in a circle. In the case of electricity, it is the electrical current which goes round; this carries electrical energy from the cell to the bulb. [From Latin *circum*, meaning round.]

Ovary. Oval, ovum, from the Latin *ovum*, an egg – hence egg-shaped and egg container.

Electricity. *Electron* is the Greek word for amber, the yellow fossil resin that traps mosquitoes that once sucked dinosaur blood. When rubbed it acquires a static electric charge, and so it came to represent the new phenomenon of 'ambericity'. Interesting, but on this occasion of no help to children.

Evaporate. Vapour is another word for gas, especially if it condenses easily. [From Latin *e-, ex-*, meaning 'out of'.]

Igneous. Ignite = set fire to, so igneous rocks are from fire. [From Greek *igni* and Sanskrit *agni*, meaning fire.]

Insulate. Insular means 'cut off' (a peninsula is almost cut off, as penumbra is almost a shadow) so insulate means to protect or cut off from. [From Latin word for island, *insula*.]

Mammal. Mammals have mammary glands for producing milk. The same 'Mmm' sound used by babies has come to be used as the word for their mother – Mam, Mum, Mom – hence, mammal. [Also from Latin *mamma*, meaning breast.]

Month. The moon circles the Earth once in every 'moonth' (this helps with spelling too).

Vaccination. From Jenner's work on cow pox – French *vâche*, a cow.

Volatile. Does not mean reactive and dangerous in its scientific meaning, but rather 'to fly away'; compare with the tennis word 'volley' – literally to let fly. Volatile simply means a substance that evaporates easily, like water, wax and the smell of wych-hazel. [From Latin *volare*, meaning to fly, as in French *voler*, Spanish *volar*.]

Box 4.5 Scientific meanings of everyday words (see Table 4.2, p. 36)

Animal. *Extended*. In science, an animal is a multicellular consumer that relies on other living things for nutrients. In everyday life it has a meaning closer to *mammal* (though humans are not normally classed as animals), as in 'There are animals, birds and insects living in the forest'; in its scientific meaning birds and insects are animals (see Chapter 14).

Current (electricity). *Different*. In science this refers to the flow of electrons or coulombs round a circuit, and is measured as charge, in coulombs, per second (= amps). In everyday life it has a meaning closer to energy or power, as in 'How much current does this drill use?' (see Chapter 13).

Energy. *Different*. In science energy has two meanings: a quantity, measured in joules, that remains the same throughout a change, and a measure of the ability a system has to do useful work (properly called *free energy*). The everyday life meaning is closer to the free energy idea, as in 'I've had a huge energy bill this quarter because I've used so much'. Joules cannot be used, but their usefulness does go (see Chapter 13).

Force. *Restricted*. In science it is measured in newtons and, when unbalanced, causes objects to change their state of motion. In everyday life it has a much broader meaning, as in 'She forced me to do it' (see Chapter 13).

Fruit. *Extended*. In science a fruit develops from a fertilised flower (carpel), and contains the seeds of the plant, such as pea pods, hazelnuts, rose-hips and tomatoes. In everyday life the term is restricted to fruiting bodies that are soft, (sweet) and edible (see Chapter 14).

Growth (of living things). *Extended*. In science growth is concerned with differentiation and development of specialised cells as well as increasing the number of cells. In everyday life it is usually used to indicate something gets bigger (though this often entails more complexity too).

Plant (life). *Extended*. In science plants are one of the major kingdoms of life – comprising multicellular life-forms with roots, stem and leaves, that obtain their nutrients from inorganic sources, through photosynthesis. In everyday life *plants* tend to be kept in pots, and are different from trees, flowers and vegetables (see Chapter 14).

Power. *Restricted*. In science power is measured in watts and is a measure of how fast energy is transferred – *joules per second*. In everyday life it is used very generally covering ideas of energy ('What is this powered by?') and social hierarchies. The word *powerful* contains the essence of the scientific meaning, 'able to deliver energy fast'.

Table (of results). *Different*. In science, a place to write your results. In school, a place on which pupils sometimes scratch their names.

CHAPTER

5

Elicitation: Children's Ideas of the World

Chapter overview

It is difficult to teach children new ideas until we know the existing ideas they hold – these often appear to conflict with accepted scientific ideas and are described as 'misconceptions' or 'alternative frameworks of belief' (Driver *et al.* 1994). Chapter 4 showed that there are many grains of truth in these 'alternative ideas'. We extend this discussion in this chapter where we will pay careful attention to what children say about their ideas in science.

Children's alternative ideas

Methods of teaching science which are based on the idea that pupils build up, or construct, ideas about their world are often called *constructivist* approaches. If we want pupils to understand and use scientific ideas their existing beliefs need to be challenged or extended. We cannot always replace these naïve ideas, but we can encourage pupils to use the scientific ones when appropriate, and to show them the inconsistencies in many of their existing ideas. This chapter looks at ways to probe and display their ideas. In Chapters 6–11 we look at active learning approaches that allow pupils to reconstruct the scientific ideas we present to enable them to make them their own.

The small sample of questions given in Figures 5.1–5.12 have all been used in schools to probe children's understanding. They are very basic – indeed so simple that we might wonder how older pupils could ever answer them inappropriately. Before you read the commentary on the questions try to answer the questions yourself at your own level and then as you think a child may see them. Better still, try them out on small groups of pupils across the age and ability range. What alternative ideas did you predict and find? If you are trying them with children, it is best to have the actual materials with you – for example, for the first question use two blocks of ice and wrap one in a hand-towel.

41

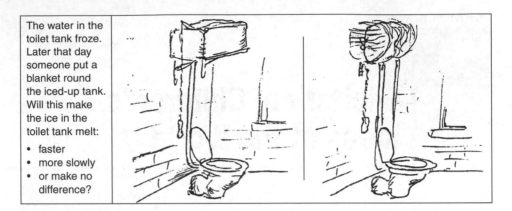

The water in the toilet tank froze. Later that day someone put a blanket round the iced-up tank. Will this make the ice in the toilet tank melt:

- faster
- more slowly
- or make no difference?

FIGURE 5.1 Frozen tank (from Ross 1998, p. 70)

Predict the temperature of the water in each cup after either sharing or mixing:

(i) When water at 60°C in a jar is shared between two cups

(ii) When water at 10°C and 70°C from two cups is mixed

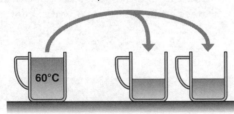
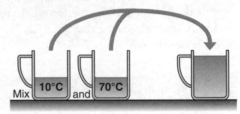

FIGURE 5.2 Temperature (after Stavey and Berkovitz 1980)

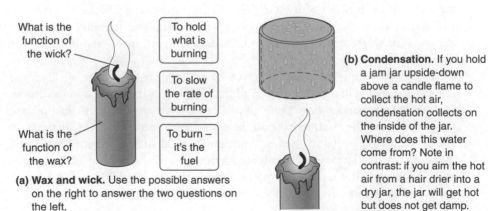

What is the function of the wick?

What is the function of the wax?

To hold what is burning

To slow the rate of burning

To burn – it's the fuel

(a) Wax and wick. Use the possible answers on the right to answer the two questions on the left.

(b) Condensation. If you hold a jam jar upside-down above a candle flame to collect the hot air, condensation collects on the inside of the jar. Where does this water come from? Note in contrast: if you aim the hot air from a hair drier into a dry jar, the jar will get hot but does not get damp.

FIGURE 5.3 Candle

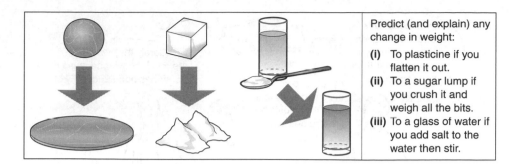

Predict (and explain) any change in weight:

(i) To plasticine if you flatten it out.

(ii) To a sugar lump if you crush it and weigh all the bits.

(iii) To a glass of water if you add salt to the water then stir.

FIGURE 5.4 Weight

What do **you** think?

FIGURE 5.5 Football (multiple choice question in the form of a Concept Cartoon™ after Keogh and Naylor 2009)

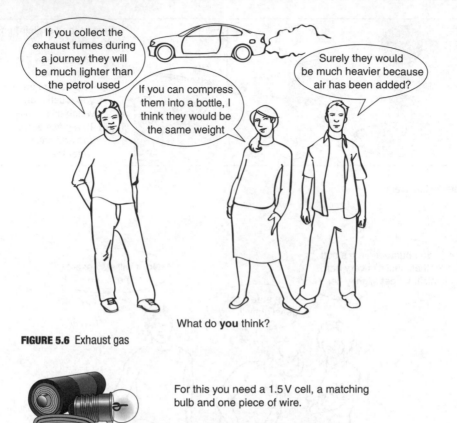

What do **you** think?

FIGURE 5.6 Exhaust gas

For this you need a 1.5 V cell, a matching bulb and one piece of wire.

Can you make the bulb light using just the cell and a single piece of wire?

FIGURE 5.7 Cell and bulb

This activity is best done by making a set of cards with labelled pictures of the following:

person	**fire**	**car**	**cow**
daffodil	**tree**	**fish**	**whale**
spider	**bird**	**grass**	**cabbage**
cat	**seeds**	**frog-spawn**	**fly**

• Sort the cards to show those that are *alive*, *dead*, *never lived*. Are there any left?
• Now sort the cards into *animals* or *not animals*.
• Now sort the cards into *plants* or *not plants*.

FIGURE 5.8 Living – plant – animal (after Osborne and Freyberg 1985, p. 30)

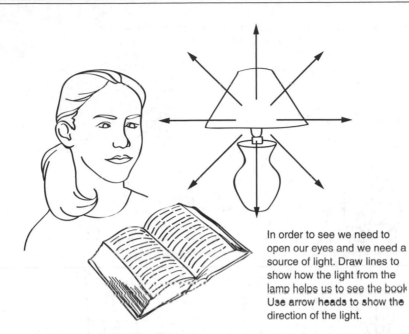

In order to see we need to open our eyes and we need a source of light. Draw lines to show how the light from the lamp helps us to see the book. Use arrow heads to show the direction of the light.

FIGURE 5.9 Seeing (from Guesne 1985)

The children are standing on the Earth.

They are all holding stones.

They let go of them.

Draw lines to show where the stones all go.

FIGURE 5.10 Gravity (from Nussbaum 1985) R. Driver, E. Guesne and A. Tiberghien, *Children's Ideas in Science*, © 1985. *Reproduced with the kind permission of Open University Press. All rights reserved.*

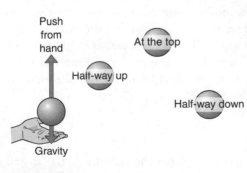

A ball has been thrown up, away from the Earth. The first picture is the ball being pushed by your hand against gravity. The other three show the ball on its way up, at the top of its flight, and on its way down. For these three pictures, draw arrows to indicate the size and direction of any forces that you think are acting on the ball. The longer the arrow, the larger the force. Label the force(s) as we have done on the first example. Before you rush to answer this, consider what is happening to the speed of the ball – is it getting slower, or faster, or staying the same?

FIGURE 5.11 Force

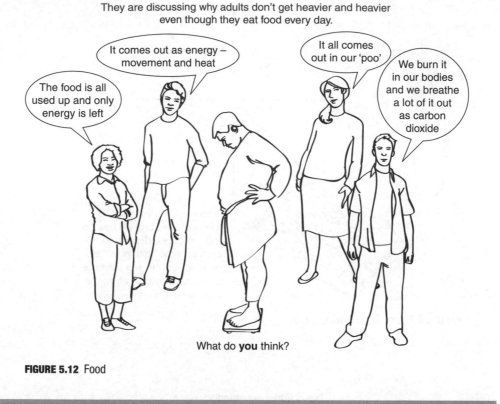

They are discussing why adults don't get heavier and heavier even though they eat food every day.

It comes out as energy – movement and heat

It all comes out in our 'poo'

We burn it in our bodies and we breathe a lot of it out as carbon dioxide

The food is all used up and only energy is left

What do **you** think?

FIGURE 5.12 Food

Discussion of the questions

Children's responses to such elicitation questions show they have a range of 'alternative' ideas which may remain unaffected by teaching *unless we take them into account* in designing the activities we ask the children to do. The following commentary on the questions gives a flavour of the extent of our problem as science teachers.

1. Frozen tank

Many answer this by saying the blanket will make the ice melt faster because blankets feel warm to their own bodies. But blankets and duvets are not warm themselves; instead they stop heat generated by our bodies from escaping. The word *insulation* in everyday life has come to mean 'keep warm' or even 'make warm'; for example, 'our new insulation makes our house very warm'. The blanket placed round the iced tank will, in contrast, slow down the rate at which heat energy can enter from the surroundings and so the ice will melt more slowly. It is for this reason we used to wrap ice-cream in newspaper (Newell and Ross 1996).

2. Temperature

Younger children tend to add the temperatures (so the mixture is 80°C) or halve them (so each cup is 30°C). Those that realise that 70°C and 10°C will not make 80°C often go for 60°C (if we don't add, then perhaps we subtract?). The idea that temperature measures the *degree of hotness* is difficult because 'hot' and 'cold' are used in everyday life as if the human body was a sort of zero point. This makes the use of a single scale of hotness difficult. If the cups at 10°C and 70°C have equal amounts of water in them, the temperature will be half way between them, that is, 40°C. Children need time at Key Stages 2 and 3 to gain this sort of experience of temperature as an intensive property, by practical activity. They have no problem if the questions are asked using qualitative descriptions of temperature rather than numbers, that is, mixing *hot* and *cold* water or sharing *hot* water into two cups (Stavey and Berkovitz 1980).

3. Candle

(a) Many pupils think the wax slows down the burning of the wick. But candle wax is simply a solid fuel (they were once made of animal fat) – the wick, just like in an oil lamp, is there to allow the fuel to get hot and evaporate, so allowing it to join with oxygen in the air as it burns. So it is the *wick* that holds the fuel and the *wax* that burns. (b) Many people explain the condensation from the hot fumes above a candle the same way they explain why a bathroom mirror steams up. But why is there no condensation from hot air from a hair-drier? In fact quite the opposite happens – a damp jar will lose its condensation when heated, like damp hair, or a damp rear car window. The hot air coming from a burning candle contains the products of combustion – hydrogen in the hydrocarbon wax fuel combines with oxygen from the air to produce water which condenses on the relatively cool sides of the jar. We need to stress the importance of air during burning, and to take note of the products of combustion (see 6. Exhaust gas, and 12. Food, below, and Chapter 12 for further discussion).

4. Weight

These questions get increasingly confusing for children. Only the very young will think that shape change or crushing will alter the mass (flattened plasticine looks bigger, crushed sugar feels lighter). However, even some children in secondary school will think that the salt disappears completely, as it dissolves, so adding nothing to the weight (Driver *et al.* 1994, chapter 8). Research shows that infants are more likely to get this right, because they have not yet experienced dissolving (Figure 5.13). The conservation of matter is not obvious from everyday experiences, and until we have a model for matter constructed from indestructible particles (Chapter 12) it is easy to understand why these pupils have problems.

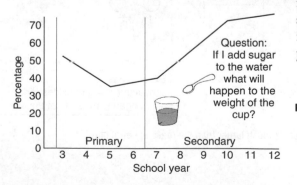

Question: If I add sugar to the water what will happen to the weight of the cup?

FIGURE 5.13 Graph showing the percentage of survey pupils who conserved mass/weight of sugar when it dissolved (from Holding 1987)

47

5. Football

It is not obvious that air is a *real substance*, except when it is moving (wind) or trapped as bubbles in water. The air around us cannot sink because we live in an ocean of air. But if it becomes less dense, for example by expansion from heating, the surrounding denser air can buoy it up. Similarly if we compress it, as we do when adding air to a football, it will be denser than the air it displaces, and so will sink, pushing ordinary air out of the way. This is well worth demonstrating to children, using a sensitive balance. Since gases are about 1000 times less dense than condensed forms of matter (solids and liquids), even if you double the pressure in a 5-litre football the mass, measured through weighing, will only increase by a few grams. (See Ross *et al.* 2002: CD – Atmosphere).

6. Exhaust gas

(a) *Much less*: many people will say, wrongly, that the exhaust is lighter, either because they don't believe gases weigh very much if anything, or because they think some of the petrol has been used, or turned into energy to make the car go. (b) *About the same*: here people may realise that you cannot destroy matter, so what goes in must come out, but they forget that the burning process involves combining fuel and air. (c) *Much heavier*: these are the people who realise the importance of oxygen. Since oxygen atoms are much more massive than hydrogen, and a little more massive than carbon, the increase in mass of the exhaust gases over the original hydrocarbon fuel is significant – in fact they have *more than three times the mass* of the petrol. Even then we have neglected the nitrogen that is mostly unchanged during the process, but forms the bulk of both the incoming air and outgoing exhaust. Once again we need to stress the importance of air in burning, and take note of the material products of combustion. See Figure 5.14 and Chapter 12. (See Ross *et al.* 2002: CD – Energy).

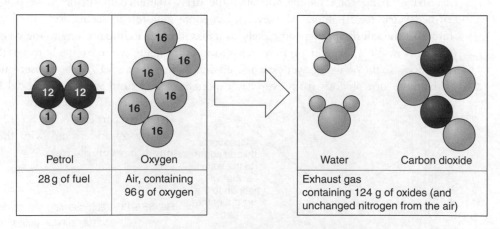

Petrol	Oxygen		Water	Carbon dioxide
28 g of fuel	Air, containing 96 g of oxygen		Exhaust gas containing 124 g of oxides (and unchanged nitrogen from the air)	

FIGURE 5.14 The mass of car exhaust is much larger than the mass of petrol burnt

7. Cell and bulb

Many pupils will try to connect only one terminal on the cell to one on the bulb. Even when they use both ends of the battery they do not appreciate that the bulb, too, has two terminals. Electric *current* must be able to flow through all components, allowing electrical *energy* to be transferred from the cell to the bulb. Young children see a single mains wire going to appliances at home, and later, when we give them bulbs in holders, they see the bulb apparently 'sitting' on the wire. All circuit work should start with 'naked' bulbs, and the presence of two terminals on all normal electrical equipment can be pointed out (see Chapter 13). (See Ross *et al.* 2002: CD Energy and Home).

8. Living – plant – animal

In Chapter 4 we mentioned the problem of using these everyday words in a scientific context where their meaning becomes much broader.

Living. Pupils may think fire or a car is living (but is it made of cells that divide?). They may also think that seeds and frog-spawn are dead (but they are made of cells that can divide and have the potential for life).

Plant. Pupils may have a very narrow view of *plants* – that they grow in pots on the windowsill. They may say a daffodil is a 'flower', a tree is a 'tree', a cabbage is a 'vegetable', seeds are seeds. In the list, to them, only grass might be a plant. If we are to use the word *plant* to represent multicellular organisms (with true roots, stem and leaves) that feed through photosynthesis, we need to make this clear to pupils in our classes.

Animal. Pupils may select only the land mammals (cat and cow, but not whale or person). This is the everyday meaning of *animal*: 'furry with four legs'. Person, bird, fish, spider and fly are also animals in a scientific sense. Frog-spawn belongs to the *animal kingdom*, but it is difficult to argue that it is *an animal*. We need to take care how this question is asked.

The concept of producers and consumers is difficult to convey if pupils use the words 'plant' and 'animal' in their restricted everyday sense (Osborne and Freyberg 1985, chapter 3).

9. Seeing

Many pupils even at Key Stage 4 will unthinkingly show light coming from the lamp and into our eyes and then from the eye to the book. The idea of *sight rays* is a consequence of words such as *look* and *notice*, that suggest the eye is an active seeker. Many ancient cultures (e.g. Greek and Indian) had this idea of active eyesight. Drawings which show light from the lamp scattering from the book with some rays entering the eye follow the scientific idea of the eye as a receptor. This was recognised by the Islamic school in the eighth century who actually dissected the eye and realised it was a receiver of light (Butt 1991; Guesne 1985). We should, however, remember that *observation* is an active process and in order to make any sense of the light entering our eyes, we must match this input with ideas generated from our memory (see also the discussion in Chapter 4, pp. 31–2).

10. Gravity

This problem is usually solved by the time children enter Key Stage 3, but younger children do find it difficult to imagine gravity acting towards the centre of a spherical Earth. They prefer to retain a notion of 'absolute up and down', allowing the stones to fall off the bottom of the page. This may be due also to their inability to see the picture as representing the land on which they are standing (Nussbaum 1985).

11. Force

Most people are stuck with Aristotle's view that moving objects have a force travelling with them, an idea more akin to the physicist's *momentum* (Gunstone and Watts 1985). Certainly this *seems* more sensible than Newton's idea which says that objects moving at a steady speed in a straight line require no force. If an unbalanced force does act, the object will change speed or direction, so with the introduction of the force of friction the object slows down. In our question, the hand forces the ball up with a force greater than gravity, so the ball accelerates up. However, as soon as it leaves the hand, the only force now acting (neglecting air resistance, which is very small) is from gravity. This acts against the motion so slows the ball down, bringing it to rest at the top of its flight. But gravity still acts exactly as before so the ball accelerates downwards gradually picking up speed. You can show this in school by attaching a length of elastic to a tennis ball and throwing it horizontally along the bench. It comes back, just like a ball thrown upwards, but now everyone can see the need of a backward (or downward) force to slow then reverse the ball's motion. The Newtonian answer will show just one downward arrow on each ball, exactly the same length as the gravity arrow on the first picture. (See Ross *et al.* 2002: CD – Atmosphere).

12. Food

This is a difficult question to ask. It requires people to make a separate account of the matter which makes up all materials (atoms), and the energy associated with them (joules).

Matter (atoms). All the carbon, hydrogen and oxygen (and other) atoms of the food we eat have to be accounted for – they are not destroyed, as many will have us believe.

Energy (joules). Energy can be stored by pulling matter apart against the electromagnetic force of chemical bonds. For example, when sunlight pulls oxygen away from the hydrogen in water during photosynthesis (see Chapter 11 and Ross *et al.* 2002: CD – Energy and Agriculture) energy is stored. This is released again when the fuel (containing the hydrogen) and oxygen recombine in our bodies during respiration.

Let us consider the four alternative answers to the original question, which asks about matter (atoms) not energy.

- *The food is all used up and only energy is left.* No – the atoms are still there. Although energy is transferred during respiration we asked only for an account of the *matter*, the stuff that would make us heavier if we did not lose it in some way.

- It all comes out in our 'poo'. No. This is a popular response, but only 5–10 per cent of our food is undigested and comes out as faeces. Most of what we eat enters the blood and is used as the fuel for respiration – a little (e.g. amino acids) is used for growth and repair, and leaves the body in many different ways (e.g. dead skin drops off).

- It comes out as energy – movement and heat. No. Since matter in the form of atoms cannot be destroyed they have to come out of the body somehow – and movement and heat are not made of matter, and thus do not weigh anything. Energy is transferred during the respiration process to be available for the body to use, but energy is not stuff which can be weighed.

- We burn it in our bodies and we breathe a lot of it out as carbon dioxide. Yes – this is the best response. The carbon and hydrogen atoms of the fuel rejoin with oxygen we have breathed in, forming carbon dioxide and water. This transfers energy (joules) to the cell, the reverse of the photosynthesis reaction. The matter leaves our body in the form of 'exhaust gases' in our breath. Note that this question is almost identical to question 6 – for combustion now read respiration. Since our food contains a considerable amount of water, we should include urine and perspiration along with breathing out as the way we get rid of the food we take in.

The need to elicit children's ideas

It may be somewhat depressing to find out how many pupils reach GCSE and even A-level standard and still answer questions like those above in a naïve way. However, experience shows that these naïve ideas are built up through common experiences and they can be very persistent. We need to find out what these ideas are and devise learning techniques that will challenge or reconcile the two views – the naïve and the scientific.

The remaining chapters in Part II take a closer look at how, as teachers, we can help pupils build ideas and concepts into their minds. Before that we look for ways we can uncover children's naïve ideas, using *elicitation* techniques.

Finding out children's ideas

Words mean different things to different people at different times so it is vital for a teacher to know what children mean by the words they use and the ideas that lie behind them. However, research has already shown us what many of these are likely to be (Driver *et al.* 1994), and if we spend too much time in class eliciting ideas from children we will have no time left to challenge or extend their ideas – instead we may simply reinforce the misconception.

Elicitation of ideas is important for two reasons. Teachers need to know what stage in their conceptual development their pupils have reached, and pupils need to compare their existing ideas with the new ideas they are being taught (cognitive conflict), thereby enabling these new concepts to be built firmly into their (new) understanding. Previous research will tell us what we might expect, but not what is actually the case in our class. So what is needed are ways to bring ideas quickly into the open, so they can be built on or challenged. Educational research may use time-consuming methods that probe more deeply, but, as teachers, we need to make use of the outcomes of this research, rather than repeat it.

Probing the cognitive structure of the whole class

Whenever a teacher asks open questions (see Chapter 8) they will be probing their pupils' understanding. What we discuss here are more focused methods for finding out the ideas about the topic held by the class we are about to teach.

Question, tell-each-other, vote

If previous research has already uncovered possible alternative ideas, we can use this method to provide a quick picture of where the pupils are in their conceptual development. Present the class with a multiple choice question, like those at the start of this chapter, preferably in cartoon format (Keogh and Naylor 2009), and give them 10 seconds (only) to make up their mind by explaining their choice to their neighbour (in a whisper). Now take a vote on each alternative using, for example, mini-whiteboards or hand-held interactive voting systems or simply a show of hands. This is more powerful, and quicker, than asking them to write, because talking is so much easier than writing if you need to clarify an idea. This 'tell-each-other' technique allows the pupils to make a commitment, which is now ready to be built on, or challenged. At this stage simply thank the class and say 'We'll take another vote at the end'. Assuming the class does display some misunderstandings we then need to set up discussions, videos, practical work, teacher explanations, etc. to challenge them. Every now and then we say 'Several of you thought [such and such]. Who still thinks this way?', and if necessary get other pupils to explain the problem. Take the vote the same way at the end to enable the pupils to make a commitment to the new idea (see Chapter 8, p. 71, for further discussion of 'tell-each-other').

Brainstorm

This is a similar technique, but useful if you are not giving suggested alternatives. Ask the pupils a question, allow 10 or 20 seconds for them to tell-each-other (as before) but now collect in the range of ideas. As each idea is suggested, write it on the whiteboard, and ask how many others thought the same thing (this allows a tally to be made to find the most popular responses). The important thing is to accept every idea as of equal merit, which will encourage a full range of ideas. As the lessons progress you can show the pupils how their ideas shift (we hope!) towards the more scientifically acceptable ones.

Written responses

If you want a more permanent record of the ideas of the whole class, one of the following written methods will need to replace the much quicker 'tell-each-other' or 'brainstorm' techniques above.

- *Concept Cartoons™*. Get written (or electronic) responses to the cartoon questions from individual pupils – or from pupils working in pairs or threes.

- Word associations and definitions. Get pupils to write the word/concept in an oval in the centre of a page, and write a simple definition inside the oval. Round the outside write all the words and ideas that they think are closely linked to the word. See Figure 5.15 and Sutton (1992, p. 61).

- Questionnaires. The advantage of a questionnaire is that it can be administered to a large sample, but it can require considerable reading and writing skill on the side of the pupil answering the questionnaire. If multiple choice questions are used they need to be based on interviews to generate the possible alternatives, and you need to ask pupils to give reasons for their choice(s).

- Concept mapping. This is a very powerful technique which can be used to find out pupils' initial ideas, but also can be used by them to modify or build on their ideas during learning. It is discussed in Chapter 10 (p. 86).

- Drawing, annotations, writing … All the techniques we use to help pupils make sense of their learning may also reveal any remaining misconceptions. All these active learning tasks are reviewed in Chapter 10.

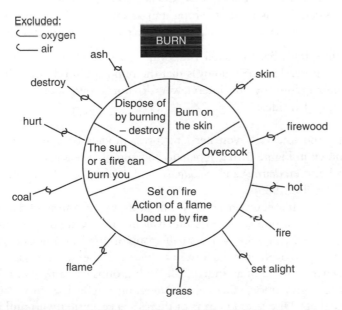

FIGURE 5.15 Burr diagram showing the way in which 'burn' was conceptualised by a group of secondary school pupils in the UK. Oxygen and air were hardly mentioned (from Ross and Sutton 1982)

- Everyday language and idiom. Listening to the way people talk can often uncover their everyday understanding. For example, in everyday English we say 'it's *burnt* away', 'no *animals* allowed', '*light* as air', '*heavy* as lead'. All of these imply meanings for the italicised words that are not the same as their scientific meaning. It is almost certain that our pupils will use these words in their everyday sense (see Grains of truth in Chapter 4, p. 36).

Please remember that, whilst it is important that these naïve ideas are brought into the open, you must not spend too long in doing so – that might serve only to reinforce the ideas. As we see in the chapters which follow, you must give yourself plenty of time to present new ideas to the pupils and give *them* plenty of time to embed the ideas into their working minds.

Interviewing small groups of pupils for research

There is a value in every teacher doing some original research at least once, for one class, on one topic, because this helps the teacher to realise the existence of these strongly held naïve concepts. The clinical interview, where the psychologist works with one child and probes their understanding (e.g. of conservation of volume), was pioneered by Piaget's work in the 1920s and 1930s (e.g. Piaget 1929, or search for 'Piaget' at http://uk.youtube.com). In their account of the interview as an evaluation tool, Osborne and Freyberg (1985, appendix A) provide a useful set of rules for potential interviewers, such as:

- Don't teach – pupils should not feel that the interviewer holds all the right answers otherwise they will play the game of guessing what you want them to say. Think of their answers not as right or wrong, but as *interesting*. Responses from the interviewer should be 'Tell me more', 'Can you explain why you think that?'

- Allow thinking time for what the pupil is saying – 10 seconds minimum wait before you ask for more. The main point is that the pupil should do the talking, and frequent interruptions by the interviewer do not allow pupils to think through and develop their ideas.

To help you conduct the interview you need pictures, models or apparatus. For example, the cards shown in Figure 5.16 will help to elicit pupils' ideas about burning – do they distinguish between *charring* and *combustion*, and do they see respiration as a form of burning (Gilbert *et al.* 1985)?

Although Piaget did his interviews on a one-to-one basis, we recommend that you try group interviews with 3–6 pupils, say in a lunch hour. The value of peer interaction, which happens when you work with a small group of pupils, cannot be overstated – and can often help to overcome the 'I want to please teacher' or 'I'm scared of saying things to a teacher' attitude of an individual. With groups some may be silent but the others tend to argue among themselves, revealing interesting information about their scientific beliefs. Discussion in pairs or threes at a computer with multiple choice (or Concept Cartoon™) questions is also valuable.

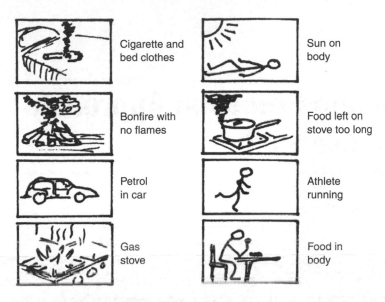

Cigarette and bed clothes	Sun on body
Bonfire with no flames	Food left on stove too long
Petrol in car	Athlete running
Gas stove	Food in body

FIGURE 5.16 The interview about instances technique – example of cards used to examine the concept 'burn' (from Ross 1989)

The importance of context

We have considered these naïve ideas in an isolated way in this chapter, but if pupils are to make use of them in understanding their world, the questions must be set into a meaningful context. Pupils may not be interested in whether ice melts faster or slower when wrapped, but they do need to understand the concept of insulation when they are householders trying to minimise their energy use at home. They may not be very interested in the weight of exhaust gases, but they need to understand the carbon footprint of using a fossil-fuelled car, and that means that they understand that the carbon in the fuel joins with oxygen in the air to emerge as the greenhouse gas carbon dioxide. Although we have illustrated this chapter with simple questions lacking in context we trust you will use them in the context of the topic you are teaching. Relevance is motivating.

Summary

Our ideas about the world begin to form when we are very young. These naïve ideas seem to serve us well – duvets do, after all, keep us warm, and food does seem to give us energy. Scientific ideas, in contrast, can often be counter-intuitive (duvets do not contain heat and food does not contain energy). However, once these scientific ways of thinking are fully embedded into our understanding they in turn become a powerful way of understanding our environment. This chapter sends a clear message that, as teachers, we need to find out what ideas are held by our pupils so that we can either build on them, or challenge them. It also warns us that if we want our pupils to take ownership of new ideas they need to be firmly related to their everyday experiences. How this is achieved is the subject of the chapters that follow.

6

A Constructivist Approach to Learning

Chapter overview

In this chapter we examine the learning process, using the exemplar of a burning candle, and compare it with the way scientists develop new ideas. There is clear evidence that children develop frameworks of belief about natural phenomena that often conflict with our accepted scientific understanding, and, just as scientists' own understandings have undergone revolutions over historical time, so children's ideas will also change.

Concept formation

Words and ideas develop and change in meaning as children get older or as science progresses over cultural or historical time. As our minds constantly try to make sense of our everyday experiences, we build up mental models which begin to fit with incoming sensory data. Consider the following example relating to gases.

Gases and vapours, to Isaac Newton, were ethereal, like light, sound and smells; they had no real substance. Such 'vapours' were classed as *imponderable* (meaning unweighable; here *pond* is the same word as *pound*, the unit of weight). Later in the eighteenth century scientists such as Lavoisier were trapping gases over water and mercury, and realising that they could be weighed, and thus came to realise that gases were real, substantial forms of *matter*, made of *stuff*, just like solids and liquids. This work led to Dalton's atomic theory in 1810, when he proposed that all matter, including gases, was made of atoms. The old idea of imponderable gases is sensible to many children and we cannot hope that they will come up with the new ideas by themselves, though some might! We shouldn't be surprised if they hold the same 'naïve' ideas of scientists of old.

It is often helpful to consider children as re-living the course of history as they grapple with the task of understanding their environment. By 'standing on the shoulders of giants' (e.g. through the input from teachers) they acquire an understanding unheard of 20, 50 or 100 years ago. A powerful way to help children with their misconceptions is to show them that other, quite learned, people saw the world very much as they do, and to show the children the problems with the old ideas and why new ideas were needed – the notion of *cognitive conflict*. Sutton (1992) suggests we should show pupils scientists' initial thoughts about a revolutionary theory, and ask, 'Well, Mary, what do you think these people had in mind when they put it that way?' (p. 80).

Not all topics lend themselves to this approach, but the principle that children need to have time and help to construct their own meanings is at the heart of modern approaches to teaching.

How we learn

By 'learning' we mean 'understanding' or taking ownership of ideas so they can be used and become part of our mental make-up. It was learning psychologists like Ausubel and Bruner who developed the concept of 'meaningful learning' (Littledyke 1998) – see the left column of Figure 6.1. In the right column we link this with the stages of a lesson developed by *constructivist* approaches to learning (Driver *et al.* 1994; Ross 2000b). Implicit in this figure is the need for the learner to be *motivated*, a necessary condition for meaningful learning. Motivation to learn will come if the class is well organised and focused, and the topics are relevant, or are made relevant, to the learner.

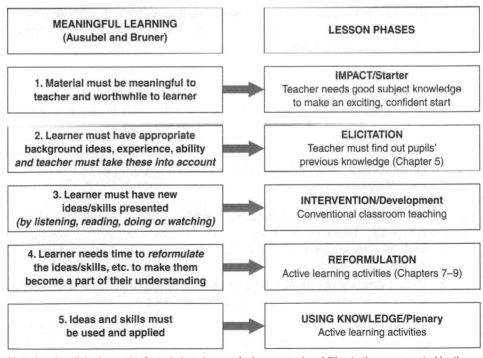

Note that the elicitation and reformulation phases of a lesson are in addition to those suggested by the National Strategy.

Note also that without **motivation** on the part of the learner meaningful learning is unlikely to take place.

FIGURE 6.1 The five conditions needed for meaningful learning

The five phases of teaching need not necessarily all occur in one lesson, but even in a coherent sequence of lessons which follows through these five phases, individual lessons will still use most of these stages (even if the emphasis is on just one or two). They have been encapsulated in the guidance provided by the Standards website (Standards 2009) for the phases that should occur in a lesson. The following is an [annotated] quotation from the site:

[Lessons should contain:]

■ a short **starter** activity, usually related to the subject of the current or previous lesson, designed to engage pupils with a short, stimulating activity [the impact and elicitation phases]

■ an introduction to the main **learning objectives** and focus for the lesson [intervention]

■ **development** of the learning (e.g. through interactive teaching, group and whole-class discussion, purposeful practical work, effective demonstration and the use of models) [a combination of intervention and reformulation]

■ **plenaries** to reflect upon and consolidate pupils' learning and to consider next steps; these can occur at the end of a lesson but are also useful when placed after any significant learning episode [a combination of reformulation and using knowledge].

To illustrate this approach, the discussion that follows uses ideas about how a candle works (see also Figure 5.3 and the related discussion in the previous chapter). The stages are illustrated in Figure 6.2 (p. 61).

Starter

1. *Impact*: Material must be meaningful to teacher and worthwhile to learner

The first step is to have material that is useful to the learner, and is understood by the teacher. Good subject knowledge by the teacher is important but more so is their imagination and sense of drama, if they are to gain the confidence and enthusiasm of the class. We need to get pupils to take notice of something, and be curious about it.

Example. Have the biggest candle you can find and also an Aladdin's (oil) lamp both burning as the children enter. It is also useful to have a bright lamp casting a shadow of the flame onto a screen. What is going on when a candle or lamp is burning?

2. *Elicitation*: Learner must have appropriate background ideas, experience, ability and teacher must take these into account

The next step is to see where the pupils are in their thinking. This was the focus of Chapter 5. Children may retain their naïve ideas right into adulthood. If we are aware of these ideas we can challenge them (or build on them) during science lessons at school.

Example. Ask the pupils, as in Figure 5.3, what the wick and wax are for. The children may think that the wick itself is burning and that the wax simply slows the burning of the wick. After all, a fat candle with lots of wax takes longer to burn than a thin one.

These two stages, impact and elicitation, have been labelled 'starter activities' by the Secondary Strategy. For science lessons this gives insufficient emphasis on the need to find out pupils' previous knowledge, hence our division of them into two sections.

Development

3. *Intervention*: Learner must have new ideas/skills presented (by listening, reading, doing or watching)

This is where traditional, but skilful, teaching comes in. We cannot expect pupils to discover everything anew as if they were inspired like scientists of old. We have already seen that pupils create, instead, their own naïve interpretations of natural phenomena. New experiences and new ideas need to be presented to the children. Teachers need to *intervene* with a new idea (or clarify an idea suggested by some of the pupils). However, to be effective, intervention must be embedded as part of this whole teaching and learning sequence, if possible by setting up 'cognitive conflict' where pupils' ideas are directly challenged by evidence.

Example. Pupils need to realise that their initial idea may not work. We could start by letting pupils burn a length of string (the wick) to see how quickly it burns and how little energy it produces. Teacher intervention gives them an alternative. 'Since fatter candles contain the same amount of wick as thin candles, yet give out much more light – couldn't the wax be the fuel, just like the oil in this Aladdin's oil lamp?' Give each pair of pupils two wax tapers which they light. They should blow out one taper and then use the other one to try to ignite the white 'smoke'. They will see the flame jump back and re-light the taper. This provides the pupils with powerful evidence: the wax from the blown-out taper evaporates from the still-hot wick, re-condenses as a smoke trail and ignites. They can then collect some molten wax on the tip of a wire (held in a wooden handle). When this is placed in a flame the wax burns – *without a wick!* But if pupils still prefer the *wax-is-a-flame-retardant* idea, they may only 'see' the wick re-lighting and will decide to reject the *wax-is-fuel* idea – to them it may still seem sensible that fat candles burn slowly because there's so much wax to melt out of the way. If we left teaching at this point pupils may 'learn' by heart that 'wax is a fuel' and get marks in teachers' tests, but still believe in *their* reality that 'wax is a flame retardant'. If teaching stops here pupils may remain trapped in their naïve ideas, and the science they 'learn' in school would simply enable them to pass exams and then be promptly forgotten.

Plenary

4. *Reformulation*: Learner needs time to reformulate the ideas/skills, etc. to make them become a part of their understanding

If you tell something to a pupil the chances are they will forget. They need time to translate from your intervention (teaching) into ideas that belong to *them* – the idea of *ownership*. Many times we are tempted to ask a class 'Do you all understand?' and we get back the obliging chorus of 'Yes'. The 'nod of agreement' from pupils hides a chasm of misunderstanding. The best way to check if we understand an idea is to communicate it to someone else or to apply our understanding to an alternative situation. The act of explaining is only possible if you understand it properly yourself. This is why so many teachers say 'It was only when I started to teach that I fully understood', and why good understanding of subject knowledge is essential for good teaching. We need to give pupils this same opportunity to teach new ideas to others, or themselves. How teachers can enable this to happen is the topic of the rest of Part II (Chapters 7–11).

Example. Pupils could be asked to explain why a candle and oil lamp both need a wick but a Bunsen burner doesn't. Hopefully they will now realise that the wick allows the fuel to get hot and evaporate so allowing it to mingle with and then react with the air. Alternatively, pupils could write and illustrate the life story of 'Walter the wax particle'; some will need to be told that the wax is a hydrocarbon – made of hydrogen and carbon atoms.

5. *Using* and *reflecting* on *ideas*: Ideas and skills must be used and applied

However well an idea is understood, it is likely to fade in the memory if it is not used. The idea of a spiral curriculum, where topics are revisited frequently, is obviously important, but in every topic we must make links to previous topics and everyday experiences. Pupils should see topics in science not as isolated things that they have 'done' but instead as a part of a network of interconnected ideas. Concept mapping is a powerful way to encourage the making of links (see Chapter 10, p. 86). Metacognition is also important here. The pupils need to reflect on their learning process.

Example. At the end of the lesson we need to do two things: pupils need to reflect on their learning and they need to apply it to wider issues. So we need to ask them: 'How did we find out how the candle works?' 'What did you think at the beginning of the lesson?' 'What do you think now?' 'What made you change your mind?' 'Which bit did you find difficult?' 'How can we make sure you still understand it next lesson?' And then we need to ask: 'Can we use these ideas to help us understand another scientific idea?' For example, candles used to be made of *tallow*, which is animal fat, used as a fuel store for the animal. So there is a topic link to respiration where food (our fuel) and oxygen combine forming carbon dioxide and water, and where energy stored in the fuel–oxygen system is transferred. It links with history in the way we used to live, and with birthdays and power-cuts where candles are used. These cross-curricular links are so important in making the science 'real' for the pupils – they allow them to use and apply their scientific ideas. It also links to our use of fossil fuels, and the way they join with oxygen in the air as they burn to build up carbon dioxide in the atmosphere.

Concept formation over historical time and through teaching

It is useful to compare the stages in this constructivist approach to learning and teaching with the process of how science works that we developed in Chapter 2. For our pupils we need to compress the concept formation process that has taken place over many centuries by scientists, into just a relatively few years of schooling.

Figure 6.2 repeats Figure 2.1, but with added help from a teacher. Instead of waiting for the inspiration of scientists through the ages to generate more universally applicable ideas, our own pupils can benefit from their teachers' knowledge. Without this help pupils are likely to remain in the first cycle of naïve knowledge at the top of the figure. Without the opportunities we give for *reformulation*, akin to scientists *publishing* their ideas, pupils may, at best, learn the new ideas by rote, long enough to pass examinations, but not to become a real part of their mental make-up.

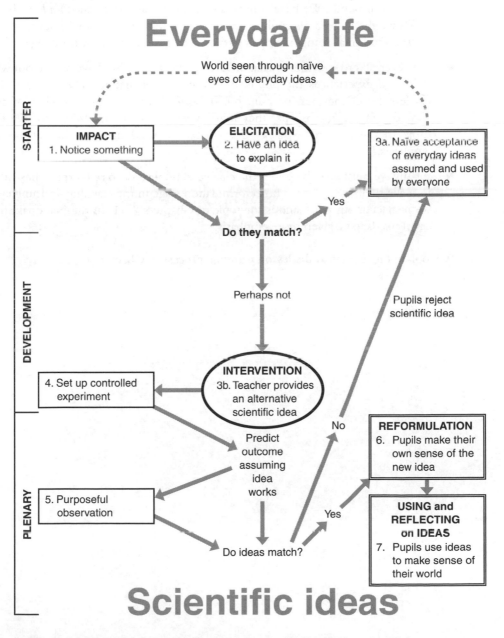

FIGURE 6.2 A constructivist approach to teaching (compare with Figure 2.1, pp. 11–12)

Summary

We have added five stages of a constructivist approach to learning (Figure 6.1) to our model of how science itself works (creating Figure 6.2). Our job, as teachers, is threefold:

■ Inspired by the creativity of great scientists we need to present their revolutionary ideas to our pupils. We have almost always done that – it is called *teaching*. In the 1960s we thought pupils could discover everything afresh, but without this *intervention* pupils may remain trapped in the naïve cycle of everyday thinking.

■ However, in order to know what intervention is needed we have to find out what ideas and experiences the pupils already have – elicitation. These might need challenging or they can be built on. In some cases (e.g. the existence of cells viewed under a microscope) they might need to experience things for the first time. In the National Strategy this elicitation phase needs to be given more emphasis.

■ Finally we must give the pupils the chance to publish or to reinterpret these ideas to make them their own. This reformulation stage in the teaching–learning cycle we neglect at our peril, and is the topic of Chapters 7–11. In the National Strategy it needs to be given more emphasis.

We look in more detail at the lesson planning process in Chapter 16.

7

Active Learning Techniques

Chapter overview

We teach science to help our pupils understand their environment. With human activity now making such a negative impact on the natural world our task as science teachers becomes ever more important in helping children understand how these changes can be countered. Evidence abounds (see Chapters 4 and 5) that children retain some of their naïve ideas about the world despite our best endeavours to teach them new scientific ones, and these are a real barrier to their understanding. This chapter introduces techniques of *active learning*, where pupils are given time to restructure their thinking to accommodate the new ideas. We may think we have successfully taught these new ideas, but unless we give children time to make sense of them they will forget everything very soon (especially after their exams!), and they will be left with little scientific understanding to help them make sense of and look after the world they live in.

Active learning

We are now ready to respond to the range of pupils' alternative ideas by using *active learning* techniques. Our teaching has elicited the ideas held by our pupils, and there are many who hold a naïve view (see Chapters 4 and 5). We *intervene* by challenging this view and presenting a scientific alternative. If teaching stopped there, we may produce a picture of the world in pupils' minds illustrated by the horticultural analogy in Figure 7.1.

School science is sometimes built up as a system of separate ideas, like a carefully weeded garden uncontaminated by the natural ecosystems of everyday life. Children learn about heat and temperature, atoms and molecules, fair testing and Bunsen burners, but do not build them into their everyday understanding. At best they have a scientific system that is good enough to pass examinations, but after harvesting the crops, the land is bare, the ideas are lost, and everyday life is unaffected (Figure 7.2).

FIGURE 7.1 School science (from Ross 1990)

FIGURE 7.2 Harvesting school knowledge (from Ross 1990)

FIGURE 7.3 The gate of active learning (from Ross 1990)

If school science is to be of lasting use, pupils must constantly make links, challenge their everyday ideas and see how their new ideas can be applied to understand the complex forest of experience that surrounds them every day. That is the task of active approaches to learning. We need to open the gate between school science and everyday life (Figure 7.3).

Learners need time to *reformulate* their ideas to make them become a part of their understanding. This has to be done through working with ideas and words, so-called *word work* (Sutton 1992). Figure 7.4 summarises the techniques available to science teachers.

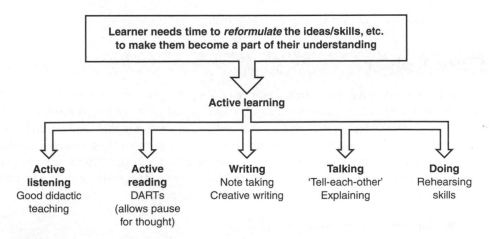

FIGURE 7.4 Active learning techniques

Active learning is not pupil-centred learning

We must be careful not to equate *active learning* with *pupil-centred learning*. Active learning doesn't usually give autonomy over organisation of the learning to the learner – many active learning tasks are very directional and specific; the main point is that they are impossible to do unless the children *think*. We cannot expect pupils to reinvent the whole of science, so their task instead is to take over the stories/ideas that scientists have used to explain the world. This may involve pupils having to modify their own ideas; think about things they have never thought to question; or develop ideas about phenomena they have never experienced before. In all cases they need time to *reformulate* and thus take ownership of ideas.

When we wrote this book we didn't write the finished text in one go. There were discussions, several drafts, and proofreading, before the final document. We were *reformulating* our experiences of teaching science in an attempt to make them clear to others. The process begins with talk – the easiest language medium to work with. One idea sparks off another. Everything is fluid. So it should be with teaching. Pupils need to be given the opportunity *to talk things through* before being asked to write – so our next chapter explores pupil talk; it also examines the power of role-play and *doing*, as a means to make sense of ideas. Reading should be easier than writing, but if the text is full of strange words, the reader may make no sense of what they read. Chapter 9 explores the activities we can devise related to texts to make the reading meaningful. In Chapter 10 we look at ways to help pupils write creatively and in Chapter 11 we look at numeracy.

A sample lesson

We can put these ideas into practice (refer back to Figure 6.2) by using the following structure for a typical lesson. We use 'force, gravity and motion' for a year 9 class as an example.

Aim: To revise the idea that when an unbalanced force acts (e.g. on a ball) the speed (or direction) of motion will change.

(See opposite and overleaf for the lesson plan.)

Pearls of wisdom

From the smallest grain of dust, oysters produce pearls (this idea seeded *The Pearl Project*, developed by Gloria Coleman, a much travelled and now retired Gloucestershire primary teacher). Her pupils found a 'speck of dust', an 'instant in time' and researched it to produce *pearls of wisdom*. It is a wonderful approach to developing subject confidence across the curriculum – a way of *using* and *applying* scientific ideas. Here are some grains of dust and some incidents in time, which can be grown into pearls – a chance to use the concept of force (or energy, particle, cell...) to explain everyday phenomena.

- You can see your breath on a cold day.
- A leaf 'floats down' on an autumn day (see below (p. 69) for a commentary).

STARTER

Impact

LESSON PLAN	COMMENTARY
Show the video Adam from Aardman on YouTube (select the bits where Adam runs round the small planet and when he throws mud into orbit). See http://uk.youtube.com/watch?v=CnVMtQe-2YM Now hold a ball high between your fingers and thumb and ask the pupils to watch very carefully to see what happens when you release your grip. As if by magic it moves towards the floor, with increasing speed, even though no one had pushed it. Compare this with a similarly held ball resting on a table.	The video will make them question their ideas about gravitational attraction and will be a stimulating start to the lesson. Then asking the pupils to question what is taken for granted (the ball falling) is one of the most challenging activities; it leads very often to some very constructive learning. Later in the lesson, they will see a ball gripped on the bench but connected to stretched elastic that will accelerate it along the bench when released.

Elicitation

LESSON PLAN	COMMENTARY
Ask the pupils what force or forces act on the ball thrown into the air (Chapter 5, Figure 5.11). Use 'tell-each-other' followed by a vote to obtain a range of responses.	We need to allow time, at the start of a topic, to take account of pupils' ideas and to respect them. Within each lesson we need to activate children's ideas so they can be challenged or built upon. On these occasions our elicitation needs to be brief but significant, so the lesson time can be used for intervention and reformulation activities. See Chapter 5 for more on elicitation and Chapter 8 for further information or questioning techniques.

DEVELOPMENT

Intervention

LESSON PLAN	COMMENTARY
Tell the story of Newton who suggested that only when a force acts on a ball will it change its speed or direction of motion. A (tennis) ball thrown upwards begins to slow down as soon as it leaves the hand and stops, at the 'top' of its flight, before accelerating downwards. Thus we only need to show it has a single constant downward force on it: the force of gravity that acts between the ball and the planet Earth. Ask pupils to put their heads sideways and see the ball thrown upwards as a horizontal movement and then (to demonstrate the effect of gravity) throw a tennis ball sideways along the bench but with a long piece of elastic attached, which you keep hold of. Pupils can now see that for a ball to move away from your hand, slow, stop and return, a retarding force is needed. Show the animation of this sideways flight using Ross et al. (2002: CD – Atmosphere).	The teacher must reach by providing alternative ideas for the pupil to latch on to before any restructuring can occur. Occasionally useful ideas will have been suggested by a child, possibly from previous teaching, reading or interest, but even then they need to be clearly re-presented. Sutton (1992) suggests we tell 'stories' to children of how scientists came to believe things as they are. Children then construct these stories into their mental map. Intervention can also allow pupils to investigate practically, gaining experiences and testing new ideas, then the reconstruction, which is to come, allows them to investigate using words. In this example we have the force of gravity pulling the ball and Adam round the planet, and pulling the thrown-up ball back to the ground. We also have the elastic slowing the ball along the bench and eventually pulling it back.

Continued

LESSON PLAN	COMMENTARY
DEVELOPMENT *continued*	
Practical/demonstration	
Use an air track to remind them that with no frictional forces the trolley carries on moving without any extra force. Remind them of the video where the mud curled round in orbit because of a constant gravitational force. Without this force it would travel off in a straight line.	
Reformulation	The 'eureka' feeling, when understanding suddenly bursts through the mental fog and a difficult concept is mastered, is one of the
Oral.	joys of teaching and it is the hallmark of someone who is actively
Pupils explain to each other why the three situations (Adam's mud balls in orbit, the ball thrown upwards and ball thrown along the bench with elastic) are similar, by focusing on the force that pulls the mud ball into circular motion or that slows and brings back the (tennis) ball.	taking over meaning. It is both the excitement of learning and the reward. It is often only when you get to teach that you fully understand an idea, and so giving pupils the opportunity to teach each other (or themselves) must be at the heart of active learning.
Written.	This reformulation phase of teaching and learning is discussed
They should then be given the elicitation question again and asked to mark and label the force.	fully in Chapters 8 and 9.
Practical/demonstration	
Let the pupils experience starting and stopping forces by using a human trolley (where you push a pupil sitting on a (large) skateboard – and use another push to stop them). This is best done in the playground.	
PLENARY	The last, but perhaps most important, of all of the principles of
Reflection on learning and use of ideas	learning strategy is that ideas must be reflected upon and used. It
Show a short extract of the video again, where the mud is in orbit, and throw the tennis ball on elastic once more along the bench, and ask the pupils to reflect how their understanding of what caused the change in motion has changed in the lesson. They could now try to explain the way they feel in a car when it starts or stops suddenly. Another approach to this is to give pupils the chance to grow pearls of wisdom (see p. 66 and opposite); for example, they could think about the leaf in autumn.	is important to keep all the pupils' scientific ideas active; so, for example, the autumn leaf will be useful in getting them to use their other scientific ideas as well as the concept of 'force'. In this case air resistance is important and the idea of terminal velocity needs to be introduced. Since all motion we experience is slowed by frictional forces of one sort or another it is important that we explain why things (such as autumn leaves and motor cars) travel at constant speed despite a downward or forward driving force.

- You hear the squeal of brakes.

- You smell toast burning.

The process will help our pupils see the science in the everyday events we take for granted. It will enable them to integrate their active scientific knowledge and make use of it.

Commentary on 'A leaf "floats down" on an autumn day'

'If gravity was acting all the time the leaf should fall faster and faster, so we have to introduce the idea of *air resistance* and *terminal velocity*. Why autumn? The seasons change because of the *tilt of the Earth* and the tree has insufficient sunlight to continue to *photosynthesise*. The colours can be linked with waste products from the tree. We see colour because of the three different *colour receptors in the eye*. Autumn is coming later because of *climate change* caused by . . .'.

In this way a number of scientific ideas are used to tell the story of an autumn leaf. It allows pupils to use and apply a range of scientific ideas in everyday contexts. From the speck of dust represented by the falling leaf a whole pearl is grown, made up of a wide range of scientific ideas.

Summary

Pupils' understanding in science is strongly influenced by what they do, see and hear in their everyday lives. If school science is to make any impact on their understanding, it must first of all recognise the influence of their everyday lives. We must not expect that one lesson will revolutionise their thoughts. Instead we must provide plenty of opportunity for pupils to translate the new ideas presented to them into their own words and meanings, and to use and apply the new ideas. This will give them the chance to compare the results with their existing ideas and hopefully show that these new ideas are better. This chapter has argued that our teaching must have *reformulation* firmly embedded into it – the next chapters give more examples of how this can be done.

8

Children Learning through Talking

Chapter overview

Only recently, and only in certain countries, has there been anything like universal literacy, yet almost everyone can use the spoken language. This chapter examines the role of talking (by pupils and teacher) and listening (by teacher and pupils) in the science classroom, especially in relation to the opportunity it gives pupils to reformulate ideas to make them meaningful – an opportunity to take ownership of knowledge. We also examine the place of role-play and other *doing* activities when they are expressly concerned with allowing pupils to make sense of the ideas they are being taught. Periods of silence, though useful and welcome at the right time, are less common in the science classroom than talk. The aim of this chapter is to ensure that this talk is productive.

Teacher talk

Listening to the teacher can be active learning – children in rapt attention, making sense of what you say, as you speak. University lecturers often rely on this for their effectiveness. However, pupils and students still need time later to reorganise and store the new ideas. They make brief notes during the lecture, they discuss it afterwards with one another, they follow things up online or in reference books and they produce their own written record of it in the privacy of their study. Lectures like this may be effective for highly motivated, resourceful university students and a few pupils and sixth-form students in school. But for most of our science lessons with most pupils we can rely neither on this 'rapt attention', nor on their ability or motivation to discuss and make notes for themselves following the lesson. A general rule of thumb is that children's attention span, even when there are no issues of behaviour management, is their *age in minutes*. Listening, watching and even practical work are more likely to be *intervention* activities, where the teacher is revealing a scientific story. The real learning, *reformulation*, comes through the activities that follow. This chapter will focus on the role of talk, and role-play – these are the easiest reformulation processes for pupils, and therefore the ones we should start with. Reading, writing and maths come later (Chapters 9–11).

Pupil talk

Pupils would talk all the time if we let them. The secret is to make this talk as useful as possible. Many lessons contain question and answer sessions where the pupils listen as the teacher questions a number of pupils in turn. Except for the child actually speaking, such an activity must be classed as *intervention* – with the rest of the pupils, hopefully, trying to make sense of the flow of conversation, but not able to try things out themselves. A few pupils will be silently rehearsing answers, and putting up their hands. Many will be afraid that they'll be asked and have nothing to say. A few may not care one way or another and be ready with the response 'I don't know'.

This sort of questioning happens in many science classrooms all over the country: good 'Socratic' questioning, with one pupil talking and 29 listening. Below we see how we can improve on this so that everyone has the opportunity to make their own sense of what is being taught.

Questioning technique

Ros Driver (1975) wrote a seminal article entitled 'The name of the game' where she criticised the way teachers in those days asked *closed questions* where pupils essentially were *playing the game* of guessing what answer the teacher had in mind. We made it clear in Chapter 5 that children need to feel that their response is worthwhile (even if mistaken) and we need to use the ideas that pupils have – to be built on or challenged. *Open questions* have no right or wrong answers, though some answers may be more appropriate than others. Such questions need thinking time – pause for thought – and not just for a handful of pupils, for *all* of them. As soon as we revert to praising 'right' answers and scorning 'wrong' ones the pupils will once again *play the game* of guessing what answers we want; they will lose their enthusiasm and their own ideas will be left uncovered.

Tell-each-other (talk partners)

'Tell-each-other' is a very powerful technique for asking class questions, which engages every pupil. We introduced this in Chapter 5 (p. 52). When a teacher asks a question they will usually wait for hands to go up. Typically teachers then ask one, or a few, pupils to respond. Instead, try saying:

'Tell each other [e.g.] what you think makes the bulb light up.'

With a year 7 or 8 class you might get away with '*Whisper* to your neighbour...'. Give them 10 seconds of talk, not silence. Perhaps half the pupils will have an idea and tell their partner (a few may be off task all together). You then say 'Quiet now, please: hands up those who have an idea', or simply choose people to respond. After hearing each response, you say 'Hands up those who agree?' 'Are there any other ideas?'

In this way every child has the chance to reply. How many disappointed looks do you get when a child is 'bursting' to tell you the answer, and you choose someone else? They can now turn to their partner and nod as if to say 'I knew that, didn't I?' – or else be thankful that their less appropriate answer remained in their small circle. The pupils who are asked to reply in open class have had the chance to rehearse their answer (verbally) to their partner, before having to speak it out in class, so far more pupils become willing to put up their hands to reply.

Many books on learning theory stress the need for 'wait-time' before accepting an answer – we tend to accept answers almost immediately, but should give pupils thinking time of about 10 seconds before accepting answers. The tell-each-other technique is no slower than this wait-time class questioning, yet it involves the whole class. Its value is that it allows (nearly all) pupils to rehearse their ideas *verbally* before answering in front of the whole class – it really only works if you restrict the time to *10 seconds*. If you give more time it is better to call it group discussion, and they will be given a more structured task. The key to successful discussion (or any activity) is the *tight control of time* – set a series of short, do-able tasks.

Where to use tell-each-other

Pupil *talk* must come before an activity, be it writing, practical work or a homework task. They need to be given the chance to make their own sense of the new ideas or information in the lesson. Tell-each-other is the simplest and quickest way to do this. Here are some occasions where it can be used:

- (Elicitation) In place of (closed) and open class questions (as above and Chapter 5).

- (Intervention) After you have explained a practical or homework task, so they internalise what they have to do: 'Now tell each other what you will do with your bean seeds'.

- (Reformulation) After you have explained an idea or concept: 'Now tell each other what you think photosynthesis means'.

Following this tell-each-other you can ask, as explained above, for a few pupils to respond in open class. This is not always necessary for intervention and reformulation activities but it acts as a useful assessment tool for you to find out if they really have understood!

Structured activities using pupil talk

When pupils need more than 10 or 20 seconds for their talk it needs to be structured more carefully. Here are some examples:

- Peer-group discussion to develop an explanation for a phenomenon ('Why do you think bulbs go dim when in series, but stay bright in parallel? You have 45 seconds to discuss this in your groups.').

- Debating an issue, having been given resources to examine (as in activities you can download from the upd8 ('update') website (www.upd8.org.uk), such as the genetics debate in Box 8.1).

- Planning a group report or Microsoft PowerPoint presentation on the results of practical work or investigations ('In 2 minutes I will ask each group leader to present the findings of their investigation.' 'You have 5 minutes to prepare two or three PowerPoint slides to explain what you found out.'). Note: set strict and short time limits.

- Deciding on an explanation prior to devising further investigation (e.g. the reason why white light goes green when it hits a leaf – see Box 8.2).

Box 8.1 A genetics debate

Having grappled with the fundamentals of genetics and cell division, pupils are in a position to get their teeth into the major issues of today. These are displayed readily on a daily basis via the media. They were epitomised when surgeons crossed a major medical frontier with the transplant of a human windpipe grown from adult 'stem cells', within a month of the Human Fertilisation and Embryology Bill being passed by the government. The bill gave the go ahead for research to take place involving the implantation of human genetic material into an egg taken from another animal, for example a rabbit. Together these advances pave the way for a host of innovative possibilities including regenerative medicine – when damaged body parts are repaired *in situ* rather than being removed and replaced by whole-organ transplants, for example, brain and nerve tissue regeneration. In one technique stem cells are extracted from cloned embryos created from a patient's skin cells and used to create mature nerve cells that can be transplanted into damaged areas of the brain.

There are many social, moral and ethical issues associated with such research, lending themselves to group and whole-class debate. This however needs to be managed effectively. To ensure that pupils can contribute to such debates they should be encouraged to collect relevant newspaper cuttings or print-outs from websites on the issues to supplement classroom-based theory lessons with their own wider research. They then take part in role-play scenarios whereby they access all aspects of the debate.

The following questions highlight issues that can form the basis of detailed debate and discussion:

- Should scientists be allowed to alter people's genes? Would it make a difference if the genes they altered were faulty ones, so that an illness like cystic fibrosis could be cured? What if they could alter sex genes, so that the illness would not be passed on to the next generation but the human genetic pool would be irrevocably changed?
- Should scientists be given the potential to create half-human, half-ape 'hamanzees' or real-life creatures from Greek mythology such as the half-bull, half-human 'Minotaurs'?
- Should it be possible to patent genes? At present genes of known function can be patented – for example, the cystic fibrosis gene is 'owned' by the universities of Michigan and Toronto – but it is not yet clear whether parts of genes or those of unknown function can be registered.
- Should food crops be modified to enable greater yields to be obtained? Who should own the patents for such developments?

During a class debate the pupils could have notes to support what they say, but insist that they speak *ex tempore*, that is, they do not read from a prepared text, but speak from their understanding.

Box 8.2 Coloured light and photosynthesis

Seal two microscope slides together with a thick band of glue-gun glue along three edges of one face so your pupils can pour into this a strong solution of chlorophyll, in alcohol, which they (or you) make by grinding up grass with ethanol and filtering. *Pupil talk* at the start is needed to elicit their ideas about how this green 'filter' works – it seems to change everything green. Some may think the light is 'dyed' by the green filter; others may think that the filter removes some of the colours leaving only green. They now use a ray box and prism to make a spectrum (the physics of light and colour) and you ask each group to discuss how the contrasting ideas can be tested. For example, if the green colour *dyed* the light, all the colours of the spectrum would go green, but if only the green was allowed through and the other colours were *absorbed*, you would see that the red and blue parts of the spectrum were missing. Following the practical work (or teacher demonstration) with filters the pupils then discuss which explanation of how the filters worked best fitted the experimental results. Finally you can help them apply these ideas to ask what happens to the red and blue sunlight energy captured by green leaves.

Showing a video

Many teachers use a worksheet to accompany a video. If we use the principle that pupils need to talk things through before they write, then why not give out the worksheet beforehand, but *forbid the use of pens*? Stop the video at a few natural breaks and ask the pupils to answer the relevant questions orally using the 'tell-each-other' technique? This enables pupils to sort out their ideas first through talking. It takes less time than writing so when the video restarts (promptly) they are all able to listen and watch again.

You can then get them to return to their places, pick up their pens and complete the worksheet (in silence if you wish) at the end of the video.

Doing practical work

Practical work does not necessarily result in active learning. If the experiment is to be more than recipe-following, pupils must be involved in the planning, must know what to look out for from their predictions and discuss the outcomes. The active learning comes mainly from this discussion, because the pupils' attention is absorbed as they are carrying out the practical activities (see Chapters 2 and 18). Here are some ideas:

■ Get pupils to *tell each other* the purpose, the safety points, the things they must do before they actually start the practical work.

■ Get pupils to predict the outcome of an investigation, using 'tell-each-other' (especially when there is disagreement between pupils) – this helps to make the practical work meaningful.

■ Get groups of pupils to report verbally back to the rest of the class from a range of (practical) activities. As they are performing the investigation they can plan what they are to say and each group can then 'teach' their experiment or findings to the other groups in the class. They should report back ex tempore, using notes, not a script.

Techniques, such as these, that make practical work into active thinking activities may appear to take more time – but if pupils know why they are doing something they are likely to be more enthusiastic and carry it out more efficiently and effectively.

Role-play

Getting pupils to act out being atoms, blood cells and so on can be a powerful way of helping them internalise the scientific stories we tell them. Having acted these out, they are more able to write creatively about what they have done (see Chapter 10). Pupils who are actually engaged in the role-play don't always see the full picture, so divide the class into two and have half watch (and criticise) – then swap to give them a turn. Here are some ideas to try:

Being atoms

Change of state. Although bulk matter can change (melts, boils, etc.) the atoms making it up do not change. Line half the pupils up in three rows of 4 or 5 pupils in a packed 'squad'. Ask them to link arms and hold onto the row in front. Draw a chalk rectangle on the playground round them to define the size of the **solid**. Instruct the pupils to wobble on the spot as the solid gets hotter. No one can walk through them. Now they drop their hands and move from place to place, but *remain in the box* as the solid melts to a **liquid**. Remember they mustn't take up any more room; particles of a liquid touch – there is little change in volume on melting or freezing. Ask a 'spare' pupil to walk through the seething mass – like stirring or dissolving. Finally the pupils break free of the mass and can walk in straight lines all over the playground as the substance evaporates to form a **gas**. Don't forget to give the other half their turn! This gives a perfect opportunity to distinguish between particle words (bond, vibrate, move) and bulk substance words (evaporate, get hot, diffuse). We meet this idea again in Chapter 12 (pp. 101–7).

Chemical change. Displacement reactions can also be acted out, for example where zinc (pupils wearing dark clothes) displaces copper ions in copper sulphate solution (pupils in blue clothes each holding both hands with pupils wearing white – the sulphate group).

Respiration can be acted out with pupils holding coloured balloons (C, H and O atoms) in groups of: *white-black-red-white* (representing carbohydrate) and *red-red* (atmospheric oxygen). The pupils then rearrange themselves as *red-black-red* (carbon dioxide) and *white-red-white* (water). Photosynthesis is exactly the opposite. Help the pupils with the origin of the word *carbo*-hydrate – the black *carb*on atom joined to water (*hydrate*).

Sound waves

Pupils (they have to be sensible ones) make a line with arms on the shoulders of the pupil in front. A gentle push or pull at one end passes down the line as a longitudinal wave. If the other end of the line is near a wall the pupils can reflect the wave off the wall and it comes back as an echo.

Summary

We have argued that talk should be the first medium in which we ask our pupils to express their newly acquiring knowledge. Pupils love to talk, and we need to channel this into useful learning activities. From the 10-second 'tell-each-other' to more involved discussion and role-play activities the secret is to provide a clear structure for this reformulation that allows ideas to be embedded. We should aim to make all pupil talk purposeful, never allowing them time to chat idly and always getting them to speak from their own understanding, rather than from a script.

9

Children Learning through Reading

Chapter overview

In this chapter we look at ways to make reading a more active process for pupils. Scientific texts are not the same as the narrative of novels, which can be read from cover to cover as the story unfolds. With our texts, whether online or printed, we need to get the pupils to pause and reflect on what they are reading – to try to make some sense of it. We deal here with the transformation of reading from an activity which gives information (intervention) into one in which learners have time to make their own sense or meaning as they read (reformulation).

Directed activities related to texts (DARTs)

The aim of active learning techniques is to allow pupils to translate the ideas they receive (by watching, listening or reading) into ideas that they *own*, ideas that are *theirs* and that they can use. Often pupils can read texts and answer questions without understanding – recall the discussion we had in Chapter 4 on *markobine gando* (p. 33 and Box 4.3).

Techniques that give pupils the opportunity to interact with the text they are reading are called directed activities related to texts, or DARTs (Davies and Greene 1984; Sutton 1992, chapters 5 and 6). In essence they all give pupils the chance to think and reflect about what they are reading. The commonest examples are *cloze* procedures where gaps are left in the text, but more demanding are scrambled texts that have to have their paragraphs reordered, diagram labelling (from text), annotations and many more.

Just as we pause in our teaching to ask questions and check understanding, so, with reading, we need to give pupils the chance to make sense of what they read. We can expect mature readers to make their own notes from published or online texts, but even during post-16 studies some teachers do not trust their students to do this, and so provide them with teacher-produced notes. If this happens, when do students make their own sense of it all? Are we asking them to learn these notes by heart to reproduce them in their A-level essay questions, trading it all in for a certificate enabling them to do the same thing at university? We return to the fence in Figure 7.2 (p. 64) all over again – science fails to impact on their everyday life understanding.

Our aim is to enable pupils to become students, to show them how to make their own notes, their own concept maps, their own summaries. This process should start as early as possible, and DARTs are a useful starting point. They provide the opportunity for pupils who still find reading hard and writing harder to make a clean written record of their work, but a record that they have in some way created themselves and therefore internalised. The essence is that writing is minimised. Instead of asking pupils to copy a completed text into their books we use the time to get them to read it and reflect on it. How this reflection is done is the subject of this chapter.

Which texts do we use with pupils?

Scientific writing can be broadly classified into four types:

■ narrative (telling the story of a discovery)

■ instructions (telling pupils what to do and how to do it, including word work and practical work)

■ descriptive (describing a phenomenon, such as a volcano)

■ explanatory (giving a theory, such as using particle theory to show how rocks, once solid, can become molten).

Only the first of these can be read as a story – the rest need to be worked at and internalised. Textbooks, and web pages, can be difficult to read if these types of writing are all muddled up. Nearly all modern texts for pupils use paragraph structure and boxes to separate different types of writing. Have a look at any double-page spread in any current school science text, and notice how this is done. It is worth trying to classify the text in each box or section on each two-page spread into these four types: you are likely to find that only one class of text is used in any one place.

There are two problems with using extracts from textbooks or web pages with your pupils. First is that the subject content of the text may not match your requirements exactly. A second problem is that the writing may be too difficult. There are various formulae which attempt to measure the *readability* of texts, the simplest of which is the SMOG test (see Box 9.1). This works by choosing an average sentence, and counting the number of words with three or more syllables in it. If the text has short sentences and few long words it is easier to read, and gets a low reading age score.

Box 9.1 Testing written passages for reading age – the SMOG (Simplified Measure Of Gobbledygook) formula (from Postlethwaite 1993, p. 113)

■ Select 10 sentences from the beginning of the text you wish to use, 10 from the middle and 10 from the end.
■ Count the number of words with three or more syllables in all 30 sentences. Call this number n.
■ To obtain the Readability Score, i.e. the reading age for the text, take the square root of n and add 8 (the minimum age it detects).

Suppose you find one long word per sentence (for the 30 sentences), making $n = 30$. The reading age will then be $8 + \sqrt{30}$, or about 14.

The longer the sentences, and the more frequent the long words are, the higher the reading age will become.

Writing your own texts for pupils (which solves the first problem) can be equally problematic. When we write worksheets for our pupils, the texts need to go through several drafts to make them readable and unambiguous. This is true even when we amend texts we have downloaded.

Reading for meaning

The ultimate aim is to produce students who are able to build their own understanding from the texts they read, the investigations they undertake, the things they hear and so on. Table 9.1 classifies DARTs according to whether the published text is modified (by us) or not (straight text), and whether the texts can be reused or not. Our aim is to move towards the top left of the table as pupils become self-studying students. In the following sections we illustrate examples from all four types. Note that these activities can be done either on a computer or with hardcopy texts.

Straight texts, reusable

- *Diagram labelling/table filling.* Pupils are given an unlabelled diagram (e.g. the digestive tract). They are supplied with a text or web page that explains the parts and functions. They have to label the diagram using the text. A similar activity would involve filling in a table: for example, of the functions of different digestive enzymes.

- *Note making.* Our ultimate aim is that students are able to make their own sense of what they read and so are able to make their own notes with no further help from us.

TABLE 9.1 Classifying DARTs

Types of DART	Straight text	Modified text
Reusable texts	Making notes from textbook or a web page Labelling a diagram from text	Card sort/sequencing Loop game
Texts written on or cut up and kept by pupil	Underlining or highlighting key ideas Labelling bits of text	Cut and paste sequencing (such as Figures 9.1 and 9.2) Matching/links (such as Figure 2.4) Cloze

Straight texts, kept by pupils

- Underlining key ideas. This is what some of us do when reading textbooks. In class we can photocopy a passage for our pupils – for example, about blood circulation: ask them to underline the sentences, or use the highlighter tool, that describe where blood is flowing away from the heart.

- Labelling bits of text. Pupils could ring, or highlight, all the scientific words to do with the circulation and link them to a short definition that they write in the margin, or as an inserted comment. They could add headings to summarise what each paragraph is about.

Modified texts, but reusable

- Sequencing. This is one of the most powerful activities linked to reading. Instructions for practical activities can be written in several steps on separate cards, on a sheet to be cut up and pasted into their notebooks or available as boxes of text to be sorted on a computer screen. Pupils have to put them in a sensible order before they can undertake the activity. Figure 9.1 is the nail-tube investigation from Chapter 2, but this time pupils have to match a reason for each stage in the practical work.

- Card sort/Matching. Pink cards could show scientific words and blue cards could have an explanation of what they mean: pupils have to match them. A set of cards containing plants and animals can be sorted (see Chapter 5, question 8, p. 44 for an example). See also the variable name and meaning matching task in Chapter 2 (Figure 2.4, p. 15).

In this activity on rusting the instructions are all muddled up. We have provided a reason for each step, but these are muddled too. Before you start your practical work you need to read and cut out the steps of the instructions, and the reasons, and arrange them in their proper order.

Instructions	Reasons
Leave for one week. Which nails do you think will go rusty, and why?	This will allow the nail to be in contact with air and water.
Fill the second tube half full of freshly boiled (but cooled) water, drop in a nail, pour oil onto the water surface to form a thin layer.	This removes any grease from the nails to enable them to rust.
Take three nails and clean them with detergent, then rinse and dry them.	
Put anhydrous calcium chloride at the bottom of the third tube, push in some cotton wool to cover it then drop the nail in. Place a rubber bung firmly into the tube.	Boiling expels all the dissolved air from the water, so the nail will only be in contact with water.
Put the first nail in a test tube with 1 cm³ of water in it so the nail is half out of the water.	This is a drying agent, and it will absorb all the water vapour from the air, so the nail is only in contact with air, and not with water.

FIGURE 9.1 Scrambled worksheet with reasons

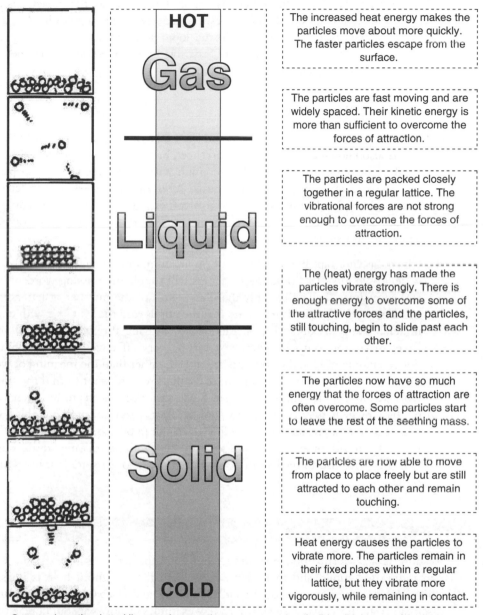

HOT

Gas

Liquid

Solid

COLD

The increased heat energy makes the particles move about more quickly. The faster particles escape from the surface.

The particles are fast moving and are widely spaced. Their kinetic energy is more than sufficient to overcome the forces of attraction.

The particles are packed closely together in a regular lattice. The vibrational forces are not strong enough to overcome the forces of attraction.

The (heat) energy has made the particles vibrate strongly. There is enough energy to overcome some of the attractive forces and the particles, still touching, begin to slide past each other.

The particles now have so much energy that the forces of attraction are often overcome. Some particles start to leave the rest of the seething mass.

The particles are now able to move from place to place freely but are still attracted to each other and remain touching.

Heat energy causes the particles to vibrate more. The particles remain in their fixed places within a regular lattice, but they vibrate more vigorously, while remaining in contact.

Cut out along the dotted lines and mount the temperature bar (solid to liquid to gas) in the centre of the page.

Cut out the diagrams and mount in the position that best describes the state of the particles (on the left of the temperature bar).

Cut out the descriptions showing what happens to the particles at each stage and stick on the right of the bar.

FIGURE 9.2 Example of a scrambled worksheet DART

- Loop game. Pupils are given cards (one or two each) that have a question on one side and an answer to a different question on the reverse, so that as each answer is given the pupil reads out the next question. However, once a pupil has had a turn (or two) they play no more part in the loop; so as an alternative try giving a whole-class set of cards to groups of, say, five pupils, who have to cooperate to make the loop on their table, domino fashion.

Modified texts, but kept by pupils

- Cut and paste sequencing. This cut and paste activity (Figure 9.2 shows an example) is also known as a scrambled worksheet, because the worksheet will be supplied to the pupils to cut up and unscramble, either on-screen or with paper and scissors or even sets of laminated cards. After the pupils have completed the unscrambling (with support if necessary) you can give out an A5 size completed version for them to stick into their books, or they can download the completed text for their record.

- Cloze. Leaving gaps in worksheets for pupils to fill in is probably one of the most widely used DARTs. Sometimes teachers will supply the missing words in a list, and sometimes they will supply the initial letter or the number of letters in the missing word. The aim is to ensure that the pupils read the sentence with enough understanding to supply the missing word. Leaving the working words (into, have, make, for) out of a cloze text can be very effective – it tests children's understanding of how the concepts are linked, rather than the meaning of words. Cloze texts suffer from the problem that pupils tend to want to find the missing word without understanding the text. Since each pupil needs to be given a copy of their own, it may be better to convert cloze passages into scrambled texts, which require a greater understanding from the pupils, and less guessing. They get to download, or keep, a neat copy of the text with no missing words, but one that they have had to read and understand in order to reassemble it in its proper order.

Summary

Reading is a powerful tool, providing rapid communication, but texts can be too demanding for pupils, and making meaning from them without help is a task we sometimes do not trust even year 12 and 13 students to do (see Chapter 21 for further discussion). In this chapter we showed a few examples of how we could break up the reading we ask pupils to do, and allow them time, through structured activities, to make sense of what they read. Further examples are given in Chapters 12–15. All the activities here give time for reading, talking and thinking, with the minimum of writing – the topic for the next chapter.

10

Children Learning through Writing

Chapter overview

We ask pupils to do writing in most lessons. There is a tension between getting a neat and accurate set of notes 'for revision' and giving pupils more freedom, with all the major headaches for teachers: it will be full of mistakes, it will take a long time to mark, they won't have accurate notes for revision. This chapter takes a candid look at the writing we ask pupils to do, and argues that their notebook has much more value as a drafting book than as a textbook – that writing should be used to make meaning for the pupils rather than to be faultless finished notes.

Traditional approaches to writing: strengths and weaknesses

Once upon a time pupils copied from the blackboard or from dictation to make a set of notes in their books, which they learnt for examinations. For bright pupils prepared to read their notes as a textbook, and make sense of them, the technique had some merit. However, lesson time spent copying is 'dead' time – wonderful for keeping the class quiet, but no good for making them think. If they have a textbook, or you have the text in a photocopiable or downloadable form, you can use this 'dead' time for a directed activity related to text (DART; Chapter 9) – the pupils not only have the text but will have begun their reinterpretation of it. You can then use their writing time more creatively.

There is some merit, however, in pupils building up an accurate written record of their work. Few textbooks will cover exactly the material at the right level that a teacher wants. In this case, unless they have kept their own record, how will the pupils review their work? An answer to this once again is for the teacher to provide 'accurate notes' in the form of DARTs, from which pupils make tables or label diagrams, and so on. The time that used to be wasted copying notes is now used to make sense of them instead.

Sometimes lesson time is spent writing accounts of 'experiments'. Once again, in order to ensure accuracy, we once resorted to asking pupils to 'write up' experiments in a standard way, often giving them help by dictating bits or writing them on the whiteboard. But it is not necessary for practical experiences to be written up in this way, even if we do include an *aim* and *predictions* to go alongside the *method*, *results* and *conclusion*. Our discussion in Chapter 2 suggests that there are many reasons for allowing pupils to experience things practically, and only sometimes is a written record going to be useful. More often the practical details are unimportant, and can cause confusion. A written record could focus on the scientific *ideas* that are being challenged or illustrated, or on the *description* of a phenomenon. Pupils don't usually enjoy writing, especially if they have no ownership of what they write. Many may happily copy things down – a task that requires little mental effort and allows them to dream happily of what they will do that evening after school. We can, however, use pupil writing more creatively, to enable them to make sense of the science they do. How this can be done is the subject of the rest of this chapter.

Moving away from teacher-as-examiner: some pitfalls and problems

We have already pointed out that published written work has to go through several drafts before going to press. The first 'draft' is likely to be a verbal discussion about what you intend eventually to write. Pupils' writing in science needs to go through the same process: begin by asking the pupils to *tell each other* what they predict, what they saw, what happened, and so on. They are then more ready to express their own thoughts in their writing.

When pupils write for us as a 'teacher-as-examiner' they will wonder if they 'have got it right'. It is therefore important to consider alternative *audiences* for their writing (Sutton 1992, chapter 10). For example, they could write for a newspaper, their younger brother, the class that follows or a web page, giving them confidence to write what they really understand and believe. This may, of course, contain misconceptions – so creative writing is a good *elicitation* technique too – but it is better that they expose their misconceptions early than produce writing that isn't theirs and that they don't understand. Pupils may need two notebooks, one for drafting and another for finished work. For those with a laptop the drafting can be done straight onto the computer, but it is worth asking them to *save their first drafts* for the teacher to see. This provides evidence that it is their work (and not plagiarised), and it is encouraging for the pupils to see the progress they made from initial ideas to finished work.

Creative writing and misconceptions

Below is an extract from the creative writing of an able Key Stage 3 pupil where they had the freedom to write about their ideas and where, as expected, a few misconceptions still remain. It is important that we praise the effort and enthusiasm put in, but also that we pick up on any misunderstandings displayed by the writing. Some of these are underlined in the extract, labelled as *1–*4 to help with the present discussion. It is doubtful if a teacher has time to identify all (or any!) of these for every pupil, but a general list of misconceptions can be given to the class after the writing has been returned and pupils can search for the misconceptions in pairs. Note how important it is for the teacher to praise these efforts – a typical teacher comment might be:

> *'This looks great and contains some good and useful descriptions (✓) but also some misconceptions – see if you can spot them from the list!'*
>   **Sp spelling error*

A Day in the Life of a Red Blood Cell

Yo, hi there! My name's R.B.C., well, it's short for red blood cell but, I don't like that name! Anyway, I'm so fit, <u>I travel round the body and all the organs about 70 times per minute,</u> [*1] impressive eh? Just think how many times I go round in a day! Well, I don't really have a beginning and an end to my day, I'm always on the move, I don't stop! As I'm your tour guide today, we'll be touring the whole body, well, I sure hope you're as fit as I am good luck!!

Off we go! We are now flowing out of the lungs through the pulmonary vein. We are taking <u>a last trip to the heart,</u> [*2] before we go round the rest of the body as I just explained. OK, we're in the heart in the left atrium, we're now going through the flap valves and into the left ventricle and wait for it LUB DUB!!! We're being pumped up the aorta and towards the body. <u>Did you know that the lub-dub pumping sound is the valves closing?</u> [✓] Ah, well, you learn something every-day, well, almost!

OK, we're travelling steadily towards the arms. As Tommy is almost continually moving, he needs <u>energy in the blood</u> [*3] to keep him going. Tommy's muscles work during exercise <u>using up the glucose in the blood and replacing it with poisonous waste products</u> [*4]. His <u>arm also uses up oxygen in the blood and replaces it with carbon dioxide</u> [*3]. The deoxygenated blood (the blood that has had the oxygen used up from it) makes <u>it's</u> [*Sp] way back to the heart through the vena cava.

Righthoe! <u>We are now travelling on to the kidneys</u> [*1]. Here the blood is cleaned. The <u>poisonous waste products of respiration</u> [*4] are filtered out and the amount of salt in your blood is regulated. Again, the <u>oxygen in your blood is used up and replaced with carbon dioxide</u> [*3] and the deoxygenated blood carries on back to the heart.

The following 'misconceptions' could be pointed out to the class – the teacher needs to make a common list from all the accounts for the pupils to find in their own and their group's writing.

*1.   The heart beats this often, but the blood only moves a short way at each heartbeat.

*2.   If you are conducting this tour going with the flow of blood you will have to return to the heart after visiting each organ.

*3.   We need to explore how glucose and oxygen 'snap' together to release energy. Their atoms rearrange to form carbon dioxide and water – see *4 – better to say 'react together' rather than 'used up'.

*4.   Carbon dioxide and water are the waste products which are removed from the lungs (see *3). Better to use 'poisons' for the materials we get from eating the wrong food or from disease. These are removed from the blood at the kidneys.

We consider this marking burden again in Chapter 17 where Assessment for Learning (AfL) must take account of these misconceptions. There is another example in Chapter 12 (Figure 12.1, p. 102).

Learning logs

Learning logs allow pupils to become aware of and evaluate their learning – a process called *metacognition*, which is an integral part of a constructivist approach to learning. Pupils' learning logs need to be honest, so they are not to be marked right or wrong. They should give us an insight into what the pupils are thinking (see Figure 10.1). As part of the plenary of a lesson it is important that the pupils reflect on what they have learnt. Following a brief 'tell-each-other', they can either write a log in the lesson, or complete their log at home.

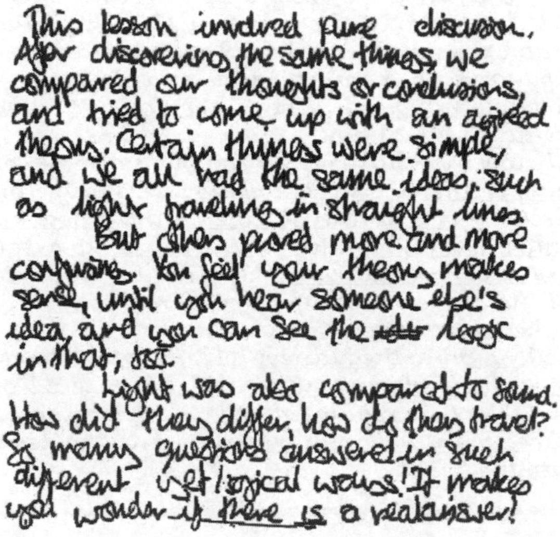

This lesson involved pure discussion. After discovering the same things, we compared our thoughts or conclusions, and tried to come up with an agreed theory. Certain things were simple, and we all had the same ideas, such as light travelling in straight lines.

But others proved more and more confusing. You feel your theory makes sense, until you hear someone else's idea, and you can see the logic in that, too.

Light was also compared to sound. How did they differ, how do they travel? So many questions answered in such different yet logical ways! It makes you wonder if there **is** a real answer?

FIGURE 10.1 Learning log written by a Key Stage 4 pupil after a lesson on 'Light'

Concept maps

Word burrs, such as Figure 5.15 (p. 53), show that there is a connection between two words, but do not explain the relationship. The real power of *concept mapping* is to label the *linking lines* (directional arrows) with verbs. It really makes you think about how the two ideas are connected. Figure 10.2 shows a map built up by someone who understands the constructive process of burning.

Pupils need to be taught concept mapping in simple stages. Begin by asking them to write a word to link two other words (concepts or ideas). Three examples are shown in Figure 10.3. Once this basic idea of linking ideas is established, additional concepts can be added to produce the completed map. When pupils construct these for themselves they can be very powerful learning tools.

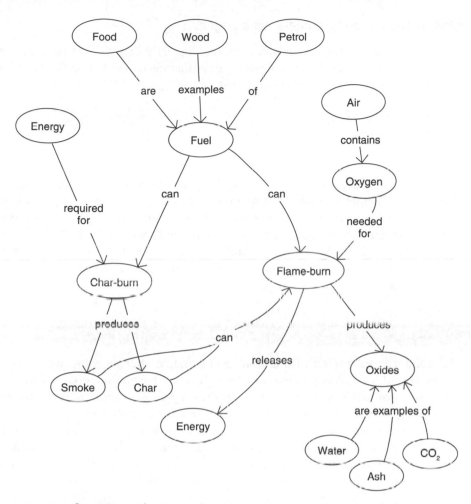

FIGURE 10.2 Concept map of someone who understands the constructive process of burning (from Ross 1989)

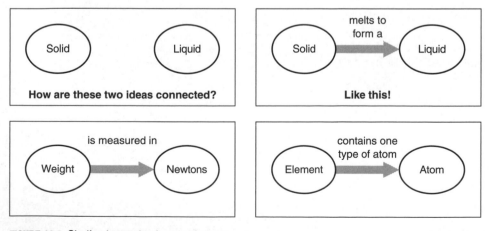

FIGURE 10.3 Starting to construct concept maps

Poems, films, cartoons, posters, web pages...

Writing poems is tough, but can have its rewards. These are the last three lines of a poem written by a year 10 student who realises that microbes, despite their bad press, are an essential feature of our environment.

> *So it's good in a way,*
> *But bad on the day,*
> *Let's love our microbes in every way.*

Creative writing provides an opportunity for pupils to express their ideas (and make mistakes). Whether you ask them to write a film script, a cartoon strip, a scientific report for a 'conference', a poster for the science room wall or a web page for the school intranet, the message is the same: pupils will be writing for an audience other than ourselves as teacher–examiner, and will take ownership of the task. However, they will make conceptual errors and we need to point these out while praising their creative efforts.

Summary

We cannot expect perfect writing from pupils straight off, so we sometimes resort to dictating notes or allowing them to copy. These are borrowed words and ideas. We need to be far more imaginative. Do we really need pupils to make a formal record of everything they do? Can we not use writing creatively, as a means to allow them to *reformulate* the ideas they receive in class, to try to make them their own? We need to make good use of word processing at home, and increasingly in school, to make the re-drafting process much easier. Just remember to ask the pupil for a print-out of their first (rough) draft to ensure it is their own work and not plagiarised!

Numeracy in Science

Chapter overview

Most scientists are numerate. When ideas are tested, data are needed, graphs are plotted, statistical tests are applied and ideas begin to have substance. In contrast, pupils often find numbers daunting and unhelpful. This chapter looks at ways to help pupils make friends with numbers, sometimes by letting the computers do the number crunching, and suggests ways in which we can introduce numeracy into our teaching to enhance the scientific understanding of our learners rather than baffle them.

Maths and science

The National Strategy urges maths teachers to liaise with staff from other departments in the school so that (a) there is a consistency of approach within the school and (b) pupils can see how important and useful maths can be in their everyday lives. You therefore need to agree with the maths team your approach (and timing) to:

- the use of units and how to get a feel for them

- how graphs are to be represented

- mathematical notation and terms to be used

- algebraic and other mathematical techniques, such as how algebraic expressions are to be simplified or how equations (especially simple proportion) are to be solved

- how and when ICT resources such as graph plotters or graphical calculators will be used.

The Strategy reminds maths teachers that almost every scientific investigation or experiment is likely to require one or more of the mathematical skills of classifying, counting, measuring, calculating, estimating, and recording in tables and graphs. Add to that: work on decimals; simple proportion, calculating means and percentages; deciding whether to use a line graph or bar chart; interpretation, prediction and calculation of, for example, rates of change in cooling curves and distance–time graphs; applying formulae and solving equations. So make friends with your maths colleagues!

Figures baffle

Temperature. Consider the example, introduced in Chapter 5 (p. 42), of mixing equal amounts of water at 70°C and 10°C. Many children simply add the temperatures to make water at 80°C, or, realising that this is hotter, subtract to make 60°C. Ask the same children what water would *feel like* if you mixed equal amounts of hot and cold water, and they will all say it would be *warm*.

> *Action*. Let pupils feel water (between 0 and 50°C) before they mix or divide it. Let them estimate the final temperature and then perform the action and measure the temperatures. In this way they can relate a temperature measurement to how hot the water feels. Eventually they need to appreciate that temperature measurement starts from 0 K so that a 10 degree rise in temperature from, for example, 10°C to 20°C is only a small increase in energy per particle. (For further discussion see Chapter 12 on rates of chemical change, pp. 117–18.)

Chemical equations. Science textbooks took to using 'word equations' to avoid confusing pupils with chemical equations. For many pupils, even at Key Stage 4, '$2H_2O$' is just a jumble of numbers and letters.

> *Action*. They can make some sense of the same thing if we use the atom pictures we see here instead of the figures. (For further discussion see Chapter 12, pp. 108–109.)

Electrical formulae. Pupils may be able to get the right answer by putting figures into $V = IR$, or *watts = volts × amps*, but how many will be able to appreciate, after that, that the higher the voltage the brighter the lamp?

> *Action*. Use the milk bottle analogy first, to help pupils get a feel for the meaning of volts, amps and watts (see Figure 13.2, p. 124).

Graphs. Even when we have translated the figures into graphs, they can be confusing. For example: which of the graphs in Figure 11.1 tells the *simplest* story of a ball thrown up into the air?

> *Action*. See the section below on *The stories graphs tell*.

In these and many more examples the numbers and symbols can obscure meaning, rather than enhancing it. This chapter aims to help you to make the mathematics *add* to the meaning not detract from it.

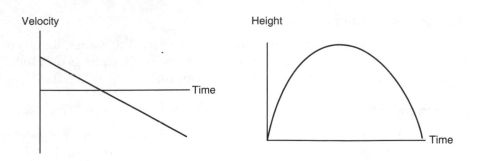

FIGURE 11.1 Graph of a ball thrown upwards

Units and measurement

Pupils will come from the primary school into year 7 with some knowledge of SI (Système International) units, but will still need plenty of experience to realise what they mean in real life. In the primary school they will often have used arbitrary, but meaningful, measurements, such as:

- Length: finger width, paces, football pitches...

- Area: squares on paper, sheet of paper, football pitches...

- Mass and weight: bags of sugar, house bricks, people...

- Capacity: jugs, juice cartons, watering cans, swimming-bath-fulls...

- Time: heartbeats, counting, 'as long as a lesson'...

These arbitrary units are not unlike the old *imperial measures*, which are still used today in the UK and USA, because these are derived from real objects: feet, stones, furlongs (the length of a ploughed furrow), barrels (oil industry) and so on. The *metric measures*, which are the basis of SI units, are more obscure, and we need to give them meaning.

The key to this is *estimation*, which plays an important part in pupils' work in numeracy in the primary school. They are taught to get a feel for what the answer to a problem will look like, so they can reject 'silly' answers (e.g. where they have moved a decimal point). In the same way, any calculation they do in science needs to have this reality. Pupils need to look at their results subjectively and pick out broad trends from their figures: 'the warmer the water the quicker the salt dissolves'; 'the closer the plants are planted the taller and more spindly they grow'. Let's look at some examples of estimation in more detail.

Force

Let pupils feel the weight of an apple – it represents a force of about 1 N. Then let them pull out newton metres to experience a range of forces. Finally, they can see if they can pull out newton metres (without looking at the scale) to achieve a particular force (say 1, 10 or 50 N). Their partners can check to see how close they are.

Length, area and volume

Let pupils estimate the *length* of the classroom (or a car...) in metres; the *area* of a room (or a football pitch...) in square metres; the *volume* of their lungs (or a bath...) in litres or cubic metres. They then take measurements.

Mass (and weight)

Suspend a full and an empty can of beans on strings from the ceiling. Let the pupils flick each can with their fingers so that they can appreciate how difficult (or easy) they are to get moving – this is a direct measure of their relative *mass*. If they are *lifted* the comparison will be between their weights (i.e. the force of gravity acting on their masses) and we are back to forces. The more mass an object has the harder it is to get moving and also the harder it is to stop – let them feel how easy it is to *stop* the empty can moving compared with the full one!

Power and energy

Try to relate all common appliances to a one-bar electric heater, which gives out a kilojoule of heat energy every second (1 kilowatt). Watts are actually one of the easiest units to experience: most pupils can see that a 100W filament light bulb (or 16W energy-saver) is brighter than a 60W (or 10W energy-saver) bulb, or hear that 40W speakers are louder than 20W speakers.

To get a feel for the unit of energy, a kilojoule (kJ), remember the electric fire, which sends out this amount of energy every second; a filament light bulb (100W) takes 10 seconds, but a 'low-energy' light bulb (10W) will last 100 seconds on its 1kJ. A person (100W) gives off this amount of energy as heat every 10 seconds, but how high must someone climb to store this as gravitational potential energy (GPE) or how much sugar and oxygen must they respire to transfer this amount of energy? See Boxes 11.1 and 11.2 for some answers.

Box 11.1 1 kJ of energy will lift us up by 2 m

A person has a mass of, say, 50 kg, and therefore a weight of about 500 N. Remember that 1 joule of energy is needed to move a force of 1 N through 1 m, so our kilojoule (1000 joules) will lift 1000 N through 1 m or 500 N (force of gravity on a person) through **2 m**.

Box 11.2 Climbing 2 m needs the respiration of only 1/20th of a gram of sugar, but living would require 500 g of fuel a day

Packets of sugar are labelled as transferring approximately 2000 kJ per 100 g when respired. So just 1/20th of a gram is needed for our 1 kJ. Our resting bodies transfer 100 joules (0.1 kJ) a second, so to keep our bodies ticking over all day we need $0.1 \times 60 \times 60 \times 24$ kJ, which is nearly 10,000 kJ. So 500 g of sugar will be OK for a day to cover our resting energy needs – about 150 sugar lumps. We normally get this fuel from our 'proper' food.

To estimate the amount of oxygen we need to respire this sugar is a little more complicated (see Box 11.3).

Box 11.3 Approximating the amount of energy transferred from the oxygen we breathe

Respiration happens (and energy becomes available) when the weak bonds in the oxygen we breathe in are replaced by strong bonds in the oxide products: carbon dioxide and water. Using values for bond strength, 300 kJ per mole of oxygen is available from respiration. (Interestingly, this value is independent of the fuel used, because the bonds holding fuel molecules together are of about the same strength as those in the oxides.)

When resting we breathe in and out about 600 cm^3 of air every breath (tidal capacity) – a cycle of about 3 seconds. Of this about 4 per cent is the oxygen we use (having reacted with the food (fuel) in our bodies during respiration it is replaced by carbon dioxide). So in 3 seconds we use (4 per cent of 600 =) 24 cm^3 of pure oxygen, which is 1/1000th of a mole (a mole of gas occupies 24 litres at room conditions). Therefore 1/1000th of 300 kJ, or 300 joules, is released in 3 seconds, or 100 joules a second – which is the figure we quoted for our resting heat output.

Clearly if we are exercising or working, we need to respire more, and we start breathing faster and deeper to provide more oxygen.

Speed of light and sound

To get an idea of the speed of light talk about how long it takes light to travel certain distances: eight times round the world in a second; 3 seconds to the moon and back; 8 minutes to the sun; 3 hours to Jupiter; 4½ years to our (second) nearest star. This also helps to give an idea of the scale of the cosmos. Compare this with sound, which travels just faster than commercial jet planes, taking 3 seconds to travel a kilometre and an hour from tip to toe of the UK. Every 3 seconds you count between lightning and thunder puts only a kilometre between you and the storm!

The stories graphs tell

In the primary school pupils will have had experience of bar charts, often for discontinuous data (Figure 11.2), and may have developed the concept of a line graph by plotting continuous data in bar format (Figure 11.3). We need to find out how much meaning they can take from graphs before assuming that they can make sense of the graphs we use in science.

They need to experience *the stories that graphs can tell*. Much fun can be had by asking children to find meaning in graphs of 'everyday' events such as eating a Mars bar (see Figure 11.4, and for an answer [only after you have had a go!] see the end of this chapter (Box 11.4)).

Once pupils understand what graphs are saying they can start constructing them themselves. However, using their own data, even class data, can lead to messy graphs with several anomalous points. It is important to account for these anomalies (see the

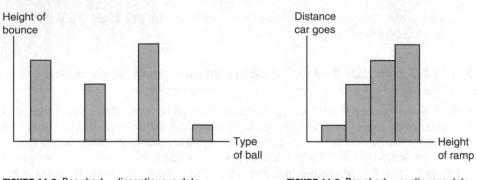

FIGURE 11.2 Bar chart – discontinuous data   **FIGURE 11.3** Bar chart – continuous data

section below on *Statistics and accuracy*) but if you want to draw a clear conclusion – for example, 'the more water you use the more salt it can dissolve' – it may be better to give them 'clean' data, or even ask them to sketch a graph from the class results to show the *trend*. In this way pupils obtain a clear *story* in graphical form instead of getting tied up counting squares in a vain attempt to plot their points on a graph. They may complete the task just before the bell goes, but there is no time left to look at the scientific ideas behind the experiment. The pupils go away with unpleasant memories of counting squares and grappling with numbers, when they should be leaving with new scientific ideas embedded, and ready to be used. Even spreadsheets can cause problems if the data are too untidy, but clearly they can be of enormous help, as we see in the next section.

Spreadsheets and data capture

There are many different skills required to use data-loggers and spreadsheets effectively:

- data input/capture
- manipulating the keyboard/data-logger
- using formulae
- producing charts, pie charts and graphs
- using graph-drawing packages within spreadsheets and data-logger packages to support the analysis of results from experiments.

There are a number of activities that can be chosen (e.g. calculation of speed and production of speed–time graphs; production of rates of reaction graphs for chemistry). The example given in Figure 11.5 was created by asking pupils to enter planetary data into a spreadsheet and then generate graphs showing the relationship between the order of the planets from the sun (*x*-axis) and their temperature, or time to orbit (*y*-axis). *Getting to Grips with Graphs* was the first publication from the AKSIS Project (*A*SE and *K*ing's College *S*cience *I*nvestigations in *S*chools). This book and compact disc pack aims to teach Key Stage 2 and 3 pupils about graphs (Goldsworthy *et al.* 1999). Their research suggests that pupils do not pick up how to construct and use

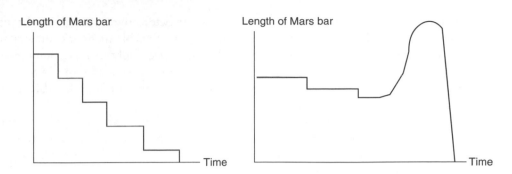

FIGURE 11.4 Can you explain these graphs of the length of a Mars bar against time? See Box 11.4 (p. 97) for an answer. Reproduced from A. Goldsworthy, R. Watson and V. Wood Robinson, *Getting to Grips with Graphs (A KSIS Project)*. © 2000. ASE, pp. 30–1

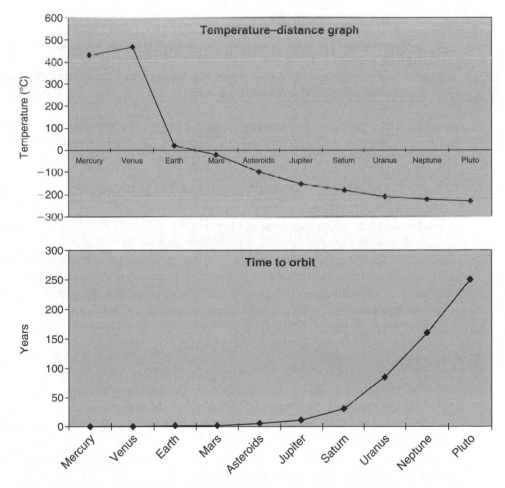

FIGURE 11.5 Production of graphs from tables (use of spreadsheets). Note that we have retained Pluto as a planet!

graphs properly, and we need to provide support before they meet them through investigations. The discs contain exercises for pupils, to enable them to overcome the major graph-drawing problems uncovered by the project; only then are pupils asked to apply what they have learnt in an investigation. Full details are on the King's College website (www.kcl.ac.uk/schools/sspp/education/research/projects/aksispubs.html); see also Figure 11.4 again.

When the data can be captured on a data-logger, pupils can see a graph of their results directly. There are several commercial systems available. One of the best sources of ideas for practical work involving data capture is Roger Frost's Datalogger-ama at www.rogerfrost.com (see also Frost 1999).

A final warning: by all means use data-loggers and spreadsheets to create instant graphs, but be very careful to ensure that your pupils understand the language of graphs.

Logarithmic scales

Consider this simple question about acid rain:

Remember that the pH scale goes from 0 (very acid) through 7 (neutral) to 14 (very alkaline).
If some acid rain has a pH of 3 and normal rain has a pH of 6, how many times more acidic is the acid rain than the ordinary rain?

Nearly half of a sample of 100 primary student teachers who had achieved a grade C at GCSE only two years previously said the acid rain was twice as acidic, and only 5 per cent realised it was 1000 times as acidic (unpublished data, K.A. Ross, University of Gloucestershire 2003).

Other 'confusing' scales are those for wind (Beaufort), earthquakes (Richter) and sound ([deci]bels). In all these a unitary change in the reading denotes a 10-fold change in the factor. Thus the change from pH 6 to pH 5 is a 10-fold change, 5 to 4 another 10-fold change, so 6 to 3 is $10 \times 10 \times 10 = 1000$-fold increase in acid concentration. This issue is discussed further in Chapter 12 (pp. 115–16). An earthquake of Richter 6 is 10 times more energetic than one of Richter 5. The famous film, book and now website *Powers of Ten* illustrates in pictures the scale of the universe by progressively scaling up or down in powers of 10 from a person having a picnic (see www.powersof10.com).

Statistics and accuracy

We often tell pupils to do repeat runs so that they get three readings, but do they understand the need for these repeats? Consider the *electricity from metals in a lemon* on p. 13. Pupils who change the distance apart but *only take one reading at each distance* may get results like these:

Distance between metals (cm)	0.5	1.0	1.5	2.0
Voltage	0.82	0.77	0.79	0.73

It looks as if there is a trend here, but if repeat results were made we would find that the variation in voltage within each distance is similar to the variation between different readings. In fact the variation may be 'real' and result from the build-up of reaction products on the metals; hence the drop-off is caused as the metals become contaminated over *time* (not because they are being placed at increasing *distance* apart).

Some investigations require calculations from data. These often involve the use of calculators or spreadsheets. We must get pupils to *estimate* the result, preferably in their heads, rather than rushing to punch figures into a calculator following some poorly understood equation. The result may have little meaning to the pupils. 'Have I got the right answer?' they might say, but when you examine their 'answer' it is quoted to six decimal places! Rounding off so that the result lies within experimental accuracy is much easier after they have estimated what it might be – don't let them quote meaningless insignificant figures.

For more help see *Developing Understanding in Scientific Enquiry* (Goldsworthy *et al.* 2000), written by the AKSIS Team – a pack of 21 units including:

■ how, when and why to take repeat readings

■ how to write better explanations and evaluations

■ how to interpret data

■ how to ask clearer questions.

Summary

It was mathematics that enabled science to develop. Dalton noticed that elements combined in simple ratios of their weights, and came up with his atomic theory; Mendeleev used atomic masses not only to build the periodic table but also to leave gaps for undiscovered elements; Mendel noticed the 3:1 ratio of types of peas, which eventually led to our understanding of genetics; and physics is often called applied mathematics. As children progress through their secondary school the science will become increasingly mathematical. We must ensure that this *supports* their understanding, by constantly asking them 'Does this make sense?' and asking ourselves 'How can I translate this into their everyday experiences?'

Box 11.4 Explanation for the graphs in Figure 11.4

The first graph is the bar being eaten in a sensible way in five bites. In the second, the person eats the chocolate off two sides, then one end, then the other two sides and the other end. They then put the bar in their mouth and pull it out (making it longer!), before plunging the whole thing in their mouth at once.

Knowledge and Understanding

Introduction

In these four chapters we cannot cover all the concepts in the science curriculum, but we can focus on some key concepts where research has identified misconceptions. We explore approaches to teaching them, explaining why children have difficulty in coming to a scientific view about them, and why the misconceptions so easily build up (even appearing in websites and textbooks – we challenge you to find some in this book!). The teaching sequence we proposed in Part II of the book relies on us, as teachers, to understand the ideas our pupils already have in their minds. We must either challenge or build on these naïve ideas, and then give learners the chance to reinterpret them – a process where pupils take ownership of the ideas and are given plenty of opportunity to use them. We resort to last-minute cramming when we fail in this deeper approach to learning. The chapters that follow show how important it is, in order for teaching to be successful, that teachers have good subject knowledge and a clear understanding of their pupils' ideas. They are exemplified by key concepts from chemistry (Chapter 12), physics (Chapter 13), biology (Chapter 14) and earth sciences and astronomy (Chapter 15).

12

Difficult Ideas in Chemistry

Chapter overview

This chapter shows how the big ideas in chemistry can be used as the basis for structuring learning. Sometimes the details blur the bigger picture: for example, pupils may learn how to balance equations but not understand that the process is an expression of the conservation of atoms, a concept closely connected with ideas about recycling our rubbish. We begin with these indestructible particles, which lead us to consider burning as a constructive process, especially important as the world attempts to move to a carbon-neutral economy. The oxides that form during burning produce acids and alkalis (the pH concept), another environmental theme. We conclude by considering the particles again in a consideration of the rates of chemical change, again putting the ideas into an everyday context.

Creating particle theories to understand how matter behaves

Consider the idea that matter is made of indestructible particles in motion: the *kinetic theory of matter*. Many pupils find this model unhelpful. Water is clearly not made of little bits, unless it is rain, and then the drops join up again. The idea that particles (atoms) persist through evaporation and burning can be hard to conceptualise: the particles imagined by the pupils are bits of real matter that 'evaporate to nothing' or get 'burnt up'. To show how difficult it is to relinquish the idea that matter is continuous, consider Figure 12.1, where an undergraduate, with A-level science, has illustrated an adventure story of a water molecule. The water molecules, HOH, are in the mouth, with salt particles (shown as separate ions, but labelled *atoms*). But note the *'watery solution'* in which the particles swim! The idea that matter is nothing *but* these particles is difficult for this student to grasp.

Matter is made of indestructible particles that do not burn away

This is from a learning log of a primary teacher in training:

> I gradually came to realise how much of a part 'atoms' do play in matter. I have always assumed that as materials go through the process of change, the atoms

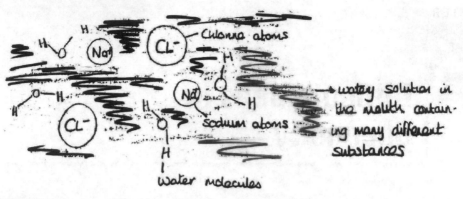

FIGURE 12.1 A watery solution (drawn by a year one B.Ed student)

from which they are made up, change too. However, I now understand that atoms are indestructible and I can look at any substance now and judge that, regardless of what change it goes through, the atoms will remain the same.

There are only about 100 different atoms, represented by the elements of the periodic table, of which about 25 make up the bulk of what we see around us. Many people leave school 'knowing' that matter is made of particles, but believing that these particles are just little bits of sugar, iron, plastic and so on. They think that the 'atoms' melt, burn, expand and dissolve, just like the materials do. One of the biggest barriers preventing people from understanding the world from a chemical point of view is the problem of seeing atoms as unchanging amid change: melting is when particles, previously in fixed positions, are able to slide past each other; burning is where oxygen atoms from the air join with the atoms in the fuel; and so on (Ross *et al.* 2002: CD – Matter). Table 12.1 emphasises this point.

We, as science graduates, already have the idea of atoms in our minds, so when we observe phenomena related to matter and materials, we see things differently from those who do not possess this idea. Our ideas influence the way we see things. As

TABLE 12.1 Bulk matter and atoms do not behave in the same way

BULK MATERIALS	PARTICLE MODEL (ATOMS, MOLECULES, IONS)
Ice melts The solid shape turns into a pool of water	Molecules once vibrating but fixed in a regular lattice are still touching but now slip past each other as they move from place to place
Wood burns The bulk of the wood seems to disappear, as gases enter the air. A solid whitish powder remains (ashes)	Atoms making up the wood combine with atoms of oxygen in the air to form oxides; most escape as separate molecules into the air, the rest remain forming a solid lattice structure (ashes)
Bulk words solid, element, crystal, temperature	*Particle words* unchanging, atom, bond, vibrate

teachers we need to help pupils to see the power of this atomic view of our world – without it they will understand few of the environmental pressures we are placing on the planet. For them petrol will burn away in cars, aerosols will disappear into thin air, rubbish will rot away to nothing.

It took decades of careful measurement of combining weights before Dalton worked out what it could all mean. His revolutionary atomic theory took several more decades to be accepted following its publication in 1810, but by 1869 Mendeleev had published his ideas about the periodic table, which we accept today. Two thousand years before all this the Greeks and, a thousand years later, the Islamic scientists both used notions of matter being made of atoms, but their atoms were not well defined and their ideas were difficult to test (Butt 1991). In the following paragraphs we highlight some misconceptions about particle theory you will encounter with your pupils in school (and maybe amongst yourselves as well!).

Be careful when modelling liquids

Consider a china cup, half full of water and half full of air. Figure 12.2 shows possible *models* for the arrangement of particles in a solid (china), a liquid (water) and a gas (air), all at room temperature. As a simplification we will consider the particles making them up as being spheres of equal size. Which of these represents the particles in a solid, a liquid and a gas? (Try answering this yourself before reading on . . .)

There is no problem in choosing A for a solid. Many textbooks and websites, however, suggest that particles in a liquid are spaced out, relative to the solid, so you may have chosen C for a liquid. But liquids are virtually incompressible and have densities similar to solids. The particles must therefore still be *in contact*, but now randomly distributed and able to slide past each other, so B is the only available choice. In contrast, gases are about 1000 times less dense than solids and liquids, so even D has particles too close for a gas at atmospheric pressure.

Be careful about how energetic the particles are

Kinetic theory suggests movement but the idea that particles of a solid are vibrating is not easy for pupils to accept. If we accept that the particles of the solid china are moving, are the particles of the water moving with less, the same or with more energy? What about the particles of gas? Remember they are all at the same temperature. (Again, try to answer this yourself before reading on . . .)

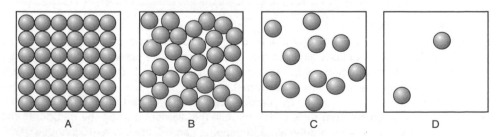

FIGURE 12.2 Which represents particles of a solid, a liquid and a gas?

Because most textbooks show ice turning to water then to steam, we have grown to believe that particles of a gas move with more energy than those of a solid at the same temperature. But the energy of a particle depends only on temperature. At absolute zero they are essentially at rest. Substances at equal temperature do not exchange heat energy (this is how 'equal temperature' is defined). That implies that their particles must also have the same average energy – otherwise the more energetic particles will knock the less energetic ones, transferring energy from one substance to the other. If particles of a gas do not move with extra energy a number of questions arise:

- Why does diffusion take place more quickly in gases?

- What makes some substances stay as a gas at room temperature when others, with the same energy per particle, remain solid?

Although the *energy* of movement is the same, the *freedom* to move is not: particles of a gas move from place to place, whereas in the condensed state movement is mostly vibrational. The state of a substance depends on the strength of the forces between its particles. Materials that are gases at room temperature have small forces; those that are solids have larger forces between the particles.

We have outlined above a number of misconceptions about particle theory – the next section suggests a way forward for us as teachers.

Review of particle misconceptions and ideas for challenging them

Misconception 1: atoms burn

Children often assume that our particles are bits of ordinary matter that melt, boil, burn and expand. But our particles are different and very strange. They can be used to explain what happens when substances melt, expand, get hot or get dirty, but the actual particles themselves remain; that is, *matter is conserved at an atomic level* (except in radioactive processes). This conservation of matter (mass) during physical and, especially, chemical change can only be fully appreciated if we consider matter as being made up of *indestructible*, unchanging particles that simply reorganise or rearrange themselves when real materials change (e.g. burning). It is helpful to recall that the Greek word that gave us *atom* means *indivisible*.

Ideas for teaching

Make a simple toy car from large interlocking children's bricks (e.g. Lego bricks or Duplo). Now make it into a different model, for example a person: the car disappears and the person appears (like bulk matter changes), but the actual bricks are unchanged, just rearranged (like the atoms).

Ask pupils what is meant by 'carbon footprint' or a 'carbon-neutral' economy. Explain that when we burn fuels which contain the element carbon the carbon atoms simply join with oxygen (from the air) and become carbon dioxide (a greenhouse gas).

Misconception 2: half-way liquids

Many pupils (and texts!) show the arrangement of particles of liquids as being 'half way' between a solid and a gas (Figure 12.2 C rather than B).

Ideas for teaching

Fill a 50 ml syringe with air and another with water. Ask your pupils to try to compress them – it is impossible to compress the water (but take care – it can squirt out!). Indeed, try suggesting that after your glass of pop is filled you could squash it down and put more in so you don't need to go back for a refill – your pupils will ridicule you. But no one will complain if you attempt to pump more air into a football that is 'full'.

Use a hair-drier to blow air gently up through a bed of tiny polystyrene balls held in a converted plastic bottle (fluidised bed *model* of liquids). The whole solid mass of balls gets no larger in volume, but sloshes about like a liquid if you gently shake the tube.

Misconception 3: fast gases

Many people (and textbooks) assume that particles of a gas must be moving with more energy than those of a liquid or solid. This is only true if the gas is at a *higher temperature* than the solid or liquid. Where the particle masses are different (as in the demonstration in Figure 12.3) the more massive particles will move at a lower speed, keeping their kinetic energy the same.

Ideas for teaching

Brownian motion: This is best viewed by the whole class using a microscope video camera attached to your data projector. Individual observations of smoke under a microscope by pupils is notoriously difficult to achieve (Driver 1983) so putting 'Brownian motion video' into a search engine will quickly give you a web version.

We can show diffusion in solids (a drop of food colouring placed on agar gel spreads out over a number of days), liquids (a drop of food colouring in hot water spreads over several minutes and faster than in cold water) and gases (set up the ammonia and hydrogen chloride demonstration (Figure 12.3), but note COSHH regulations).

Pupils can act out being particles. Use one pace per second (back and forth for solid; keeping *in contact* but pushing past each other for liquids; and pacing in straight lines until you bounce off something (or each other) for gases).

All these give evidence for, or an explanation of, *particles in motion*. The reason why diffusion in solids is slow is not because the particles have less energy, but because they vibrate essentially in one place, so these diffusion experiences will reinforce this misconception unless we are careful to link it only to the freedom to move. By showing diffusion in hot and cold water the link between faster movement and higher temperature can be seen. Solid state diffusion is achieved only because crystals have imperfections, allowing atoms to move into spaces – an important process in the heat treatment of alloys.

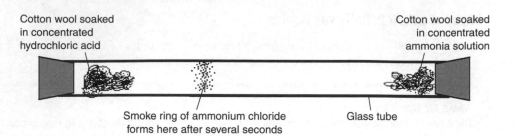

Cotton wool soaked in concentrated hydrochloric acid

Cotton wool soaked in concentrated ammonia solution

Smoke ring of ammonium chloride forms here after several seconds

Glass tube

FIGURE 12.3 Pupils might speculate why the smoke ring forms closer to the HCl end

Other ideas for teaching about particles

For all particle work we need to distinguish a *model* (trying to explain what we observe) from a *phenomenon* (something that actually happens).

For *models*, we need to remember that scientific theories are all analogies or models: none is absolutely true, all have their faults. We need to consider the good and bad points of each model we see or use in our explanations. Where is it useful? Where does it break down? Examples include:

- Comparing 'pouring' a beaker of peas with a beaker of sand to model the phenomenon of pouring water (shows that particles in contact can pour like liquid, but doesn't explain why diffusion occurs and doesn't explain surface tension).

- Using the vibrator model of gas and computer models for solid, liquid and gas (shows particles in motion but doesn't explain surface tension).

- Imaginative writing (model in the mind) such as Figure 12.1 (a good way to find out pupil misconceptions!).

- Creating a bubble raft model of metals, where bubbles can slip past each other while being attracted together (shows particles attracting each other but unlike bubbles, atoms don't pop!).

For *phenomena* we need to try to explain what we see using various particle models. Examples include:

- Look at crystals. What model is needed to explain their regular shapes?

- Place a loosely rolled 10g ball of (degreased) fine iron fibre on ceramic paper on a digital balance (reading to at least 0.1g). Ignite it with a 4.5V battery (wear safety goggles), and blow gently to keep the iron burning. What particle model is needed to explain why it gets 30 per cent or more heavier? (The iron forms the blue/black magnetic oxide at this temperature, with three iron atoms (= 3 × 56) to four oxygen (= 4 × 16), so 10g of iron becomes 13.8g of oxide.) Contrast this with most fuels which form gaseous oxides when they burn, so appear to get lighter or 'burn away'.

- Compare the hot gases from a hair-drier with those above a Bunsen flame by catching the hot gases in glass jars. Why does condensation only form inside one of the jars? Why does that same jar, when placed over a lighted candle, cause the candle to go out much more quickly than if you had used hot air from the other jar? (In this case we need to explain that the particles of the gas above the Bunsen burner are not the same as those in fresh (hot) air from the hair-drier. Methane and air (containing oxygen) combine in the Bunsen flame, producing new gases in which the atoms have rearranged themselves. No longer can we represent particles of the substances as round identical spheres. For chemical changes we need to represent the actual atoms: in our example, those that make up the particles of methane and air.)

It is interesting to survey science textbooks and websites to see how many perpetuate the myths relating to particle models discussed above. Even more interesting is to survey your pupils' ideas about indestructible particles. Refer back to Chapter 5 for more on *elicitation*.

Particle words to describe bulk matter?

What word do we use for these indestructible bits of the materials in our environment? The word *particle* causes immediate problems, since pupils rightly see them as little bits of real matter, which *do* melt, boil, burn and so on. But using the word *atom* is also problematic. What if the substance is made from *molecules* or *ions*, rather than being a giant atomic lattice (or inert gas)? How happy would you be with the pupil who labelled the *ions* in Figure 12.1 as *atoms*?

It is only at the level of atoms that indestructibility really holds, as we saw with the combustion of methane in the example above; and even then some researchers think we should refer to the atomic 'cores' (atom less its valence electrons) as the 'particle' that remains unchanged during all chemical processes (Taber 2002).

The National Curriculum uses the word 'particle' – but be warned, be careful, and always have the term 'indestructible' at the tip of your tongue. Then look out for the confusion in using bulk descriptions (particles are melting, they are getting hotter) instead of particle descriptions (particles break free from one another, they vibrate faster). We need to spend much more time emphasising that our particles (called atoms, molecules and ions) are very different from little bits of 'real' matter. See Table 12.1 again and mark it well!

Bulk materials (National Curriculum Sc3: Classifying Materials)

The matter around us comes in five forms (Ross 1997; Ross *et al.* 2002: CD – Matter) dictated by the elements that are involved.

- **Metals.** Metallic elements bond with each other or themselves to form metals and alloys, which are typically metallic structures. They deform plastically (i.e. their shape stays changed when bent or hammered), are good conductors of heat and electricity, are shiny and have a metallic 'ring'. Although most can be melted fairly easily they are hard to vaporise.

- **Volatile (molecular).** Non-metallic elements bond with themselves or each other to form small self-contained molecules, giving us volatile materials: soft solids that easily melt and vaporise; liquids like water and petrol; and all gases.

- **Ionic.** Metallic elements bond with non-metallic elements to form ionic compounds. If they dissolve in water or are melted they conduct electricity, but decompose. They have very high melting and boiling points and form brittle crystals which crack easily when hit.

- **Giant molecular – polymers and life.** Carbon, the first member of group 4 of the periodic table, forms (linear) polymers with giant chains of carbon atoms sealed along the edges with, for example, hydrogen atoms: includes all life structures, and polymers derived from petrochemicals. These are flexible and tough, and decompose if heated strongly (often forming a char and inflammable smoke), but some will soften and then can deform plastically (hence they are often called, somewhat confusingly, 'plastic').

- **Giant molecular – rocks and ceramics.** Silicon, the second member of group 4, also forms giant structures, usually with oxygen, but this time they tend to be three-dimensional and we get rocks, which are brittle and hard to melt and boil.

Our aim is to get pupils to appreciate the *bulk* properties of these materials, which make up the whole of our environment, and to begin to *model* how their particles are bonded to account for their behaviour. Note that the first three represent the reactive metallic elements (metals), the reactive non-metallic elements (volatile) and the compounds formed when they react with each other (ionic), whereas the last two are giant structures built from elements from the middle of the periodic table (mostly carbon and silicon). Note that compounds made from a group 3 and a group 5 element behave like silicon and germanium and are used in electronics – for example, GaAs and InSb.

Chemical equations

It amazes people to see molten iron emerge from a furnace where black charcoal and brown rock are heated strongly (and few will link this with the layers of rust that appear on garden tools left out in the damp). Chemical changes only become understandable when we see that beneath the outward appearance of change are the unchanging indestructible atoms – the Lego blocks of our real world – which we confidently express to our perplexed pupils in the form of equations. Balancing equations is often perceived as such a difficult task that it is only undertaken with the top GCSE sets and it is taught as an algorithm, as if the important thing is to get the right answer. One problem is that as soon as you mention numbers pupils get frightened (see Chapter 11). In consequence, lower down the school we make do with *word equations*, but these are also meaningless to pupils and so have to be learnt by heart to get marks. They simply name the reactants and products (using obscure names), and fail to provide the underlying particle model that makes everything so clear.

The solution is that equations should be taught at Key Stage 3, not using numbers, but actual atomic models or coloured circles, with the symbol in each circle. Until pupils can count the atoms in such drawings, you cannot expect them to understand balancing equations. These picture equations are easier for pupils to understand than word equations (which have little meaning). Chemical symbols can be introduced by labelling the circles, and the numbers we use in formulae can be introduced when pupils get tired of drawing out all the atoms, and need shorthand. By then they understand that a balanced equation implies the conservation of atoms.

Figure 12.4 shows a typical equation that we give to Key Stage 3 pupils in words. If coloured atoms are used it is simple to see that no matter has been lost during the marble–acid reaction and pupils enjoy counting to ensure that every atom is accounted for. It gives the word equation a whole new meaning. Balancing equations is not a tricky mathematical exercise, but a fundamental statement that atoms remain the same during and after chemical change – all they do is rearrange themselves.

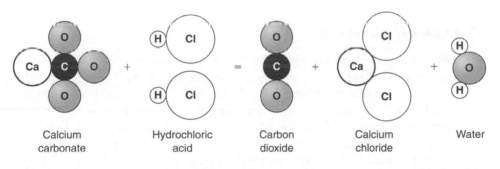

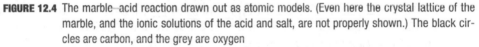

| Calcium carbonate | Hydrochloric acid | Carbon dioxide | Calcium chloride | Water |

FIGURE 12.4 The marble–acid reaction drawn out as atomic models. (Even here the crystal lattice of the marble, and the ionic solutions of the acid and salt, are not properly shown.) The black circles are carbon, and the grey are oxygen

Fuels don't 'contain' energy

If atoms are the same before and after a chemical reaction, what is the origin of the energy that is often transferred during reactions, either 'producing energy' as in burning, or 'requiring energy' such as photosynthesis? Chapters 4 and 5 are full of questions that help to show the distinction between matter (measured in atoms) and energy (measured in joules). On planet Earth, it is the matter that gets cycled, while energy degrades. The energy arrives as high-grade photons of sunlight and leaves as low-grade infra-red radiation to space. Without this energy balance the planet would not keep its constant average temperature.*

---

*Greenhouse gases make it harder for infra-red radiation to leave, so the surface temperature of the Earth has to rise to restore the balance between incoming sunlight and outgoing infra-red. Another factor we need to consider is the loss of heat from the interior of the Earth, partially replaced by energy from natural radioactive decay that occurs deep in the Earth's interior. Taking this into account, the Earth actually loses more heat each day than it gains from the sun alone.

Our use of fossil fuels has allowed us to develop a technological society. Before that we had to rely on a daily supply of energy from sunlight (which drives wind and water power and the life processes that power the muscles of beast and man, and provide wood for fuel). Careless talk suggests that these fossil fuels 'contain' energy. While it is true that the atoms within a fuel will be vibrating because the fuel is at room temperature, it is certainly not true that this supplies the energy transferred when they are *used as a fuel*. The same argument applies to food, whose packets proudly proclaim they have an *energy content*.

Let us begin with a simpler system, gravitational potential energy (GPE). Again, many will say that the water behind a dam has, or 'contains', GPE. In order to store this energy water has to be pulled away from the Earth (using solar energy). The energy is stored in the Earth–water system. Like stretched elastic, the more the two are separated, the more energy is stored. Because the Earth is 'fixed' we find it easier to measure GPE simply by how far 'up' the object has been lifted, and we say that the energy is stored *in* this object. We should say, instead, that energy is stored in *the system*.

The fuel–oxygen system

We can now apply this argument to the chemical system involved with burning and respiration. It takes energy to break bonds between atoms. The electrons attract the atoms on each side of the bond. To pull the atoms apart against this electrostatic force there must be an *input* of energy. If burning or respiration is to take place we need to separate the bonds of the carbohydrate molecules and the oxygen molecules to allow them to rearrange themselves as H_2O and CO_2. The energy transferred during respiration and burning has come from replacing the weak double bond (holding oxygen atoms in an oxygen molecule) with the much stronger bonds in the oxides. Energy is not stored 'in' the food or fuel, but it is available from the fuel–oxygen system (Ross 2000c; Ross *et al.* 2002: CD – Energy).

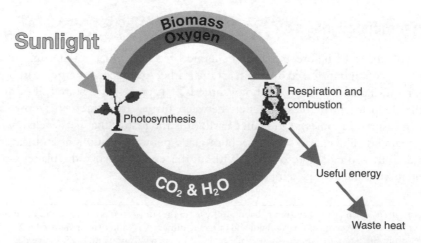

FIGURE 12.5 The fuel–oxygen system for transfer and degradation of energy (from Ross *et al.* 2002: CD – Atmosphere)

Photosynthesis and the role of oxygen

To complete the picture, we can now see energy from sunlight pulling the oxygen away from the oxides during photosynthesis. The whole process is summarised in Figure 12.5. Matter is conserved, represented by the constant thickness of the circle all the way round. Energy comes in as high-grade sunlight that 'sets' the system by pulling oxygen away from water during *photosynthesis*. The biomass produced will form the substance of living things and could be passed along food chains. When life needs energy all it has to do is to take the biomass and join it with oxygen, in a process called *respiration*. Biomass that has fossilised and that we dig up as fuels can also rejoin with oxygen, in a process called *combustion*. In both cases energy is stored in the *fuel–oxygen system*. It is important to realise that it will continue to be stored as long as the fuel and oxygen do not rejoin, so you can eat (digest and reconstruct into new cells) or fossilise the biomass and still retain its fuel value. Once you allow the oxygen back, useful energy is transferred. Eventually the energy is degraded and is radiated out into space as waste heat. Energy is degraded as matter is cycled. This matter–energy distinction is nicely made in the *saucepan model* for photosynthesis (Box 12.1)

Box 12.1 The upside-down saucepan model for photosynthesis

This 'saucepan' model helps pupils distinguish between the *energy source* needed to drive chemical change, and the *ingredients themselves* (*matter*). In a normal saucepan the *ingredients* are added, and the *source of energy* comes from the stove from below. In the leaf (upside-down saucepan) the *source of energy* comes from above (sunlight) and the *ingredients* enter, through the stomata and xylem vessels, from below.

The reason why we think of energy being stored *in* the fuel is because oxygen is freely available to us – our problem is getting the biomass. However, whales also have a problem getting the oxygen and when we send rockets out of the atmosphere, climb high mountains or go under water, we have to take oxygen with us, just as whales do.

The model fuel cell system in Figure 12.6 is a simple illustration of this. Water is split by energy from the sun – the *photosynthesis* stage. The hydrogen (equivalent to biomass) is piped to the fuel cell (like biomass carried along food chains), but the oxygen is vented to the atmosphere, as in the leaf. The fuel cell obtains the oxygen it needs from the air, just as we do during *respiration*. The energy transferred in the cell is 'used' to power the fan, just as energy from respiration powers our muscles. We need a pipe for the hydrogen – the food chain – but not for the oxygen. In this way we take the air for granted, and we think the energy is stored *in* the biomass. The prospect of 'clean energy' from burning hydrogen as a fuel (see, for example, www.altenergy.org/renewables/hydrogen_power.html) is based on the system illustrated in Figure 12.6. What many commentators fail to say is that our current source of hydrogen is from methane, a fossil fuel whose use contributes to greenhouse gas emissions. The hydrogen needs to come from a replenishable source of energy that can be used to split water.

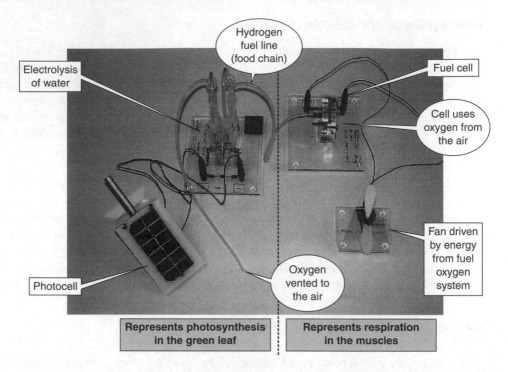

FIGURE 12.6 Electrolysis and the fuel cell representing a plant-to-animal food chain. Note that the oxygen is transferred via the air, so tends to be forgotten

Implications for teaching

It is not easy to change the habits of a lifetime, especially if the ideas we are using work so well – it is so convenient to say *fuels contain energy*. The reason why we urge a change is simple: if we fail to acknowledge the role played by oxygen, and the exhaust gases that result, we are in danger of perpetuating the myth that matter, at an atomic level, can be destroyed. Few people gain any real idea of the material nature of greenhouse gases, or of the other products of combustion such as the gases that cause acid rain. Once children appreciate the simple picture of the cycling of matter using energy from the sun (Figure 12.5 again), the carbon cycle becomes as simple as the water cycle, and the meaning of our *carbon footprint* becomes clear.

Note carefully what the Standards site says about energy:

> We want to avoid talking about 'energy use' and 'energy consumption', as this might cause problems later when we want to introduce the idea that energy is conserved. We can talk, however, about 'fuel use' and 'fuel consumption' without any inaccuracy. If the word energy is used, it is better to talk about 'using (or consuming) energy resources' rather than about 'using (or consuming) energy'. [...] The idea that foods are the fuel for living organisms can also be introduced here.

(National Strategies 2009)

In the sections that follow are some implications for teaching about fuels and energy.

Emphasise the distinction between matter and energy

The main problem here is the way we call biomass (e.g. cornflakes, coal, fat, wood, etc.) *energy*. Call it *fuel*, and emphasise that they only transfer energy when they combine with oxygen during respiration (except during *anaerobic respiration*, where a small amount of energy is transferred by rearrangement of the bonds in the molecules).

Emphasise that gases are the material products of combustion

Flames, hot air and exhaust gases are often considered to be forms of energy; certainly the life-world view is that they are weightless. We need to take account of where matter goes during burning, by collecting exhaust gases from above a flame and seeing the water condense, or placing them over a burning candle and seeing that it burns less well in this 'used air'. Our everyday experiences tell us that burning is a destructive process – only ashes remain. We must encourage pupils to see the exhaust gases that escape to the air as being massive, and to use this as evidence of an increase in mass as oxides are *built up*. Some five-year-olds described what happens to petrol in a car like this: 'it goes into steam and it's all warm ... 'cos every time we cross the road I can feel it across my legs' (Ross *et al.* 2002: CD – Energy). This is a rich and useful experience that needs to be built upon. Water is not often perceived to be a *product of combustion*, nor is the carbon dioxide that we breathe out often perceived as an oxidation product of the food we eat. Again, how many see the ashes left after a wood fire as oxides of the metals that were taken in as minerals during the lifetime of the tree? Only when these oxide products of respiration and combustion are given more prominence will pupils begin to appreciate these processes as *constructive* rather than *destructive*.

Use the particle concept primarily to explain the conservation of matter

If matter is created or destroyed then atoms must come and go. We need to use the *particle concept* to explain that during physical and chemical changes such as evaporation and burning the atoms are still there, in the same amounts. When chemical equations are written the use of atomic models or drawings allows the actual atoms to be counted on each side (note Figure 12.4 again).

Emphasise the role of oxygen in combustion and respiration

There is plenty of evidence that we rely on oxygen every second of our lives. It is oxygen that we take with us on high mountains, in aircraft and under the sea. We pant after vigorous exercise. The three dramatic demonstrations in Boxes 12.2, 12.3 and 12.4 show the need for oxygen (air) when fuels burn.

Box 12.2 The exploding can

Make holes in the base and lid of an empty metal 2 lb syrup tin just smaller than a pencil. Grease the lid with petroleum jelly and replace it. Have two bits of tape ready to cover the holes after filling with natural gas (methane). Do this by holding the rubber gas tube (from a Bunsen burner) over the top hole, and waiting for 10 seconds as the methane displaces the air out through the bottom hole. The sealed tin is now ready for the demonstration. Place the tin on a tripod, remove both tapes and light the gas that comes out of the hole in the lid. The flame is initially yellow, like a Bunsen with the air hole closed. Pure methane is coming from the tin. As the methane is burnt, air enters from the base. Only when there is enough air in the air/methane mixture in the tin will the flame spread into the tin. The flame acts like the spark in a car engine cylinder full of a petrol/air mixture. The bang blows the lid into the air, there is a flash of flame and the can gets hot. Ask your pupils why the gas in the tin did *not* burn when you first lit the flame.

Safety: Do not try this with bottled gas, which is too dense.

Box 12.3 Using methane to extinguish a candle

Fill a large gas jar with methane, and have another 'empty' one (i.e. it has air in it) ready. Light a candle perched on the top of a pole and lower the air-filled jar over it. It burns normally. Ask the pupils to predict what will happen to the flame if you lower the methane-filled jar over it. When you do lower it over the lighted candle (see safety note below) the methane will ignite, but the candle will go out. You can lift and lower the jar several times, and each time the candle re-lights then goes out, and the methane continues to burn up into the jar. Point out the condensation inside the jar (water is a product of combustion).

Safety: Hold the jar containing methane at a slight angle, down and away from you, so the flame doesn't come up over your hand. Do not try this with bottled gas, which is too dense.

Box 12.4 Dangerous powder/air mixtures

Hold any powdered food (custard, milk, flour...) on a spoon in a Bunsen flame, and nothing much happens (see safety note below). Sprinkle the powder from high over the flame, and the result is spectacular. The difference is that the sprinkled powder is mixed with air, so there is oxygen available for the combustion reaction. Gear wheels in flour mills were never metal on metal to avoid making sparks that could ignite flour dust. Ask your pupils why the powder on the spoon did not burn well.

Safety: All must wear eye protection, keep pupils well away, have the Bunsen burner in the middle of the bench and sprinkle from a spoon that is tied onto a pole to avoid your hand being above the flame.

Avoid the use of the term 'high-energy bond' in ATP (at A-level)

The third phosphate group in adenosine triphosphate (ATP) is weakly bonded to the rest of the molecule. ATP is therefore a reactive molecule. By breaking this weak bond and replacing it with a stronger bond, energy is made available to do useful things in the cell. To reset the system, energy from the glucose–oxygen system is used. Energy is not released when the 'high-energy' bond breaks, but comes, instead, when stronger bonds are made, replacing the easily broken weak bond.

Teaching acidity and the pH concept

The word 'acid' comes from the Greek '*oxys*' meaning sour, the acid taste. Pupils will be familiar with some natural (organic) acids, such as citric, lactic and acetic, found in lemons, sour milk and vinegar (literally *vin*, wine, and *egar*, sour, from the same root as *acrid*), but they are likely to associate acids with danger and burning. All acids will sting if you have an open wound, but it is the mineral acids, associated with acid rain and derived from non-metal oxides, that cause most damage.

If you can gain access to the food technology area of the school you can set up a tasting exercise where pupils can use solutions of sugar (sweet), citric acid (sour), salt (salt) and coffee (bitter) to detect areas of the tongue that are sensitive to the four tastes. If sodium bicarbonate is provided as a powder, they can try adding a little to their tongue while the citric acid is there, and notice that the acidity is neutralised or 'cured'. Sugar *appears* to do the same thing, but it is only the sensation that is masked; the acidity is still there, as you can see if you use a pH indicator.

Indicators from red cabbage

Many plant pigments act as indicators, but red cabbage must be one of the best and is certainly very easy to make. Keep sachets of red cabbage in the freezer and when required smash them with a hammer when still frozen. Boiling water or cold methylated spirit (hazard) can be used to extract the colour using a pestle and mortar.

Pupils can put samples of common household products (ash, lemon juice, bicarb, washing soda, Epsom salts, aspirin, ammonia, vinegar, etc.), adding water if necessary, into labelled pairs of test tubes arranged in two test-tube racks opposite each other. The red cabbage extract is added to one rack, and full-range indicator (for which a pH colour card is available) to the other. Pupils can then rearrange the tubes in order of pH, according to the full-range indicator, thus making their own pH colour chart for their home-made indicator. All subsequent experiments can use their own indicator, now that they know the pH corresponding to each red cabbage colour (Ross *et al.* 2002: CD – Atmosphere).

The pH concept: telling the story

At first pH is going to seem a rather funny numbering system: from 0 to 14, with neutral being 7. To make sense of this requires knowledge of the ionisation of water and hydrogen ion concentrations. This is beyond the comprehension of most pupils at Key Stage 3, but it is possible to show them that the scale is logarithmic (see Box 12.5). For every change of one unit on the scale, the acidity changes by a factor of 10. There are many such logarithmic scales used in science, and all need careful introduction (see Chapter 11 for further discussion, p. 96).

Box 12.5 pH is a logarithmic scale

Give pupils a boiling tube with a tenth molar solution of either hydrochloric acid or sodium hydroxide. They should have a pH of 1 and 13 respectively. Pupils can then take $1\,cm^3$ of the original solution and add $9\,cm^3$ of water, making it 10 times less concentrated. The dilution can be done once or twice more. Using their red cabbage indicator (or a pH meter), they will see that each 10-fold dilution changes the pH by approximately one unit.

Acid rain

Oxides of sulphur and nitrogen which enter the atmosphere dissolve and cause acid rain. Most books and websites start the story from the burning of fossil fuels and consider the damage done to ecosystems. But we need to go further back than that to find the origin of the nitrogen and sulphur. Setting the science in an environmentally important context motivates pupils to want to understand.

Sulphur and nitrogen are essential elements to life, brought into plants through sulphate and nitrate minerals in the soil. During the conditions of high temperature and pressure of fossilisation much of the oxygen and nitrogen in the organic molecules becomes detached, but the sulphur atoms remain bonded. Millions of years later they are released as sulphur dioxide when the fuel burns (animated in Ross *et al.* 2002: CD – Atmosphere).

Nitrogen oxides on the other hand are produced from car exhausts. The cylinders of internal combustion engines are filled with a little bit of vaporised fuel but mostly with air – and this is mostly nitrogen, with some oxygen. Under the conditions of high temperature and pressure in the cylinder, similar to a lightning flash, small amounts of nitrogen join with oxygen, forming small amounts of nitrogen oxides. The nitrogen and sulphur in acid rain are beneficial – it is the hydrogen ions that cause the damage.

Rates of reaction

This topic is another example of how we conspire to make things difficult for pupils. We give them reactions to perform that are obscure and unrelated to everyday life (e.g. marble and acid, thiosulphate and acid) in order to teach them something about how chemical changes progress.

All around us are the slow reactions of life, waiting to be examined and explored. Our aim is to share with pupils our ideas about what makes a chemical reaction sometimes go fast, and at other times go slow. Following these everyday examples of chemical change we can develop the *collision theory* model to explain why reactions go faster when we increase the surface area (of a solid reactant), the concentration (of a reactant in solution) or the temperature. We do not need to resort to test tubes and strange chemicals to experience these effects.

Particle size – the smaller the size the faster the reaction

- Cooking provides us with the easiest set of examples. Small potatoes, or cut up potatoes, cook more quickly than large ones (whether boiling, baking or making chips). Eggs cook faster when scrambled rather than poached, or when made into an omelette rather than fried.

- Warm-blooded mammals need to digest their food quickly, so they have crushing and grinding mechanisms called jaws and teeth to ensure the food is in small bits. Warm-blooded birds use stones in their gizzard. Contrast this with a snake, which swallows prey whole and needs to wait for days for the digestion process to reach the inside of the animal it swallowed.

- Small twigs burn more quickly than large logs, because the oxygen from the air can reach them more easily.

Concentration – the higher the concentration (of a solution) the faster the reaction

- Bleach is more effective and works faster (and is more dangerous) when used undiluted. This is true for all cleansing solutions.

Temperature – the higher the temperature the faster the reaction (usually)

- For every 10°C rise in temperature the rate of slow biochemical change approximately doubles. Trees in the tundra (5°C) take 40 years to mature, trees in our temperate woods (15°C) mature in 20 years and in the tropics (25°C) they take 10 years.

- Milk left in the fridge (5°C) lasts six days, in a cool room (15°C) three days, in a warm room (25°C) a day and a half, and at body temperature (35°C) less than a day. A similar situation occurs with other food 'going bad'. Microbial action doubles for each 10°C rise in temperature. Because these reactions are controlled by enzymes there is a maximum temperature above which the enzymes are denatured, and no reaction occurs. This allows us to sterilise food by heating it above this maximum (boiling is usually sufficient).

- Cooking – compared with simple boiling, potatoes cook more quickly at the higher temperatures in hot fat (chips) or under pressure (pressure cooker).

Collision theory

It is easy to see why a doubling of the surface area or concentration is likely to double the rate of a reaction: we are doubling the number of collisions, and reactions can only occur between two chemicals when their molecules collide.

There is a problem in explaining the effect of temperature. Many books use the idea of an increased collision rate to explain why chemical reactions go faster when the *temperature* is raised. This does not go anywhere near explaining what we actually observe. We have seen that for reactions that are slow at room temperature, a 10°C rise in temperature causes a *doubling* of rate. According to collision theory this suggests there are twice as many collisions at 20°C as there are at 10°C, but also twice as many again at 30°C as we had at 20°C. Clearly this is not the case.

What is the link between particle movement and temperature? At absolute zero (−273°C) particles essentially do not move. Their movement energy is proportional to absolute temperature. So if we want to double the energy of our particles, in a substance that is at room temperature, we need to work out its absolute temperature and double that. Room temperature is roughly 300 K. So doubling that we get 600 K or about 330°C. But our 10 degree rise in temperature, from 300 to 310 K, is only a 3 per cent rise in temperature, so we should expect only a 3 per cent increase in the rate for this tiny temperature rise, not the doubling we actually observe.

A better explanation is not easy. We need to realise that not all molecules will be moving with exactly the same energy. Some will move slowly, others faster than average. The reason why reactions between molecules are so slow at room temperature is that very few collisions are successful. Existing bonds must be broken before the next ones are made. If every collision resulted in broken bonds, the substances would be highly reactive and unstable. Bonds can only be broken (allowing a reaction to occur) if a collision is particularly energetic. Such energetic collisions are very rare, making the reaction slow. A 10 degree rise in temperature only increases the average energy of the molecules by a few per cent, but it can double the number of these particularly energetic molecules, which every so often, and by chance, have an energy perhaps 10 times the average. This is sufficient to break bonds and start the reaction. It is the doubling of the population of these very energetic molecules caused by the slight temperature rise that gives a better model for what is happening.

Should we use an erroneous model with our pupils if the better explanation is too complex? As long as we always warn pupils that our models and explanation are never 'true', but are there to attempt to make some sense of our experiences, pupils may be willing to accept ideas, but will be ready to develop and modify them as time passes.

Summary

In the original Key Stage 3 strategy *particles* were identified as one of the key ideas. Without this idea of indestructible atoms all other explanations in chemistry become a closed book. We need to test our pupils continually to see whether they have grasped this idea and are beginning to use it. In a similar way it is no use explaining the constructive (building up of oxides) approach to combustion and respiration and the need for a distinction to be drawn between matter and energy, presented in this chapter, in one lesson only, if you later talk about 'food contains energy' or 'energy in a crisp' (say 'food provides *fuel* for the body') or 'oil contains energy' (say 'oil is a fossil *fuel*'). Nor should ideas of acids and rates of reaction be confined to bottles of chemicals in laboratories. Instead they should be used as a concept to help us to explain how everyday chemical changes happen in the kitchen, within living things and in our whole environment. We must give our pupils much more time to reinterpret, use and apply the ideas they meet in their science lessons. Otherwise they will be learnt for the exams, harvested as a 'good' GCSE grade and promptly forgotten.

13

Difficult Ideas in Physics

Chapter overview

Physics has taken a large number of words in daily use and given them specific meanings. This is one reason why misconceptions with physical concepts are very prevalent and hard to remove. In this chapter we look at how the everyday meanings of words used in physics have helped to spread confusion as children try to understand scientific models in these concept areas. Our focus is on two key ideas from the schemes of work for science: *energy* and *force*. Our solution is to urge teachers to get pupils not to use the words only in the scientific sense, but to realise that the words stand for different ideas depending on context. In this way they will be able to see their world in new ways.

Energy

Popular use (and misuse) of the word *energy* has led to confusion between matter and energy – the issue of the origin of energy transferred when fuels burn and food is respired. We resolved this in Chapter 12 (pp. 110–15) by our focus on the *fuel–oxygen system*.

In this chapter we deal with a few more confusions:

■ in how the word energy is used in everyday life and by physicists

■ between the extent (heat energy) and intensity of energy (temperature)

■ about the words we use to measure and describe electrical energy and circuits

■ (in light) about the words used to describe colour.

Confusion in how the word *energy* is used in everyday life and by physicists

The word *energy* is used spontaneously even by five-year-olds – it is a part of our everyday language. Not so long ago, in school we did experiments where 'work' was turned to 'heat' by friction; we could calculate the number of joules that were *equivalent* to 1 calorie. Later we learnt that heat and mechanical movement were both forms of 'energy' and could be measured in the same units.

Nowadays, the word *energy*, in its everyday meaning, has come to represent an ability to do something *useful* and is best represented in science by saying something has 'fuel value'. As this 'energy' is 'used' it degrades into waste heat, so we have to come back for more. In this way energy can be seen as a flow: from high-grade, useful sources to scattered waste heat. This is unlike the matter cycles we met in Chapter 12, where matter (at an atomic level) cannot be destroyed, meaning that we have to develop cycles for all those materials we use that cannot be recycled by natural means. These material cycles (extract, transport, manufacture, recycle, etc.) need to be fuelled by an energy source, but in this case the energy becomes degraded so we need a continuing *energy* supply from the source.

In everyday conversation we might say, 'Energy is being used up, so we must conserve it, and use it wisely'. A physicist, on the other hand, might say, 'When something happens the total amount of energy does not change, so the amount of energy in the universe is constant – it is conserved'. Can both be true? The problem is that the words *energy* and *conservation* mean different things in both cases. We need to consider the laws of thermodynamics to understand this.

What the physicist says agrees with the *first law of thermodynamics*, which is the law we tend to teach first in school: the amount of energy remains the same, energy cannot be created or destroyed. If you measure the joules at the start of a change there will be the same number at the end. Thus chemical energy from burning the petrol in your car is transferred into movement (kinetic) energy and heat (thermal) energy. A useful analogy is money – at the end of a transaction there is the same amount of money (joules) as there was at the start – but see below for more comment on this.

In contrast, what our everyday use of the word *energy* says agrees with the *second law of thermodynamics*: that 'energy degrades to waste heat as it is *used*'. Thus, once the petrol has been burnt in the car engine, the energy has become scattered as waste heat and movement of air, and it cannot be *used* any more.

We see this progression from concentrated useful resources to scattered waste all around us. Rooms become untidy, bath water becomes dirty, electricity lights up our homes and the energy becomes scattered waste heat. It is the *second law* at work: the universe becomes less ordered; everything spreads out over time. An input of high-grade energy is required to prevent this descent into chaos and to maintain order. For example, for a room to remain tidy, there has to be an input of energy (muscle power or a vacuum cleaner) so that instead of the matter in the room becoming scattered the energy you *use* is degraded. The money analogy can be extended: a £20 note is useful, worth picking up if you see one, but once it is scattered into two thousand 1p coins hardly anyone would go looking for them all. However, unlike money that circulates and becomes collected up again in places called banks, energy, once scattered into outer space, has to be replaced by a fresh source of high-grade energy if useful work is to be done.

Science courses on energy at Key Stage 3 often start with an energy 'circus' in which pupils realise the 'interconvertibility' of energy. We need to acknowledge, at this time, that pupils will be saying that energy gets *used up*. In every energy change the useful energy we get out is never as much as we put in, because of 'losses'. Sometimes these losses are a nuisance, as in the waste heat in a car or our bodies, which we have to get rid of (through the cooling system or through sweating). This energy (measured in joules) is not used up, but its usefulness has gone, and in that sense it has been *used*. There is more than a grain of truth in what the pupils say.

When dealing with energy changes we suggest you use Sankey diagrams (see Figure 13.1). The boxes represent energy, and the connecting arrows are labelled by the process or object that causes the change. This makes a clear distinction between the objects, like the plants or light bulb, that cause energy to be changed, and the energy itself. In addition, the boxes are drawn so that their size represents the amount of energy. With the first and last boxes being equally tall you can show that there is *no loss in joules*. You can then show, at each stage, what proportion of the energy is transferred *usefully*, and what fraction is 'wasted' as heat. In Figure 13.1 it is the white boxes that represent the useful energy transferred to the next stage. The grey boxes are waste heat, but they all add up in the end to equal the useful energy we started with.

To make things happen, high-grade energy has to become spread out and dissipated as waste heat. Thus, in a 100 W old-style filament light bulb (giving out 100 joules per second) high-grade electrical energy is transferred into light (5 joules per second) and waste heat (95 joules per second). You can replace this with a 15 W *energy-efficient* light bulb, which also transfers 5 joules a second as light, but only wastes 10 joules as heat and so is about seven times cheaper to run.

Energy cannot be *renewed* once it has dissipated, but we can *replenish* it by burning more fuel, or waiting for more sunlight to arrive (Ross *et al.* 2002: CD – Energy).

Teaching point. Don't assume your pupils will use the word *energy* in the same ways as you do. Find out their meanings through elicitation.

Teaching point. Explain that when energy is 'used' it degrades – it is still there but scattered and useless.

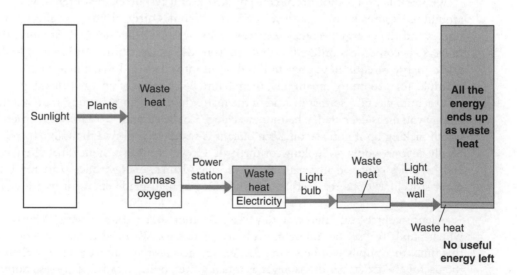

FIGURE 13.1 A Sankey diagram: the degradation of energy

Heat (thermal energy) and temperature

Pupils in school, and the public at large, often confuse temperature and heat (thermal energy). Such terms are used interchangeably in everyday life, but it is important to realise that one (heat energy) represents an *amount* of energy, which may have to be paid for, and the other (temperature or hotness) applies to the *intensity* of the energy. You can have a red-hot nail at the same temperature as lava flowing from a volcano, but the amount of energy in the nail is negligible in comparison.

Energy that is at a high *intensity* can be linked with danger: a high temperature, a high voltage, a fast-moving mass (e.g. a bullet), a short wavelength electromagnetic wave (e.g. X-rays), a raised mass (e.g. a loose tile) and appropriate mixtures of weakly bonded chemicals (e.g. a firework) are all dangerous. But how much useful work they can do depends on *quantity*, as well as intensity. A red-hot nail plunged into a cold mug of coffee will not do much to make it drinkable, but a red-hot poker (same temperature, more heat energy) will do the trick. However, the red-hot nail can do more damage than the hot coffee. Temperature measures the amount of energy *per particle*. High temperatures are dangerous, but may not 'contain' very much energy. A spark has a high temperature, but very little heat energy.

Heat (thermal energy), on the other hand, is associated with payment. To make your bath water hot requires buying fuel (the oxygen is free). The amount of fuel you need to burn depends on the amount of heat energy needed, which, in turn, depends on three things: the amount of stuff you are heating; the material it is made of (in this case it is water); and the required rise in 'hotness' (i.e. temperature rise). Heat (strictly 'thermal energy') is the total amount of energy transferred into your system, so we add up the energy given to all the particles (of water).

Teaching idea

■ Try asking your pupils this question: You add 10 kettle-fulls of boiling water to some cold water in a bath to make it warm. (a) Which has more heat energy in it – the kettle of boiling water, or the bath full of warm water – answer: the bath (b) Which has the higher temperature (which is hotter?) – answer: the kettle. See also the discussion of question 2 in Chapter 5 (p. 42).

The word *electricity* has two meanings: current and energy

When we use the word *electricity* in everyday life we usually mean *electrical energy*: 'It works by electricity', 'It uses electricity'. However, it can also mean electric *current*, and there lies the confusion.

For example, people might say that electric *current* (measured in amps) is 'used up', so less *current* flows back to the battery than went out to a bulb, because they think of *current* as electrical *energy*. But a physicist will say the *current* remains the same all the way round a series circuit. To understand the concept of current we need to think about why there has to be a *return* wire, and what it is that is conserved when the ammeter reads the same wherever it is placed in the circuit.

The *milk bottle analogy* is helpful (see Figure 13.2). The milk (representing energy in joules) is delivered in bottles (the *coulombs*, which measure the number of energy carriers or electrons) to the house (bulb). The actual current is the *flow rate* of energy carriers – bottles per day (coulombs per second, or amps) – and it must be the same all the way round, since used bottles return to the dairy (and electrons return to the cell). How much milk (energy) is carried by each bottle (coulomb) depends on how full the bottles are – the *milk per bottle (joules per coulomb*, or voltage). In the case of electricity the energy is transferred by the repulsion of neighbouring electrons: the more packed together they are the higher the voltage, the more they are able to push and the more dangerous (or useful) each packet of electrons is. See www.science issues.org.uk/screens/u5energyscreen.htm for an animated version of this analogy (from Ross *et al.* 2002: CD – Energy).

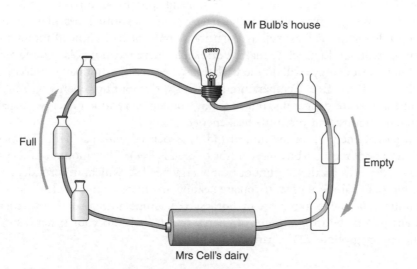

FIGURE 13.2 The milk bottle analogy for an electric circuit

We probably teach ideas about electricity in the wrong order, and introduce current too soon. Although it appears to be a complex unit, *power* is easily recognisable in everyday terms (see also Chapter 11, p. 92). Power tells us the *energy transferred per second*, and is measured in *watts*, which are *joules per second*. We can all see that a 3 kW kettle boils water more quickly than a 2 kW kettle, and that a 100 W bulb is brighter than a 60 W bulb. In the milk bottle analogy *power* is represented by the amount of milk you get each day (joules per second or watts). To find this out you need to know how many bottles you get a day (the current, coulombs per second, or amps) and multiply this by the amount of milk in each bottle (joules per coulomb, or volts). If volts and amps are introduced too early they just get muddled into a vague idea that 'they measure the amount of electricity'.

So *electricity*, in common parlance, means electrical *energy*, which is transferred (and dissipated) during changes involving electrical appliances; *power* is a measure of how quickly that energy is delivered; *current* is the flow rate of a 'carrier', which needs a complete circuit; and *voltage* shows the danger (how highly charged with energy each carrier is).

Teaching point. Don't use the word *electricity* on its own: say either electrical *energy* or electric *current*.

Colour vision and pigments

If all light is absorbed by an object it will appear black, and the light energy will be transferred to heat energy, but if only some light is absorbed the surface can look coloured or grey. Pigments are therefore *selective absorbers* of light.

Children find it hard to believe that white light is composed of a spectrum of colours – seen as a rainbow when raindrops cause light to become separated (dispersed). Pigments work by selectively absorbing some colours from the white light. That is why you must look at colours in daylight to appreciate them properly, and why a blue door (which only reflects blue) looks black in sodium vapour street lamps at night. Since the sodium vapour light has no blue in it, which is the only colour the pigment on the door will *not* absorb, all the light from the street lamp is absorbed.

Colour mixing by subtraction and addition

To understand colour vision, and mixing of pigments and lights, you must appreciate that the artists' primary colours – *red (magenta)*, *yellow* and *blue (cyan)* – are not single wavelength (rainbow) colours like the scientists' primary colours of *red (close to the artist's orange)*, *green* and *blue (close to the artist's purple or rainbow indigo)*. There are six colours here, not four, and the names given to them by artists and some teachers are not the same as those given by photographers, printers and scientists (see Figure 13.3).

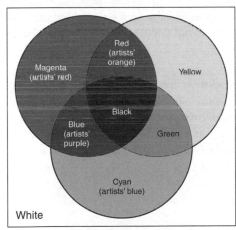

Artists: colour mixing by subtraction

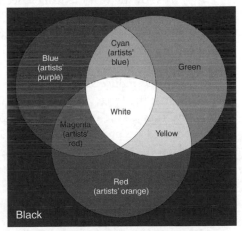

Scientists: colour mixing by addition

FIGURE 13.3 Artists' and scientists' primary colours

Force and motion

Once again we are struggling against common usage of language. Everything in shops is weighed in kilograms, yet kilogram is a unit of mass. How do we separate out the ideas that the mass of an object stays the same but its weight is produced by the effect of gravity (or acceleration) and is a changing force, measured in newtons? See Chapter 11 (pp. 91–2) for a brief discussion of how to overcome this in your teaching.

A more serious misconception is that objects that are moving 'have a force' in them. No matter how many times we refer to Newton's laws of motion, pupils will insist that as well as gravity affecting moving objects they also have a *force of momentum* driving them and the objects stop when this force 'runs out'. They cannot see that the object slows due to the force of friction and that without this friction the object would continue forever. The problem is that there are no common examples relevant to them where there is no friction. When we push a trolley we need a driving force to keep going, only because of friction. Skating on ice comes nearest to experiencing frictionless motion – you have to dig your skates in to create a friction force in order to stop.

We began to address this in Chapter 7 (pp. 66–8) with a teaching sequence that developed the idea of 'force, gravity and motion'. Here we suggest a scheme that starts the *intervention* phase with an air track demonstration and then uses the ideas which develop to understand the motion of cars and footballers.

Air track demonstrations

The air supply to the track should be regulated by having a hole in the air line that can be gradually closed, allowing air gradually to push the trolley off the track and reducing friction essentially to zero. A very weak, stretchy length of elastic is used to pull the trolley, so pupils can estimate the pulling force. You begin (with no air blowing) by showing that the trolley needs to be constantly pulled to make it go. As soon as you stop pulling the trolley stops. We explain this by saying that there are two horizontal forces, which are in balance: your pull and friction. The more the friction the more you have to pull, but if the pull is greater than friction the trolley will pick up speed.

We now reduce friction in stages by closing the hole in the air feeder tube and show that the force we need to pull the trolley (as indicated by the amount of stretch in the thin elastic used to pull it) gradually drops to zero. When friction has been eliminated no pulling force is needed to maintain the speed of the trolley. We still need a force to get it going, of course, and we also need another force to stop it. This laboratory-based discussion can now allow us to reconsider everyday events.

Cars, football and skidding

Ask a pupil to run and stop. Talk about the need to get a grip. Talk about icy roads, wet floors and football boot studs. The idea is: to change the motion (slowing down, getting faster, changing direction) you need a force. If a footballer, or anyone else, needs to change their motion they need to get a good grip. It is only when you attempt to change your motion and can't get that grip that skidding happens.

People often associate skidding, or slipping, with turning corners, and it is true that it is during cornering (or trying to start or stop) that cars and footballers skid. But a skid happens when there is reduced frictional force from the ground, so your attempt to slow down or turn a corner fails, and you carry on in the same direction that you were going. With no frictional force (or grip) there can be no change in motion.

What force causes hot air to rise?

Air is made of atoms, which have mass, so air is attracted to the Earth by the gravitational force. If you pump air into a football the ball gets heavier (a 3-litre pop bottle with a bung and valve is easier to deal with in class, and its mass will increase by about a gram when pumped up with a cycle pump, an increase which can be detected on a top-pan balance). This leads to the important idea that our atmosphere is 'heavy' and is attracted to the Earth by gravity. Why is it, then, that hot air and helium move *away* from the centre of the Earth – that is, why do they rise? They are both made of atoms so must be attracted downwards to the centre of the Earth!

To illustrate this, we can compare air and water in a demonstration. Fill a tank with water at about 35°C. A red balloon filled with very hot water is released half-way down. It will be buoyed up as the cooler water around it takes its place – this is 'hot air rising'. A blue balloon filled with ice-cold water sinks, displacing the warmer water surrounding it upwards. It is no different from a block of wood (less dense so buoyed up) and a stone (more dense so sinks). [Caution: make sure the balloons have no air trapped with the hot or cold water.]

Accounts of the weather frequently describe convection currents as being caused by 'hot air rising allowing cold air to rush in'. What they should say is that the cold, dense air moves in, buoying (pushing) the less dense hot air away from the Earth against gravity. Gases are real, massive forms of matter and we need to appreciate that if they rise, something more massive must be pushing them upwards.

Summary

We have focused on two major concepts in physics – energy and force – to show how our everyday use of words and our experiences often go against the scientific understanding we are trying to share with our pupils at school. Once again we have shown the importance of knowing pupils' firmly held everyday ideas if we are to enable them to go through a real revolution and adopt our more widely applicable scientific understanding.

14

Difficult Ideas in Biology

Chapter overview

We begin this chapter by looking at the big ideas in biology, in particular the notion of being alive and the characteristics of life itself, then explore these ideas using plants as examples. These are sometimes neglected in our teaching and many misconceptions build up about how life works. We take a brief look at some other problems facing learners, many of which we have mentioned earlier in this book. Unlike physicists, biologists tend to invent new words when they need them, usually based on classical origins. This means that biology can be filled with strange long words, but uncluttered with everyday meaning. We conclude with some examples of the opposite: confusion that occurs when biology takes over existing words for its own use.

Big ideas in biology

Biology is the study of living things. These are usually cellular but a few are acellular (for example many fungi) in organisation. It is therefore appropriate that the Secondary National Strategy has recognised the 'organism' as one of the key concepts underlying an understanding of the world around us. It is interesting to note that since viruses share the same nucleic acids and proteins as cells, they are often regarded as biological systems but not usually as organisms. 'Organisms, behaviour and health' is the biological strand in the Strategy's science content: organisms are interdependent and adapted to their environment; this adaptation and its associated variation can lead to evolutionary changes; and it includes life processes (including the role of microorganisms and immunity) and the more complex ideas of genetics. All life starts as a single cell, and the overarching characteristic of an organism is that the single cell can divide, making copies of itself. So we look first at the characteristics of life and then at cell division.

Mrs Gren: characteristics of life

At the basis of all biological studies are the characteristics of life itself: what makes something living as opposed to something that is inanimate and, indeed, something that has never lived? The 'Mrs Gren' mnemonic, representing the characteristics of livings things, is very popular, but is only a memory aid, and gives no deeper understanding. We need to start further back and 'invent' the characteristics of life afresh with our pupils. The overriding feature of life is that it can make copies of itself – it is self-replicating. We need to add, too, that it evolves. What would something need to enable it to reproduce by itself? Houses are not alive, but it is useful to think of how they come into being. They need an open space, plans (in time and space), materials, tools and energy.

- Space. Without space into which they can grow, living cells could not reproduce.

- Plans. These are held in the DNA in most life-forms, providing instructions not only on how to make the parts but also on how the parts function and fit together.

- Tools. Life's tools are enzymes – the proteins which are manufactured from the coding instructions in the DNA. The enzymes enable chemical reactions to take place in cells and allow structures to be built and function.

- Materials. Some forms of life (e.g. plants, the producers, the autotrophs) are able to use non-living materials: carbon dioxide as their source of carbon, water and minerals. Others (e.g. animals, the consumers) need to take in their materials ready made: for example, as carbohydrate, amino acids (protein) and nucleic acids (DNA) from other living things.

- Energy. Autotrophs need sunlight as their primary energy source (except, for example, in the case of vent communities at mid-oceanic ridges, which use reactive chemicals). This energy 'sets' the fuel–oxygen system by building up biomass in the living organism and releasing oxygen to the atmosphere. Once this energy is stored, all living things can use it in a process called respiration. In turn this sets smaller 'springs' such as the ATP–ADP system to provide energy in manageable chunks where it is needed.

If life needs these things and it has to do everything for itself a number of characteristics must be present, which children can devise for themselves. If a living thing has to make a copy of itself, what must it be able to do?

M – Movement. Needed to get to empty space, to find materials and to reproduce.

R – Respiration. Recombining oxygen and biomass to provide energy. Historically this has been described as 'internal respiration' and breathing as 'external respiration'. It is worth noting that some schools completely disassociate the process of 'breathing' (gaseous exchange) from the cellular activity of respiration so as not to confuse the two. They are both vital components of the same process and without the first aerobic respiration could not take place, though many organisms get their oxygen by direct diffusion from the air (or water).

S – Senses. Living things must have ways of telling which way is up or down, where light is, how to find other living things.

G – Growth. Growth occurs by adding cells, which is the same process as asexual reproduction. This is the 'purpose' of life. These cells (in multicellular organisms) differentiate as they mature, becoming specialised and more complex.

R – Reproduction. Sexual reproduction allows a range of characteristics, which might become useful one day, to lie dormant in a population, so allowing them to respond to changes in their environment. Without this, evolution, as we know it, could not take place.

E – Excretion. Materials need to be taken into cells, but after being processed wastes are inevitable. They have to be excreted.

N – Nutrition. Getting materials for growth and to use as a fuel.

Elicitation tasks such as question 8 in Chapter 5 (p. 44), where pupils have to sort cards into life or not-life and animals or plants, become more straightforward after these seven characteristics are explored. See Box 14.1 for more teaching ideas about living and not-living.

Box 14.1 Probing pupils' ideas about living things

1. Ask groups of pupils to identify what processes the living things go through when they are alive, when they are decaying and when they are changed by people into other things. Make a list or mind map of ideas about 'living'.

   Questions such as the following can act as prompts:
   - What is different between something that is living and something that has never lived?
   - What makes a (once) living thing alive or dead?
   - When does death occur?
   - Is fire a living thing?
   - Are seeds living?
   - What is the link between the living and the non-living worlds?
   - What are microorganisms and are they alive?

2. Make use of key vocabulary in your plenary session: habitat, adaptation, food chain, consumer, producer, predator, ecosystem, decay, decomposer, herbivore, carnivore, life cycle, pollution, energy transfer.

3. As a homework exercise get pupils to design a 'sun' machine (producers) that only needs air, sunlight and rain to enable it to work, and then to design 'robber' (consumers) machines that rely on using parts of other machines to work. They will put sensors and wheels on the 'robbers' but not on the 'suns' until they realise that the suns need to escape from the robbers. They may also decide to protect the 'suns' using spikes (thorns).

Human biology

Following the outline above we can get pupils to think about our own body design.

- How do we get the materials to build new cells where they are needed?

- How do we get fuel and oxygen to all our cells?

Rather than telling pupils about our circulation system, why not let them design it?

Ask the pupils to outline a 'balance of duties' for the heart and circulatory system – that is, identify exactly what the heart and circulatory system has to do – before considering the various components.

- How many would think of a four-chambered heart, or come up with the artery and capillary system to allow bulk transport followed by distribution to all the cells?

- Would they come up with the design for the lungs or gut, or think of putting a liver-like organ immediately after the gut to deal with undesirable material that might get in?

Too often pupils see the alimentary canal as one long tube, which takes food from mouth to anus. It is the big idea, not the details, that needs to be emphasised. The purpose of digestion is to get food into the blood (see Box 14.2).

Box 14.2 A simulated 'gut'

Collect all the ingredients you would need for a simple meal, for example breakfast: milk, cornflakes, banana, sugar, bread, butter, marmalade, orange juice, coffee and any other soft food you can think of. Discuss briefly what is happening to the food in the mouth. A knife can be used to cut the food (the incisors) and a meat pounder to grind it (the molars). Now pour/spoon all these foods into a polythene bag to represent the stomach. Get a pupil to crunch and grind it up using their hands on the outside. Vinegar can be added to represent the stomach acid. Using a prepared pair of tights (one leg placed into the other and toes removed to give a single tube) explain to the pupils that you are now going to allow the food to enter the intestines. Cut the lower corner of the polythene bag (stomach) to make a hole in the bag and squeeze the contents so they enter the top of the tights. The food has now moved into the small intestine. By squeezing the mixture you will get it to move along the tube (peristalsis). Twist the tights so that the mixture becomes compact and collect the juices in a drip tray. These juices represent the 'goodness' passing into the blood for use by the body. Squeeze the remaining (undigested) mixture towards the toe of the tights and let it 'plop' into a bowl (the toilet) to show egestion of faeces. Emphasise that the aim of all this is to get the liquid goodness into the blood so the body can use it.

When pupils write creatively about the journey of our food, they usually say that the food (having said goodbye to the good bits) leaves out of the anus. Why not say goodbye to the indigestible bits and begin the real adventure as the blood carries you round? You then leave minutes or hours later as carbon dioxide at the lungs, or falling to the floor as dead skin some weeks later, having contributed to the growth of new skin cells. This approach helps to avoid confusion between *egestion* of faeces, which have never entered the blood, and *excretion* of wastes that accumulate in the blood and have to be removed by the lungs, kidneys or as sweat. This path of food is animated in Ross *et al.* (2002: CD – Health).

We must try to see the body as an integrated whole, not a lot of independent parts. It is this independence that leads to another serious misconception that many text-books perpetuate. It is the idea that food 'contains' energy, rather than saying that energy is transferred when food is respired: this is a topic that we discussed at some length in Chapter 12 (pp. 109–15).

How can two make one?

As mentioned earlier, one of the key characteristics of life is that it can reproduce itself, and this means that cells must be able to divide. But cells divide for a variety of reasons, namely:

- growth

- repair

- reproduction.

Division requires one cell yielding two cells, which must be identical. This is the process of asexual cell division known as *mitosis*. This process has many advantages:

- it is quick

- it is reliable

- it has a low energy cost

- the offspring are always the same.

It is of course the process involved during growth, when a fertilised egg develops into an adult organism. By selectively switching genes on and off, each new cell can become increasingly specialised.

A major misconception associated with cell division relates to the structure of chromosomes. A single chromosome (obtained from either one of your parents) in a typical diploid cell, observed during the normal lifetime of the cell (interphase), would appear as a single strand of DNA capable of active protein synthesis. During the lead-up to cell division, this molecule makes an exact copy of itself so the genetic/DNA quota for the cell doubles. The chromosome takes on the more characteristic two-pronged structure, with its two chromatids being held together at the centromere. To prevent excessive loss of material, the chromosome appears to contract, becoming shorter and fatter as it winds around the nucleosomes. During division, it is the chromatids that separate, breaking apart at the centromere. The resultant daughter cells contain a chromatid from each replicated chromosome, thus retaining the original genetic/DNA quota.

This is all very well for growth and repair, when you want more of the same thing, but consider survival in a changing environment. All the offspring are identical and therefore susceptible to the same environmental influences.

This is where sexual reproduction takes the upper hand. It does not display any of the advantages of the above, but it does ensure that variation can arise, enabling the organism to respond to environmental effects in different ways – a factor crucial to the evolutionary process. In genetic terms, sexual reproduction causes a potential doubling of genetic material, as two cells fuse to form one. A reduction division is therefore required for the production of the sex cells, each containing half the total genetic quota and each with the potential to be different. *Meiosis* is the process by which this is achieved. Reduction is achieved by the initial separation of homologous chromosomes, which then undergo a further division to separate the chromatids. As these chromatids separate they become intertwined with one another and at the 'cross-over' points breakages and recombinations occur. This results in additional variation within the genetic make-up of the individual.

By emphasising the role of the chromatid during cell division, we can give pupils a greater appreciation of the process and how the two types of cell division can achieve the desired end results.

A teaching sequence about plants

This section outlines a number of conceptual problems associated with plants, and suggests some active learning activities for pupils.

What is a plant?

The Secondary National Strategy does not refer to plants specifically – indeed, it would be very easy to concentrate purely on animals (especially humans) and associated microorganisms and forget about plants completely. This would serve to ignore a significant proportion of life on Earth and contribute to our increasing lack of basic knowledge and understanding about this important kingdom. In the past, curricula have focused on 'Green plants as organisms', with particular reference to nutrition, growth and the role of respiration; however, one of the most pressing issues is what constitutes a 'plant'. In the *elicitation* phase of the lesson, ask a group of pupils what they think a plant is: they are likely to come up with a very restricted view that begins with 'pot plants' and may extend to vegetables, flowers and trees. The more adventurous answers include (wrongly according to modern classification systems) lichens, fungi and seaweed.

It is at this stage that you need to *intervene*. Taking the definition that plants photosynthesise, it is possible to eliminate one of the above. Fungi appear in a wide array of vivid colours, but 'chlorophyll green' is not one of them. They excrete enzymes into the surrounding medium, digesting cellulose, glycoprotein and starch before ingesting the substrate. They are saprophytes, living off dead organic material.

Confusion: germination of the seed and growth of the seedling

It is important to distinguish between the conditions seeds need to germinate and the conditions needed for the seedling to continue to grow. We discuss this towards the end of this chapter (pp. 136 and 137).

Misconception: 'Plants respire at night, but breathe in carbon dioxide in the day'

Pupils and adults alike hold this common misconception, but we need to appreciate the broader picture. There is clearly a grain of truth here (see Chapter 4) – plants are net users of carbon dioxide during the day, and net exporters of it at night; however, respiration goes on *all the time*.

When a plant photosynthesises it uses sunlight energy to split water and reduce carbon dioxide. The end products are glucose and oxygen. Plant biomass (its overall structure), however, is made of more than mere glucose. As well as carbohydrate, they need proteins, DNA and many other chemicals. By combining the glucose with minerals available from the soil, the plant produces these components of biomass. This process, however, requires energy. Some of the glucose will have to be combined with oxygen to release the energy associated with this fuel–oxygen system. This is respiration and it takes place all the time in every part of the plant.

'But plants only respire at night!' say the pupils. During the day the plant uses carbon dioxide in the photosynthetic process, and far more is needed than is produced through respiration. As the question in Figure 14.1 shows, many children do not appreciate that plants get their main structural material, carbon, from the air, and respond by saying the plant's mass comes from the water and the soil.

Now consider oxygen. Only some of the oxygen produced during photosynthesis is used in respiration, and the remainder is released. At one stage, referred to as the 'compensation point', the amount of gases produced equals the amount of gases required and there is no net production or release (see Box 14.3). In the night, when light is not available, the export of oxygen stops and the carbon dioxide from respiration has to be released to the air.

A small tree is planted in a tub.

After 20 years it has grown into a big tree, with an increase in mass of over 70 kg.

The level of soil in the tub has hardly changed over the 20 years.

The only substance added to the tub over the years has been rain water.

Where do the extra 70 kg come from?

Explain your answer as fully as you can.

FIGURE 14.1 Tub tree elicitation question (based on van Helmont's famous experiment)

Box 14.3 Photosynthesis: A role-play activity

Introduce photosynthesis by talking about the word itself, and getting the pupils to investigate other 'photo' words to see if they can understand what the prefix 'photo' actually means. Once the connection with light is made, pupils begin to understand its importance in the plant world.

Give each pupil a molecule model of either water (HOH) or carbon dioxide (OCO). As the teacher narrates the pupils role-play the photosynthetic process. Use a row of stools to depict the plant stem. The benches by the window can be the leaves. Water molecules (pupils carrying water model) enter the plant through the roots and move up the stem to the leaves. Light photons (from the windows) enter the plant through the top of the leaves, and the molecules of carbon dioxide enter through the leaf bottom. A reaction takes place between the molecules, and the pupils rearrange the atoms to form carbohydrate (HCOH) and oxygen (OO) – the end products of photosynthesis. At this stage you need to point out to the pupils that no growth has yet occurred in the plant. Most of the carbohydrate will need to be converted into other molecules to help build the plant and the spare oxygen will be given off to the atmosphere. This building process requires energy through respiration – provided by the few remaining sugar molecules and the oxygen molecules, which now recombine (re-forming HOH + OCO). This is what happens in daylight: plants become net exporters of oxygen. When no further photosynthesis takes place (i.e. at night) only respiration takes place so the plant becomes an exporter of carbon dioxide and water.

Teaching point. Note that plants respire all the time (plants and seeds die when their roots have no access to oxygen in the soil, e.g. when waterlogged).

See also the 'saucepan model' and related discussion in Chapter 12, Box 12.1 (p. 111).

Roots, stems and leaves

Another clearly defined characteristic of plants is that they possess true roots, stems and leaves. Seaweed contains a simple arrangement of cells forming a 'holdfast', stipe (primitive stem) and various fronds. They photosynthesise effectively but, owing to their simple specialisation and undifferentiated cell structure, are not classified as plants. They are in fact algae and classified alongside other single-celled structures such as *Amoeba*, *Euglena* and *Paramecium*. Pupils often describe single-celled plant-like and animal-like organisms as being true plants or true animals. Lichens are a result of a symbiotic association between two groups of organism – fungi and algae – and are not classified as plants either. However, it is useful to see all photosynthetic organisms, whether single-celled or true plants, as 'producers' on which 'consumers' depend.

Transport of materials in plants

The rooting system of the more advanced plants is complex, with a central taproot and a series of radial, lateral roots. Root hairs serve to increase the overall surface area of the system. Water and mineral salts are absorbed from the soil into the roots by osmosis. The water and minerals pass through a network of cells into a series of hollow tubes, the *xylem* vessels. These connect the roots to the rest of the plant.

Teaching point. Take time to question pupils about what they think the small quantity of ash is that remains after plants are burnt. All the carbon and hydrogen are returned to the air in carbon dioxide and water vapour, so the ash represents the minerals taken up by the plant from the soil. That is why wood ash is such a good fertiliser.

There are many excellent traditional ways to demonstrate the transpiration process, such as:

- celery or carnations in coloured water showing water uptake via xylem vessels

- leaving several leaves to 'dry', some coated with petroleum jelly on the top side, the underside or both sides to show that water loss is greater from the underside of the leaf

- observing condensation inside a polythene bag tied around some leaves of a plant.

Owing to their underground existence, roots are excluded from the light and are therefore unable to photosynthesise. Food needs to be taken to them via a second series of vessels, the *phloem*. This provides material for growth as well as fuel for respiration, but to release energy, oxygen is also required. This comes from air pockets in the soil, which the roots have access to. If the roots can't get this oxygen, for example when the soil gets waterlogged, the plant will die.

Teaching point. Compare roots with germinating seeds. They cannot photosynthesise and so need fuel and oxygen. Both have a store of carbohydrate (and roots are continually supplied from the leaves) but both need access to oxygen from the air. Try germinating seeds (a) left dry (no water), (b) left on damp cotton wool so they have air and water and (c) under water (no air). Only (b) will germinate.

The stem links the whole plant together, surrounding the xylem and phloem and supporting the leaves and any flowers. This support is achieved by maintaining high water pressure (turgidity, like air in a football) within its cells or by forming the woody *lignin*, present in larger plants such as trees. The stem offers a continuous transport system from roots to leaves, while the transpiration stream ensures that water is continually drawn into and up the xylem by capillary action, and out through the leaves by evaporation.

Teaching point. Discuss leaf wilt and the function of lignin in supporting a plant. An analogy with blowing air into an inflatable toy is useful.

Teaching point. Discuss why some trees (deciduous) shed their leaves in the autumn whilst others (evergreen) appear not to do so. In fact evergreen trees (e.g. most conifers) shed their leaves or needles throughout the year but it is not as noticeable as the bulk 'leaf-shedding' of the deciduous variety. Leaf fall is closely related to light intensity and day-length. It is an ideal means by which toxins and other waste products can be effectively removed from the plant.

Everyday words with special meaning

We began this chapter by saying that biology is full of its own invented words, like testa, xylem and ovary. We end by addressing the opposite. Below we consider some everyday words that are also used for a special purpose in biology.

Growth

We often ask pupils to investigate the conditions necessary for the growth of seeds, but we need to distinguish between germination and growth. Most pupils would agree that water and warmth are required. Many would suggest that light is also necessary. But this is not so for germination (although, in some cases, for example poppies, it acts as a regulator, like frost, in triggering germination). Seedlings require light to photosynthesise once the seed has produced its first leaves. Until this stage, light is of little use because there is no chlorophyll available for photosynthesis. The seed needs oxygen to respire its food reserves in order to germinate and then to grow. When pupils set up conditions for plant growth investigations, we need to be clear whether they are investigating the growth of seedlings (light needed) or germination of seeds (light not needed).

Teaching point. Seeds can be collected from trees in the autumn. Some can be put in the freezer for a week, and others left in the classroom. All seeds are then planted in warm, moist conditions, and pupils can see which germinate most successfully. They can also consider the advantage of germinating only after a big freeze.

TABLE 14.1 Fruit, vegetable or seed?

FOOD	PART OF PLANT	SCIENTIFIC CLASSIFICATION			KITCHEN CLASSIFICATION		
		Vegetable	Fruit	Seed	Vegetable	Fruit	Nut
Tomato	Ovary (fleshy)						
Rhubarb	Stem						
Cucumber	Ovary (fleshy)						
Potato	Stem						
Onion	Leaf – bulb						
Plum	Ovary (fleshy)						
Beetroot	Root						
Apple	Receptacle (fleshy)						
Carrot	Root						
Melon	Ovary (fleshy)						
Coconut	Seed						
Hazelnut	Seed						
Runner bean	Ovary (fleshy)						
Sweetcorn	Seed						
Cauliflower	Flower						

Fruit, seed or vegetable?

These words, especially fruit and vegetable, have different meanings in the kitchen from those they have in biology. Show the pupils a range of fruits and vegetables and ask them to identify the part of the plant from which they came and whether they are 'fruit', 'seed' or 'vegetable'. You will need to recognise, biologically, that a fruit is a fertilised ovary, seeds reside inside the fruiting body and a vegetable is any part of a plant used for food, other than the fruit. How many in Table 14.1 are classified differently in the kitchen and in science?

Summary

By using the 'organism' as our conceptual focus, we have highlighted problems with technical and everyday biological vocabulary. We have once again stressed the importance of thinking about the fuel–oxygen system, keeping ideas about material (atoms) and energy separate. We have concentrated on the common misconceptions held by pupils and many adults, several of which are associated with plant classification and plant metabolism. Some suggestions for practical and word work activities to overcome the misconceptions have been made.

15

Difficult Ideas in Earth Science and Astronomy

Chapter overview

This chapter deals with the big ideas in earth science and astronomy: the origin of the universe and solar system; the relationship between the Sun, the Earth and the Moon using the phases of the Moon as an example; and the formation and cycling of rocks – an area that is often tackled superficially owing to its seemingly 'dry' nature. We follow a teaching sequence on the 'rock cycle' and explore the origins of the words we use. The potentially difficult ideas here emanate from the fact that the content either presents itself as an illusion of the real thing (e.g. phases of the Moon) or is explored from our short human time frame (e.g. the rock cycle).

Big ideas and misconceptions in earth sciences and astronomy

Astronomy is the study of the stars and the universe. Humans have been trying to make sense of the stars and planets since our earliest ancestors attributed mythical shapes to them and described the constellations we still talk about today. They used the perceived movement of the stars for navigation purposes and sowed and reaped their crops in accordance with the changing position of the Sun and the phases of the Moon. Indeed our whole understanding of time and the language associated with it is directly associated with the movement of these heavenly bodies. Just as the sky appears not to change from one year to the next, so the mountains and rivers appear static to pupils. The timescales involved with the evolution of the universe and of planet Earth are difficult to comprehend.

The Standards website has listed some common barriers that could prevent understanding if we don't acknowledge and challenge them. Pupils may think that:

■   the Sun is not a star – stars are small and cold

■   day and night are caused by the Sun orbiting the Earth

■   the phases of the Moon are caused by the shadow of the Earth (confusion with eclipses)

- it is hot in summer because the Earth is nearer to the Sun then (but the northern summer happens when the south has winter!)

- the planets and the Moon give off their own light

- light years refer to time rather than distance.

And for rocks and soil, they may think that:

- erosion is the same as weathering

- minerals are 'precious rocks', or they are linked only to mineral water, minerals and vitamins

- Earth is molten except for the crust

- continents do not move

- humans and dinosaurs co-existed and humans are responsible for the extinction of dinosaurs

- the rocks, mountains, and other geographical features formed instantaneously.

(Based on the Standards website: http://nationalstrategies.standards.dcsf.gov.uk/node/102666 and 102661)

Scientific ideas on the origins of the universe

To answer these questions of origin we need to go back in time, some 14,000 million (14×10^9) years ago. But before we do, think about your own understanding of the formation of the universe and try the following elicitation questions:

- What is the currently agreed view of the origin of the 100 or so elements that make up the world?

- Why does this suggest that the Sun is a fairly recent star?

- Is it possible that we are all made of 'stardust'?

- What is the difference between a star, a planet and a moon?

Current scientific understanding is that the entire universe began by being squashed up; far smaller than the dot on this 'i'. There was a massive explosion creating space as we know it. Over the billions of years of expansion since the 'Big Bang' the energy associated with the explosion has been stretched to microwaves, which are detectable in space as background radiation. These were only discovered in the early 1990s. Reiss quotes the news as it was reported in the *Independent* on 24 April 1992:

> Fourteen thousand million years ago the universe hiccuped. Yesterday, American scientists announced that they may have heard the echo. A NASA spacecraft has detected ripples at the edge of the Cosmos which are the fossilised imprint of the birth of the stars and galaxies around us today.

> (Reiss 1992, p. 26)

Matter as we know it began to form 300,000 years after the Big Bang forming hydrogen and some helium atoms. These atoms then gravitated together to form stars and galaxies.

The Sun, the Earth and the Moon

The Big Bang theory explains our scientific understanding of how the universe as a whole developed and how the very first atoms might have been produced, but we need to look at what happens in the stars to find out how the 100 or so elements of the periodic table were formed. So picking up the story from where we left it...

Some stars 'grew' greatly in size by engulfing matter drawn towards them by increasing gravitational forces. As the size of the star increases so more nuclear fusion reactions begin. Small stars, like our Sun, only fuse hydrogen to helium, but in larger ones the fusion reactions build elements up to iron, always releasing energy to make the star 'shine'.

So a star can be described as an 'element factory' from which energy is released as more massive elements are synthesised. The elements remain trapped in the star unless it is big enough to end its life as a super nova. As the star collapses in on itself elements heavier than iron are formed, absorbing energy this time. The whole lot rebounds and is scattered into space as the star explodes. Since our own solar system contains the full range of elements we must belong to a second generation of stars that have been formed from dust produced from previous super novae. Outside the solar disc the material condenses into planets which orbit the Sun – some of which acquire moons which orbit the planets.

Pupils of all ages are fascinated by space and the make-up of the universe. Being abstract, it is a difficult subject to grasp. Stannard has presented it in an exciting and stimulating manner:

> 'Tell me something interesting, Uncle.' Gedanken lazily trailed her hand in the water.
> 'Something interesting?' replied Uncle Albert. He pulled the oars aboard. 'How about: You are made of stardust!'
> 'What does that mean?' asked Gedanken.
> ...Uncle Albert smiled ... 'After the fusion, some of the stars explode.'
> 'Explode?'
> 'It all happens when the stars get very, very old ... the materials thrown out of the exploding star went to form further stars – like our Sun, and the planets – like the Earth. And some was used to make people.'
> 'People?!' Gedanken looked down at herself, and at her hands. 'You mean all this came out of exploding *stars*!'
> 'That's right – the raw materials. You're made of stardust.'
>
> (Stannard 1991, p. 59)

A teaching sequence about the Moon

It always helps to introduce this topic from first-hand experience. Set the following homework at least a month (in winter when the nights are long!) before you plan to introduce the topic; this may take some organising, but is worth it! Ask the pupils to complete Table 15.1 to record the time of moon-rise and moon-set and its appearance by watching the morning, evening and night sky. Remember the Moon tracks the same path across the sky as the Sun, rising in the east and setting in the west. If they can't see the Moon it may be that it is too cloudy, or they will have to wait for the Earth to turn round, because the Moon is on the other side of the Earth. They can use newspapers or the internet to get the exact rising and setting times. Look out for a waxing moon in the afternoon and evening, and a waning moon before dawn and in the morning.

Having discussed the changes in the shape of the Moon over the month, an explanation for what we see needs to be developed. Once again, first-hand experience always helps. The following activity gives just that. It is best carried out in small groups in turn.

TABLE 15.1 MOON CHART

DAY OF LUNAR *MOONTH* (MONTH)	DAY 1	DAY 7	DAY 14	DAY 21	DAY 29
Description of Moon	New moon		Full moon		New moon
Drawing of how Moon appears					
Moon-rise	Dawn (with Sun)		Dusk		
Moon-set	Dusk		Dawn		

Tennis ball moon – demonstrating the phases of the Moon

Each pupil stands in a beam of light from a projector (the Sun's light) holding a tennis ball (the Moon) on a stick at arm's length from their head (representing the Earth as they look up at the Moon). They slowly rotate on the spot towards the left, arm outstretched, so the 'Moon' goes right round the 'Earth'. Remind them not to let the ball go into the shadow of their head (that would be a lunar eclipse); it needs to be lifted up a little higher than their head.

Note that one half of the ball is always lit up, but they don't always see the whole of that lit face – in fact that only happens at a full moon when it is on the opposite side of their head to the 'Sun' (light source). Notice then that the Earth is in darkness so this full moon is high in the sky at midnight. As the Moon goes round encourage the pupils to notice how the lit part of it gradually disappears and eventually looks like a crescent. The rest of the group can follow this but will need to take turns in the light beam to really appreciate the phases properly.

Remind the group that they are looking straight up at the Moon in this model, so this will be when the Moon is at its highest point in its path across the sky. Notice what 'time of day' it is when you see the Moon. For example, when you see the Moon waning as a half moon you will be looking at right angles to the beam of light just as the 'Sun' is coming back to dazzle you, so the Sun will be just rising. The waning half moon will be highest in the sky at dawn, rising at midnight and setting at midday.

Eclipses

An eclipse of the Moon occurs when the Moon passes into the shadow cast by the Earth. This can only happen when the Moon is full, when it is exactly opposite the Sun. It can be seen by everyone experiencing night and lasts for several hours. Many pupils use this explanation for the phases of the Moon, so you need to identify this possible misconception. An eclipse of the Sun occurs when the Moon's shadow is cast onto the Earth. When this happens people see the Sun blocked out (or with a bite taken out of it). This can only be seen at particular locations and times on the Earth's surface. As the Moon's shadow moves across the Earth's surface the Sun appears obscured for only a few minutes, allowing a thin line of locations on Earth to experience a total eclipse, each lasting a few minutes.

These are best demonstrated using a working model of the Sun, Earth and Moon (an *orrery*). Notice that the orbit of the Moon is not exactly in line with the plane of the *ecliptic* (i.e. the orbit of the Earth round the Sun). This means that the Moon usually passes under or over the Sun during a new moon, and under or over the Earth's shadow during a full moon. However, when the Moon's orbit crosses the ecliptic it can block the Sun (solar eclipse) or it can enter the Earth's shadow (lunar eclipse). If, using the orrery, you allow the Earth to make one complete orbit of the Sun and count the number of orbits the Moon has made it will not be a whole number. This is why religious festivals that depend on the phase of the Moon (such as Ramadan and Easter) move from one year to the next.

Somewhere between a rock and a hard place...

There have been many models of planet Earth put forward over the centuries (e.g. a flat disk carried on the back of seven giant turtles on a vast ocean). Ideas have been suggested and refuted but the following is based on our current understanding of a planet which still has many secrets.

Any acceptable model of the Earth's structure had to satisfy several well-researched observations based on both mathematical and scientific calculations:

- Materials below the Earth's surface must have a higher density than that on the surface. Surface rocks have densities of between 2 and 3.5 times that of water. The whole Earth has a density of 5.4 times that of water.

- Earth has a magnetic field that has reversed its direction many times during the lifetime of the planet.

- Earthquakes and volcanoes only occur in certain regions around the Earth.

- Seismic waves sourced on one side of the Earth are not detected in certain regions on the opposite side. If the Earth were a homogenous, uniform solid sphere, the waves would be transmitted through it.

- Fossil records, mineral deposits and coastline shapes suggest that the continents were once joined, suggesting that whole continents are capable of moving across the Earth's surface.

Begin any teaching sequence about the structure of the Earth by asking pupils what they think is beneath their feet. Unsurprisingly their answers may be limited to what they can see – the flooring and soil or dirt and possibly rocks. A few may have heard of the mantle and core. You could use 'half an apple' as a model for the suggested make-up of planet Earth. The skin represents a thin crust, the flesh the mantle and the core, the core.

Plate tectonics

The 'plate tectonics' model of the Earth's structure, which suggests that the crust is composed of 12 major plates closely aligned, answers the five observations outlined above:

- Materials below the Earth's surface are of a higher density than that on the surface; the mantle and the two parts of the core are all of a higher density than the crust. A good picture is of the continents existing for the lifetime of the Earth 'floating' or transported about on denser oceanic crust which is continually being created at mid-ocean ridges and being re-melted at subduction zones.

- Earth's magnetic field is derived from movement in the liquid iron outer core.

- Earthquakes and volcanoes only occur in certain zones around the planet especially at plate boundaries as the plates separate, slide against each other or move together (in which case mountain ranges form).

- The transmission of seismic waves through the different layers of the Earth accounts for the seismic 'shadow' as secondary (or sideways) S waves are absorbed by the liquid outer core.

- Movement in the mantle drags the crustal plates carrying continents apart, resulting in continental drift. This explains peculiarities within the fossil record.

When introducing plate tectonics try asking the following elicitation questions:

- Could the dinosaurs have walked from Europe to America?

- Why are they believed to have died out so dramatically?

See Box 15.1 at the end of the chapter (p. 146) for answers.

A teaching sequence about the rock cycle

The best website for help in teaching about rocks is that of the Earth Science Education Unit based at Keele University (www.earthscienceeducation.com). What follows here is a brief overview.

When we look at a mountain or a large cliff face it is easy to think that rocks are permanent and will never change. However, rocks do change and new ones are formed all the time. If we lived for millions of years we would be able to see the ways in which one rock is gradually produced from another.

Although rocks appear to be static and never changing, they form a fundamental part of the evolution of the planet. Igneous rocks are weathered (broken into bits) and eroded (carried away); the weathered bits eventually settle to form sedimentary rocks mostly at the bottom of lakes and the sea. Tectonic movements may help to bury them deeply below the Earth's surface and they can become changed by heat and pressure, metamorphosing into new rocks which can become uplifted to form mountain ranges. These in turn become weathered and eroded and so the cycle continues…

The rock cycle

First establish your pupils' understanding of the terms 'rock' and 'mineral' – remember that rocks are made of minerals. Each rock is usually composed of several minerals mixed up as small grains or crystals. In sedimentary rocks the grains are usually rounded and glued (cemented) together loosely, making them porous and crumbly. In igneous and metamorphic rock the grains are interlocking, making the rocks harder and impervious to water. Minerals have been used by humans ever since the discovery that a piece of flint made an excellent tool.

To set the rock cycle in context try asking the following question:

■ What is the link between granite, sand, clay, mudstone and slate?

Begin your explanation by introducing volcanoes (use a DVD clip or download one from a website). Let the pupils examine a piece of granite and ask them to describe it. They should note the large light-coloured crystals of quartz, the darker feldspar. Granite is an *igneous* rock. [Note: explore the origins of the word 'igneous' – ignite; to do with fire (see Chapter 4, p. 34).] The crystals in granite are relatively large which indicates slow formation and slow cooling, suggesting that granite cooled from magma that never reached the Earth's surface as a volcano. There is opportunity for practical work on the formation of crystals here.

Inform the class that quartz is silicon oxide, the same as *sand*, and feldspars are complex aluminium silicates, the same as *clay*. So once granite has been broken down (weathered) by a series of physical and biological means the resulting grains will be carried away (eroded), usually by water, and deposited on beaches or river beds as *sand* (quartz) and *clay* (feldspar). If they shake any soil sample with water in a jar and leave it to stand they will see those two minerals – first the *sand* settles to the bottom, followed by the *clay*. These sediments become compacted by geological processes to form sedimentary rocks such as sandstone (silicon based) and mudstone (a derivative of the finer feldspar particles; clay, mud and silt). [Note: explore the etymology of 'sedimentary', similar to sedentary; to settle.] This is also an ideal time to explore and examine fossils, their formation and means of distortion, fragmentation and preservation.

As time goes by these sedimentary rocks become covered with more sediments, compacting them further. The heat and pressure sometimes causes changes in their chemical and physical make-up and the rocks begin to 'cook'. Shale and slate are examples of a rock transformed (metamorphosed) in this way from clay/mudstone.

Other metamorphic rocks, such as marble (from chalk and limestone) and quartzite (from sandstone), have been subject to even higher temperatures caused by being within close proximity of the mantle either through subduction of the plates or by being along a fault line. Discussion of the term 'metamorphic' will bring in cross-discipline uses such as the life cycles of insects [*meta* = from Latin and Greek, meaning to transform; *morph* = Greek, meaning form].

Human impact and the earth sciences

Planet Earth has withstood a turbulent history of geological upheaval and meteorite attack resulting in periods of extreme but natural climate change. However, it has become increasingly evident over the past two decades or so that the human race is having a profound effect on this natural environment and its physical and biological components. The scale and magnitude of our impact on the environment is well documented. As we saw in Chapter 3, our role as science teachers is fundamental to ensuring our pupils develop into informed citizens, able to make use of the knowledge they acquire and develop through their learning. To enable this they need a clear understanding of the complexities of the planet we inhabit and share with other forms of life on Earth.

Summary

In this chapter we have explored some of the conceptual problems facing pupils when trying to understand the scientific history (i.e. formation and development) of the universe and our Earth. We began with the chaotic beginnings of the Big Bang, the evolution of the elements in stars, our solar system and the development of early Earth. We explored a range of teaching sequences on various aspects of the earth sciences, and concluded with the hard-hitting reality of our human impact on this planet. See also Ross *et al.* 2002: CD-Transport.

Box 15.1 Responses to the elicitation questions on p. 144

Could the dinosaurs have walked from Europe to America?

Geological evidence suggests that at the time when the dinosaurs first evolved, approximately 310 million years ago, the continents were 'huddled' together forming one supercontinent called Pangaea. By studying a diagram of this continent it is possible to make out the future continents of North and South America, Africa and southern Europe. Approximately 250 million years later, these sub-parts of Pangaea had moved significantly apart and the gaps between them filled with ocean. The new arrangement of the continent began to take on the appearance we recognise today. So, early on the dinosaurs could have walked from Europe to America, but by the time they died out the continents had moved far enough apart to make movement between them impossible.

Why did the dinosaurs die out?

There are two major theories as to how and why the dinosaurs died out so dramatically in geological terms. The first theory posits a meteor strike to the Earth just off the coast of Mexico approximately 63 million years ago; the second a string of associated basalt lava flows erupting at around the same time. Whichever theory you uphold the outcome was the same: dust and smoke spumed into the atmosphere, causing darkness on a large scale for months or even years. Deprived of sunlight to raise their body temperatures and to fuel their food supplies, the dinosaurs were faced with certain doom.

IV

Planning, Assessment, Teaching and Class Management

Introduction

This part addresses the requirements set out in the Professional Standards, especially Q11–13 and Q22–33. In Chapter 16 we discuss some different approaches to planning in both the medium and short term which can lead to the effective tracking of progression. Being well prepared for the class does not guarantee success but failure to plan usually ends in disaster.

In Chapter 17 we show the importance of assessment *for learning*. We consider the role of questioning and discuss the benefits of peer and self-assessment. The chapter also covers marking pupils' work and the formative use of summative tests. Chapter 18 looks specifically at the assessment of *How science works*.

In Chapter 19 we look at classroom management in a science lab. There is no magic formula that guarantees success when applied, but there are approaches that nearly always fail (like confrontation). It is important to note that certain strategies only work when the relationship between the pupils and the teacher has matured to a level where the group will accept something new. So if something does not work in the early days, do not abandon it for ever: bring it out and dust it off later in the school year. You will find some useful tips on 'what to do in the event of' situations and on learning names.

In Chapter 20 we discuss the practicalities of resourcing and teaching in a science lab with a close eye on our health and safety responsibilities.

Finally, Chapter 21 has a focus on teaching and learning with the older student, but we advise you to retain strategies that worked well with the younger pupils.

16

Planning for Progression

Chapter overview

This chapter outlines the process of planning an effective lesson by moving from a medium-term plan to a detailed lesson plan. We look at how choosing suitable learning objectives and outcomes for the lesson can assist tracking of pupil progress.

Medium-term planning

Many schools make very good use of published teaching schemes these days and this can make life much easier for a training or new teacher. However, it does mean that the learning process of developing such a scheme has been done by someone else and therefore much of the thinking-through of the topic is left out. We would argue strongly that there is much to be gained from developing from scratch sections of a National Curriculum programme of study or exam board specification into a sequence of lessons.

Let us look at two different approaches.

Approach 1

- Read the scheme of work.

- Complete each task in the order presented.

- Plan each lesson with an appropriate activity to achieve the outcomes required.

- Set a mini-quiz or test.

- Record the class test results.

- Compare results from test to test.

Approach 2

- Locate electronic versions of the relevant pages from the school's scheme, the Qualifications and Curriculum Development Authority (QCDA) teaching scheme or exam board specification and National Curriculum requirements for the topics being covered.

- Identify learning objectives from all of these and specific tasks from the schemes that will enable pupils to develop their knowledge and skills and show progression.

- Copy and paste these sections into a sequence of tasks that you feel comfortable to follow and that will allow you to cover the objectives in a sensible, progressive order.

- Create a grid (perhaps in Microsoft Excel) of specific tasks that you will use to assess a specific focus or outcome.

- Divide this sequence into a series of lesson-sized chunks in order to plan the series of lessons. Identify appropriate activities to achieve the outcomes required, starting with an elicitation session.

- Share the sequence of objectives for the topic with the class.

- At the end of the sequence mark the tasks against the grid using the appropriate level descriptor.

Approach 1 is an entirely satisfactory approach as long as the lessons are 'good'. It does mean that your medium-term plan has been done for you as you are following a pre-planned route through the topic. The three disadvantages are:

- you are trying to follow someone else's progression of ideas and links through a topic from their start point

- there is a danger that you will have to adjust the level and content of the lessons part way through the topic

- you may get too involved in the process of getting through the topic and only discover at the end that little progress has been made by the pupils.

Approach 2 has more work at the start of the topic but has three major advantages:

- because you already have your tracking grid set up it is easy to see whether progress is being made

- because you have planned your elicitation, you are more likely to identify a better starting point for the group in front of you

- because you are constantly in dialogue with the group regarding progress, there is a more natural flow as you respond to the needs of the group and adjust your future lessons accordingly.

Progression

As long as you have started from a sensible point that the pupils can relate to, and the *shared* outcomes are met, then the pupils will make progress. If they have been *engaged* in the learning then new knowledge is more likely to stick and they will also be able to apply this knowledge more effectively. When the pupils have learnt new ideas or have a better understanding of the topic and can move up the rough guide to attainment, we can say they have *progressed*. Checking previous attainment and elicitation at the start of the topic are key to finding the sensible point to start from and to identify, later, if progression has really taken place.

Measuring attainment is done in a variety of ways: at Key Stage 3 there are National Curriculum levels from 3 to 8 and at Key Stage 4 there are the GCSE grades from G to A*. The recent introduction of Assessing Pupil Progress (APP) ensures that attainment can be measured as National Curriculum levels in five Assessment Focuses (AFs) that cover every aspect of becoming a scientist. The AFs are generic science skills rather than content-driven knowledge and understanding; use of these can simplify the measurement of pupils' progress from Key Stage 2 into Key Stage 3 and ultimately through to Key Stage 4.

It is useful to compare some of the published methods for guiding and measuring standards. For example, Bloom's taxonomy (Bloom 1956) is a well-known hierarchical list of skills that pupils might develop as they progress. Table 16.1 combines these with some National Curriculum level descriptors and the APP assessment criteria to produce a list of words that can help teachers and pupils to understand how to progress.

Record keeping

Every school has plenty of pupil data available electronically; you will need to keep your own records of pupils' achievement, progress and effort so that you can identify pupils who are not meeting targets and of course to write reports. For example, in Key Stage 3, the requirements of APP mean that you need to keep a list of tasks or activities and the level achieved by each pupil in each of the five AFs; each school will have a different system for recording this information centrally.

From medium-term to lesson planning

Now that you have your lessons in your own preferred sequence, the next task is to 'flesh out' each lesson into a detailed plan. The essential first step is to identify clearly the objectives of each lesson and the desired learning outcomes for pupils working at different levels: exactly what do you want the pupils to learn? There are many styles of lesson-planning proforma but they should all contain the same essential elements as discussed below; an exemplar for a year 7 lesson on 'Energy' is shown in Figure 16.1 at the end of this chapter (pp. 156–7).

- Learning objectives (some schools use 'We Are Learning To....' or WALT). Taken from your medium-term planning exercise or from a prepared scheme, these outline what the pupils are going to learn in the lesson. Sentence starters could include: know that...; understand how...; develop...; be able to...; be aware of...; explore..., etc.

- Learning outcomes (some schools use 'What I am Looking For...' or WILF). These are statements of what the pupils will be able to do by the end of the lesson. Differential targets are good, and 'all must', 'some should' and 'a few could' statements can help. Sentence starters include: use; identify...; describe...; explain...; compare...; summarise..., etc. These become even better if they are written as differentiated statements for the pupils to use as targets. Notice that they should follow Bloom's taxonomy in their level of demand (see Table 16.1).

■ Prior knowledge. What have the pupils learnt in previous lessons or key stages? Make sure that such learning is not repeated for the sake of 'completeness' as this undermines the work of previous teachers or schools, but it is important to build into your lesson some elicitation exercise that allows pupils time to recall and reflect.

■ Provision for pupils with Special Educational Needs (SEN). Named pupils may need additional resources to be prepared.

TABLE 16.1 Useful words for progression

BLOOM'S TAXONOMY	NATIONAL CURRICULUM LEVEL (APPROX.)	SIMPLE MNEMONIC: IDEAL	BRIEF DESCRIPTION	USEFUL WORDS FOR LEARNING OUTCOMES
Knowledge	3	Ideas	Pupils describe, record and recognise simple patterns.	describe; name; sort; select; label; match; record
Comprehension	4	Describe	Pupils use correct scientific terminology in descriptions and simple explanations; they select information and make generalisations.	define; compare; classify; summarise; present; decide; recognise
Application	5	Explain	Pupils apply ideas to new situations and begin to use abstract models; they explain scientifically.	explain; predict; construct; solve; what ... if; suggest; identify
Analysis	6	Apply	Pupils use abstract ideas to explain; they select resources and write conclusions.	conclude; plan; compare; select; explain scientifically; justify
Synthesis	7	Link	Pupils link abstract ideas from different areas; they use quantitative relationships.	calculate; combine; generalise; predict (quantitatively)
Evaluation	8		Pupils evaluate evidence from different sources.	evaluate critically; judge; recommend; develop; interpret

- Adult support. Any teaching assistants in the room may need to be provided with support materials or guidance.

- Homework. This should be an integral part of the lesson rather than an add-on (see Chapter 18 for more detail); this is easier to achieve if it is planned here.

- Resources. A list of paper (worksheets, etc.) and practical (equipment) resources is useful here to ensure that you have everything ready for the lesson. For most practical lessons you will need to have ordered these from the technician in plenty of time! (see also Chapter 19).

- Health and safety. It is essential to do a risk assessment for every aspect of the lesson; an activity that is safe to do with a responsible year 8 class may not be possible with an immature year 11 class. List the possible sources of risk and your chosen methods of reducing the risk (see Chapter 20).

Only when these sections are complete is it possible to plan the lesson activities. With the lesson outcomes firmly in mind, you can now design a sequence of activities which will enable the pupils to achieve those targets. You will need to build into the lesson continual opportunities for assessment so that you can measure the pupils' progress. The different stages of a lesson have been discussed thoroughly in Chapter 6; an exemplar for the year 7 lesson on 'Energy' is shown in Figure 16.2 at the end of the chapter. This book contains several fully worked examples of effective lessons for you to study – in Chapter 1 (on density, pp. 5–7), Chapter 6 (on burning, pp. 58–60) and Chapter 7 (on gravity, pp. 67–8). It is obvious that there is no magic plan that always works, but there are some common ingredients to include.

Start with *impact* – something to attract their attention – then an *elicitation* exercise. Find out what they know and are interested in and you may be able to 'create' a task together for future lessons. While activities are in progress you have the opportunity to talk to each group, confirm their level of ability and help them to move on in their understanding. Provide support (*intervention* activities) and give them time to make sense of it all (*reformulation*). The plenary session can be driven by you from the front: for example, by getting each group to share their findings in turn. Remember that a plenary session does not have to be at the very end of the lesson. As you monitor the pupils' work from lesson to lesson you can complete your markbook/tracking grid very easily. Give them plenty of chance to work and research on their own for homework so ideas get *used*. You have pre-planned the learning outcomes and will be able to assess the progress made by the pupils. Retain high expectations for each group, but don't make them unreasonable lest you fail to get any progression, because the tasks and concepts are too demanding.

Summary

By writing or modifying schemes of work you will develop a better personal understanding of the progression of concepts and skills through a topic. This can then be developed further into individual lesson plans with objectives and outcomes that enable you to assess pupils' progress.

Name	School	Date	Teaching group	Period and duration	No. of pupils	Room	Signature of class teacher
J. Bloggs	High School	3rd March	7Y (mixed ability)	1 hour	15 boys 15 girls	S1	

Pupils with SEN

Amy is partially sighted – will need enlarged copies of nutritional information on food packets.

QTS Standard/personal target for the lesson

Q26a to make effective use of peer assessment to assess pupils according to Assessing Pupil Progress (APP) AF1

Prior learning

Pupils have studied the forms of energy and energy transformations. They have burnt different fuels and have been taught that energy is measured in joules.

Ref to NC & level	
NC 4.1 Levels 3 to 6	QCDA Topic 7I Energy

Learning Objectives: We Are Learning To

Know that energy is measured in joules and kilojoules.

Recognise that different foods release different amounts of energy when respired and that this energy is needed for all animals to live.

Explore how the energy available through respiration of food depends on its constituents, and requires the intake of air (oxygen) like burning.

Begin to calculate the energy available from meals.

Learning Outcomes: What I Am Looking For

All pupils will:
- state the unit of energy
- know that 'burning' food in our bodies is called respiration and supplies the energy for all animals
- be able to identify the energy available on food labels
- know that air is needed to enable us to respire food.

Most pupils will:
- know that 1 kJ = 1000 J
- recognise which foods have the highest energy available per 100 g
- understand how the energy available is displayed on food labels.

Some pupils will:
- understand why fat and sugar release more energy
- be able to do simple calculations using energy in joules
- explain where the body releases energy and uses energy (in cells).

Strategies for differentiation

Different food containers/packets given to different groups.
Table proforma for slower pupils to complete.
Extension tasks for faster pupils – internet search.

Resources

Large variety of food wrappers including sweets, sugary drinks, drinks from school vending machines, fats, pizza boxes, etc. (could be brought in by pupils)
Chocolate bar in wrapper
Table proforma   John Tyndall worksheet

Language for learning

energy; joule (J) (kJ); fat; sugar; (calorie), respiration

Role of additional adult/s

TA should work with Amy to ensure she can read nutrition labels.
Also work with Mike's group to keep them on task.

Health and Safety/Risk Assessment

Very low risk. Pupils should be warned not to eat any food remaining in wrappers.

Cross-curricular expectations: literacy/numeracy/citizenship/ICT

Questions could lead to discussions about obesity and anorexia; need to be sensitive to pupils in class.

Set/Due in/Length/Other Requirements

Need to decide on marking criteria in lesson so that they can peer assess next lesson.

Homework

Pupils design one meal and calculate the energy available using information from lesson and kitchen cupboards. Use double-page spread in their books to present the evidence. Choice of presentation but could include diagram/photo, table of foods, etc.

FIGURE 16.1 The first stage of planning a lesson on 'Energy associated with food'

Time	Teacher Activity	Pupil Activities including differentiation	Formative Assessment Strategies
9.00	**Starter:** Hand out variety of food wrappers so that each pupil has at least one. Remind pupils that this is an energy topic and (*Elicitation*) ask them to find the link between their burning topic (air needed) and respiration of food (air needed) in order to release energy. Use *tell-each-other*. Discuss how the energy information is presented. (*Elicitation*) What do we need the energy for? Does exercise 'give' us energy or 'use' it? Which words should we use? Use *tell-each-other* again.	Pupils study packets and ask 'what is this for?' They discover the energy available in nutritional information and discuss values. TA helps slower pupils to find nutrition 'box'. Pupils spot that energy is per 100g and start to discuss. Pupils discuss what we use energy for and contribute answers, developing correct language. Note that energy comes from respiration using air (oxygen) which happens in cells after the food is digested and has entered the blood to be carried round the body.	I, the teacher, notice how many pupils have realised the link with the Energy topic; have they realised that energy is the same thing in this context? Have they recognised that both burning and respiration need air (oxygen)? Link with panting after exercise?
9.10	**Main:** (*Intervention*) Display learning outcomes for lesson and discuss. Explain the homework task. Explain kJ, kcalorie, calorie, respiration, etc. Ask pupils to design a good way of surveying the energy available from a wide range of the foods, display their results and spot patterns.	Pupils write homework in their planners. (*Reformulation*) Pupils discuss process and design tables to record data. Pupils carry out survey and look for patterns.	Discussion of correct language (and asking pupils to check that I, *the teacher*, always use it) allows me to assess pupils' language development. Discussions with groups and careful questioning reveals their development in spotting patterns and their level of understanding about what the energy is used for. Provides useful information for APP AF1.
9.20	Circulate and support weaker pupils. Stimulate higher-ability pupils with questions and direct towards internet research.	Weaker pupils use table proforma from worksheet. Faster pupils spot patterns and research why fat and sugar have high energy available (and other questions) using the internet.	
9.30	Give 5-minute warning to finish collecting results and spot patterns.	Many pupils have completed their tables and start looking for patterns.	
9.35	**Plenary:** Ask named pairs of pupils for one of their results and observations, patterns, etc. Explain that a typical person needs about 10,000 kJ each day; link to fat and sugar content of different foods.	Pupils need to choose observations that have not already been given by other pairs.	Skilful questioning gives opportunity for the weaker pupils to contribute whilst challenging the more able to think of something new.
9.45	Show the 100g chocolate bar in its wrapper. Tell the story of John Tyndall (he calculated that the only needed a ham sandwich to climb the Matterhorn so that's all he took!). The chocolate bar would enable a pupil to climb about 4 km! What are the energy transformations here? Why was JT wrong? We need energy to keep our body systems going.	All pupils guess the energy available; one reads it out. All pupils guess how high the bar's energy would lift a pupil – and are very surprised by the answer! Pupils link back to lesson 1 of this topic (burning), display higher-order thinking, check the learning outcomes for this lesson and contribute ideas for assessment of homework and write the details in their planners.	Their answers indicate their concept of energy available. Their answers indicate their understanding of energy and ability to use ideas in different contexts.
9.50	Refer back to the learning outcomes. Discuss the homework task and assessment.	They clear away and leave the room.	Their review of the learning outcomes and choice of assessment criteria for homework encourages them to take control of their own learning.

FIGURE 16.2 Lesson structure – the final stage of a lesson plan on Energy associated with food'

17

Assessment for Learning in Science

Chapter overview

Assessment of pupils' learning is an essential process. In this chapter, we study how assessment can be achieved in ways that not only give the required statutory information (summative assessment) but, more importantly, provide learners with useful guidance to help them progress further *and* provide teachers with the tools to help them to do so (formative assessment). It covers the Professional Standards for Teachers Q11–13 and Q26–29.

Formative and summative assessment: the differences

Summative assessment is the necessary process of testing that draws a line under a topic or whole subject and publishes the results for the benefit of pupils, parents, employers and other educational institutions. The data are absolutely essential for informing everyone what the pupil has achieved at each stage of their education. Currently, parents can expect National Curriculum levels to be reported at the end of Key Stage 3, GCSE grades or diplomas at the end of Key Stage 4, AS-levels at the end of year 12 and A-levels (and other qualifications) at the end of Key Stage 5. In addition, most schools report an attainment level or grade at least once every year.

Formative assessment is an on-going process that should guide every aspect of each stage of learning. Often referred to as 'Assessment for Learning' (AfL), it has been defined as 'the process of seeking and interpreting evidence for use by learners and their teachers to decide where the learners are in their learning, where they need to go and how best to get there' (Assessment Reform Group 2002).

It allows teachers to challenge their pupils' understanding as they learn and to check the breadth and depth of their subject knowledge; it allows the pupils to check their understanding and improve it by appropriate methods. Above all, it informs teachers and pupils alike about how to make the next steps. Consider the example in Box 17.1.

Box 17.1 The importance of formative assessment to inform your teaching

A teacher has been teaching about photosynthesis for several lessons.

A GIRL ASKS: Why do we spend so much time on photosynthesis?
ANSWER: Because it is the way plants grow and they are important to us.
THE GIRL: How are they important?
ANSWER: We eat them.
THE GIRL: Don't be silly, we don't eat plants!
ANSWER: Yes we do, we eat carrots, potatoes, peas and tomatoes and things.
THE GIRL: They are not plants. They are vegetables!

This little scenario shows the importance of the elicitation phase of a lesson, which we developed in Chapter 5 (see question 8: Living – plant – animal). Now the teacher must incorporate an appropriate activity into this lesson that helps the pupil (and any other pupils with the same misconception) to appreciate the scientific classification of living organisms. To simply 'tell' her or plough on regardless is pointless: the girl will not learn the new material effectively and the lesson is wasted. To avoid frequent occurrences of this problem, it is essential to elicit and clear up misconceptions as we launch into a new topic. If we do not then pupils will fail to accept new ideas or block them because they are not relevant, or they do not fit with their existing model. Chin (2003) provides a useful comparison between deep thinking and surface learning. Formative assessment needs to recognise and reward deep thinking.

Formative assessment has many strands, including:

■ teacher questioning

■ marking

■ peer and self-assessment

■ formative use of summative testing.

A series of good lessons incorporates all of these plus many more: the teacher can incorporate AfL strategies throughout the lessons to such an extent that the lesson plans are continually modified to take into account the feedback from the pupils. We will consider each of these in turn.

Teacher questioning

This is the most important and commonly used teaching tool; teachers do this all the time and pupils understand the 'game' that they must play in answering (after all, the teacher knows the answers so why is she asking?). At its simplest level, the teacher can select appropriate closed questions which reveal how much the pupils know. Skilful teachers can develop methods of asking these questions; by asking the pupils to write their answers on small whiteboards, they can see how *many* of the class know the answer. They can also increase the richness and complexity of the questions to reveal more complex misconceptions and to stimulate higher-order thinking. Figure 17.1 shows how the complexity of a question can be increased.

Increasing complexity and richness

1. Which is the process that plants use to make their food: photosynthesis or photovoltaic?

2. What is the name of the process by which plants make food? It begins with P.

3. How many chemical products are made in this process?

4. What are the two chemical products of this process?

5. What happens to the two chemical products of photosynthesis?

6. Why is this process so important for *all* life (not just the plants)?

7. Some people think that a plant makes its food from the soil; how could you prove that they are wrong?

8. There is an 'old wives' tale' that says that you should never keep a pot plant in your bedroom at night but it is okay during the day. Is this true or just superstition?

FIGURE 17.1 Questions in order of complexity and richness

In a class of mixed ability, start by asking straightforward, closed questions and take answers from less able pupils first. As you increase the difficulty of the questions, move from hands-up to a no-hands strategy to avoid some pupils becoming complacent and lazy. To compensate for this new regime, allow more thinking time (at least 10 seconds and longer for more complex questions) and offer the opportunity for pupils to discuss their answers (remember the 'tell-each-other' technique in Chapter 8, pp. 71–2). To stimulate a broader discussion of a high-level question, choose several pupils to answer, then ask another pupil (perhaps one who could not answer an earlier question) to select the best answer and give a reason.

It is useful for all teachers to make a list of key questions related to the learning objectives, prior to each lesson. The route taken through these questions can be adapted to the revealed knowledge and skills of the pupils.

Marking

Marking a pupil's work provides an opportunity for the teacher to respond to each pupil as an individual and to provide feedback and guidance at exactly the right level – this is a perfect example of personalised learning through differentiation. Using suitable tasks and comments on the work, it is possible to elicit a response from the pupil that results in a change of thinking and working. In other words, the pupil is able to continue learning because they understand how to improve *and* they are motivated to do so.

Figure 17.2 shows an able pupil's inadequate response to a task, with the annotations of two teachers. The task was to explain the physics of the cover-picture on Keith Johnson's book *Physics for You*, published by Nelson-Thornes.

Teacher A has only succeeded in alienating the pupil thus ensuring that she will not increase her effort next time. Teacher B has encouraged her to improve her work, given clear guidelines for doing so *and* given a deadline for the work to be done (it is essential that the teacher makes a note in their markbook to remember this deadline!).

It has probably taken Teacher B about 2 hours to mark the work of a whole class; it is certainly not possible to mark every piece of work to this level of detail every

Teacher A's annotations

~~Canon~~ Cannon

E   Not finished, poor effort

Teacher B's annotations

You have made a good start Suzie, with a clear description of what happens in one section of the picture.

Now you need to finish the account. I will collect it in next Monday.

Remember to:

1. Check the spelling of 'canon'.
2. Write **explanations** of the processes
3. Use **scientific** words in your explanations

Here is an example: 'When the match strikes the box, friction causes it to get ...... and start ......'

Able pupil's inadequate homework attempt at describing a picture scientifically.

Professor Messer wakes up

The boy pushes the newspaper onto a tray which is connected to a hammer, by a rope. The hammer knocks the canon ball onto the ledge which rolls down and starts off the wheels. Three wheels are connected. Connected to one is a box of cornflakes. When the wheel turns they fall out of the box and into the bowl. Connected to another of the wheels is a pint of milk which also falls into the bowl when the wheel turns. On the edge of this wheel is a match which strikes the box as it turns, then lights the candle. The candle then boils the water in the kettle above, which goes through the funnel and filters into the cup.

FIGURE 17.2 Teachers' annotations on a piece of homework

week! But the benefits are so great that this *should* be done when you first start teaching a class (to set your expectations and gauge the level of the pupils) and for key tasks every few weeks thereafter (to monitor progress and effort, to reinforce expectations and to redress misconceptions).

If you have marked like Teacher B, then do allow a significant time at the beginning of the next lesson for the pupils to respond to your comments. During this time, pupils who have a small number of tasks to do can complete them while you speak to those who are further adrift from your expectations.

It has been noted (Black and Harrison 2004) that where a mark or grade is given pupils do not search the text for comments about where they went wrong; those with a high grade sit back feeling smug whilst those with a low grade close their books (and minds) in disgust. Positive comments and suggestions for improvement at the end of the piece are far more formative and thus productive.

Reducing the marking load

Not all the work produced needs to have this detailed response; you may only need to record the fact that the work has been completed on time. Many types of work can be checked in the following lesson by providing an answer sheet (perhaps displayed on the board for most pupils). Examples of suitable work for this method are:

- crossword

- sorting a muddled method

- matching words to statements

- preparation for the next lesson: research; draft design; survey, etc.

- multiple choice test paper.

Here are some other ideas for easing the burden:

- Ask pupils to hand in their books open at the correct page; this saves you time finding the work but also makes it easy to check who has not done it so that you can hold them back straight away. This instant feedback allows for a possible immediate detention if the lesson is just before 'break' or lunchtime, and makes it easy to complete the report cards of 'tracked' pupils with current information.

- Set homework at the beginning of the lesson; this can easily become the focus of the lesson and a key learning outcome. Pupils will get ahead of their work, make a start on their homework and are much more likely to complete it.

- Set homework that has clear success criteria: pupils know how it is to be assessed and will, with practice, be able to match their work to the criteria. Marking such a piece of work is much faster as you are just looking for a particular sequence of ideas and evidence; the best of these is suitable for peer and self-assessment (see below). One example of a suitable task is to draw a diagram (e.g. How could they make fresh water from sea water if they were stranded on a desert island?). The pupils have already listed the desirable features of a good diagram during the lesson (labels, sharp pencil, etc.) and are more likely to achieve them, thus making your job much easier.

Peer and self-assessment

This is very much more than pupils marking their own or another pupil's work, although that is an important ingredient. The pupils should be actively engaged in discussing the differences between *their* work and the mark scheme or an exemplar piece of work. Listen to the pupils: if they are arguing about whether a sentence qualifies for a Level 4 or a Level 5, and they use phrases like 'but that is an explanation not a description', then you know that they are truly learning from the experience.

One example of a suitable Key Stage 3 task is a level-assessed task (LAT) in which a level-ladder is supplied, stating what is expected for each National Curriculum level. At GCSE, some exemplar coursework at different grades could be provided and pupils discuss which one is the closest match to their own work.

Formative use of summative testing

Marking a set of test scripts is the most informative feedback of all for the reflective teacher: now it is clear just what the pupils have and haven't grasped! It can be thoroughly depressing to discover so many misconceptions after you have taught the topic so well – but do remember that misconceptions take a long time and much careful discussion to unravel, and that the pupil needs to reinforce their new understanding many times before it becomes embedded. After pupils have done an end-of-topic test or school exam, it is easy to just hand back the work; after all, they only want to know their marks! 'Going through' a test is one of the hardest lessons to manage as it tends to be in a didactic style and the pupils don't want to listen. With some easy modifications, this process can become formative and much more enjoyable for all. After all, this is the very best time to revisit the topic and help pupils to gain an even deeper understanding.

When marking tests, tick the correct ideas to indicate each mark gained but simply underline any incorrect answers at the relevant place without giving the correction. Annotate to provide clues to the missing information (see example in Box 17.2).

Box 17.2 Teacher's annotation of an exam answer

Exam question:
  Explain how a nuclear power station produces electricity.

Pupil's answer with teacher's annotations:
  Atoms in the fuel <u>fuse together</u> and produce a lot of heat.
  <u>This</u> makes steam and turns a turbine to make electricity.
  There is a stage missing here.

In addition to giving a percentage and perhaps a National Curriculum level or GCSE grade, it is productive to write a comment about how much the pupil has improved since the last test. When handing back the test, also hand out a mark scheme in pupil-friendly language (some exam board mark schemes are not very helpful to pupils) so that pupils can identify their errors. You might choose some key questions to go through with the whole class, but most of this work can be done by the pupils individually or in pairs. As they correct their mistakes, they should decide which category each lost mark fits into. Examples of categories are given in Table 17.1.

TABLE 17.1 Categories of lost marks in tests and exams

CATEGORY	EXAMPLE
Careless error	Missing units in a calculation Incorrect rearrangement of a formula Misspelling of two similar words
Lack of revision	Simply not knowing a fact or formula
Poor use of language	The pupil clearly knows the answer but has not used the correct terminology or has contradicted himself or has started the explanation half-way through
Lack of understanding	Referring to 'particles expanding' during heating Unable to answer a question on parallel circuits
Lack of time	The end of the test is unanswered
Poor reading of the question	The pupil answers the question they think is asked or misses a part of the question. Q: Why does the plant grow towards the window? A: During the daytime. Q: State and explain how the force will change. A: The force goes up.

At the end, they can add up the marks in each category and calculate the percentage they would have achieved, for example, with more revision or by reading the questions more carefully. Finally, they should write two or three specific targets for themselves, based on their analysis of the lost marks; they could write them on the test itself (useful to collect in and use when writing reports) and in their planners for future reference and updating.

Summary

Assessment for Learning can, and should, be embedded into every aspect of a teacher's work with pupils. From planning the objectives of the lesson, through questioning and modelling of good answers during the lesson, to marking the work produced and the use of peer and self-assessment, the teacher can help the pupils to improve their understanding by the use of carefully constructed responses and choice of further tasks. The key is to praise the pupils on what they have achieved and to encourage them to improve on it.

18

Assessment of *How Science Works*

Chapter overview

This chapter explores aspects of assessment at Key Stages 3 and 4 set within the context of *How science works*. This aspect of the Science Secondary National Strategy uses practical and enquiry skills to collect, interpret and analyse evidence. Often this is achieved through problem-solving, carried out by pupils in groups or individually. This forms only one aspect of science – supplying the evidence – but it needs ideas, theories and applications of science to provide a focus. In this chapter we look at how recent developments in assessment techniques are applied at Key Stages 3 and 4 to assess pupil progress within the broad arena of *How science works*.

Assessment for Learning and the science curriculum

As we discussed in Chapter 17, Assessment for Learning is seen as being fundamental to good teaching and learning. There is now a stronger emphasis on teacher assessment in the secondary curriculum, since the removal of the Key Stage 2 and 3 SATs. Assessment for Learning creates a common language with the potential to develop high-quality assessment beneficial to all concerned – teachers, pupils, parents and external bodies alike. Supporting this approach is a range of tools including the Assessing Pupil Progress (APP) materials developed by the Qualifications and Curriculum Development Authority (QCDA) and the National Strategies. Collectively they aim to enable the teacher to assign a progress level to individual pupils against a clear set of assessment criteria. The approach is to be developed across the Key Stages, creating a common language of assessment which will enable better transition between Key Stages and consistency in pupils' education.

The National Curriculum: *How science works*

The National Curriculum has undergone a series of revisions since its inception, the most recent being at Key Stage 4 in 2006 (implemented in 2007) and at Key Stage 3 in 2008 (with a phased implementation from 2009). Both sets of changes include and promote an understanding of *How science works*.

The current changes in science at Key Stage 4 give greater emphasis to scientific process and less to content. The thinking behind this is that sufficient basic content is covered in primary school science and at Key Stage 3. It is therefore suggested that Key Stage 4 should progress the student in other ways, with *How science works* being at the top of the list! (DfES 2006a). Controversial in its own right, this approach presents significant dilemmas and definite challenges to the teacher of science. Many teachers have never been professional scientists. Having spent much of their adult lives in education they have never lived the scientific process, except at university, and during their own training and their teaching. If they are to rise to these new challenges there is a need to re-establish links with those people who are doing it – people in industry and in scientific research (we discuss ways this might be done in Chapter 23).

The changes at Key Stage 4 not only cite a reduction in content, but also give a greater emphasis to learning strategies and making science relevant to everyday life – in particular the applications and implications of *How science works*. Here pupils learn about the use of contemporary scientific and technological developments and their benefits, drawbacks and risks. They consider how and why decisions about science and technology are made, including those that raise ethical issues, and about the social, economic and environmental effects of such decisions. They learn about the uncertainties in scientific knowledge and how scientific ideas change over time and about the role of the scientific community in validating these changes (DfES and QCDA 2005, p. 37).

This focus on *How science works* saw the end of the traditional coursework assessment. The objective is not that pupils should gain a body of knowledge but rather develop an understanding of science as a process (DfES 2006a), as a means of progressing the conceptual knowledge developed earlier in their education. Within the science curriculum the *How science works* strand is divided into four key areas:

- data, evidence, theories and explanations
- practical and enquiry skills
- communication skills
- applications and implications of science.

Data, evidence, theories and explanations

The process of science usually begins when someone notices something (see Figure 2.1); they then propose an explanation (an idea) which they can test out practically as a means of arriving at an explanation. The examples in Box 18.1 set this idea in an everyday context:

Box 18.1 Ideas and explanations – modern-day context

Stimulating pupils' ideas – thinking about more evidence

- *Lemonade fizz*. Sometimes people can be seen adding a spoonful of sugar to lemonade or cola to make it fizz more. Why do you think this happens? Is it only sugar that has this effect? What would you do to find out?
- *Pineapple jelly*. Jelly made with tinned pineapple sets, whereas that made with fresh pineapple doesn't. The tinned pineapple is superheated in the production process; do you think this might affect its performance in the setting process? What do you think might be going on here?

(For those people who need an answer, see Box 18.3 at the end of this chapter.)

Because pupils often need to go through the same revolutions in thought as did scientists in the past, it is particularly useful to use historic case studies. The following excerpt, from the history of photosynthesis, is a case in point.

When considering the evidence that exists to support our current understanding of photosynthesis, it is necessary to go back in time to the work of several historic scientists. Each made their own contribution to this evidence but it was invariably someone else's subsequent work that accepted or refuted their conclusions. (The following sections are adapted from McGrath 1999, p. 600.)

Is water the source of energy in plants?

In the 1600s Jan Baptista van Helmont, a Flemish physician, chemist and physicist, carried out a famous experiment by growing a willow tree in a pot for five years. At the end of this period the tree had increased in mass by 74 kg but the mass of the soil had changed little. Van Helmont believed that water was the source of the extra mass and the plant's source of life. John Woodward, a professor and physician at Cambridge University in the late 1600s, tried to design an experiment to test van Helmont's hypothesis that water was the source of the extra mass. In a series of experiments over 77 days, Woodward measured the water consumed by plants. A typical result was one plant gaining about 1 g in mass, while Woodward had added a total of almost 76,000 g of water during the 77 days of plant growth. Woodward correctly suggested that most of this water was 'drawn off and conveyed through the pores of the leaves and exhaled into the atmosphere'. So the hypothesis that water is the nutrient used by plants was rejected. (See also Figure 14.1, the 'tub tree' question, p. 134.)

The interaction of plants with air

In August 1771 Joseph Priestley, an English chemist, put a sprig of growing mint into a transparent closed space with a candle that used up the air (oxygen was not discovered yet) until it soon went out. After 27 days, he re-lit the extinguished candle again and it burnt perfectly well in the air that previously would not support it. And how did Priestley light the candle if it was placed in a closed space? He focused sunlight beams with a mirror onto the candle wick. So Priestley demonstrated that plants somehow change the composition of the air.

In another celebrated experiment, from 1772, Priestley kept a mouse in a jar of air until it collapsed. He found that a mouse kept with a plant would survive [Consider the ethics behind this one!]. These kinds of observations led Priestley to offer an interesting hypothesis that plants restore to the air whatever breathing animals and burning candles remove.

Plants and light

Jan Ingenhousz took Priestley's work further and demonstrated that it was light that plants needed to make oxygen (oxygen was discovered a few years earlier, in 1772 by Carl Wilhelm Scheele). Ingenhousz was mistaken in believing that the oxygen made by plants came from carbon dioxide rather than water. However, he was the first person to demonstrate that light is essential to this process and that it somehow purifies air fouled by candles or animals. In 1779 Ingenhousz put a plant and a candle into a transparent closed space. He allowed the system to stand in sunlight for two or three days. This assured that the air inside was pure enough to support a candle flame. But he did not light the candle. Then, he covered the closed space with a black cloth and let it remain covered for several days. When he tried to light the candle it would not light. Ingenhousz concluded that somehow the plant must have acted in darkness like an animal. It must have breathed, fouling the air. And in order to purify the air plants need light. (See the discussion of misconceptions about photosynthesis in Chapter 14, pp. 134–5.)

Practical and enquiry skills, applications and communications

This subsection of the *How science works* strand covers the process skills of scientific enquiry: planning; obtaining and presenting evidence (with an emphasis here on the use of ICT); considering evidence and analysing data in terms of earlier predictions; evaluating the process and data obtained; and suggesting improvements. As part of the National Curriculum pupils are encouraged to consider the following:

- The details of the procedure. Is it an investigation or is it an experiment? What is the difference? What science underpins the process (both hypotheses and facts) and what are the expected or predicted outcomes based on these?

- Significance of variables involved and fair testing. What types of variables are they and are they controlled to ensure a fair test?

- Reliability and validity of the procedures employed. How reliable the data are depends upon the nature of the process, if it can be repeated and if it is consistent. How valid they are depends upon whether or not the data are telling you what you want to know.

Whilst pupils study the four broad conceptual areas of science of the Key Stage 4 National Curriculum (organisms and health, chemical and material behaviour, energy, electricity and radiations and the environment, Earth and universe) they will also be taught the knowledge, skills and understanding of how science works. There should be an emphasis on relating science to everyday life, exploring everyday occurrences through whole or partial investigations, communicating findings and interpretations effectively and considering all aspects of health and safety when conducting such investigations. The work of Goldsworthy and Feasey (1999), which helps to make the planning and conduct of investigations clearer, was mentioned in Chapter 2 (pp. 13–15). What we need to discuss here is how this central aspect of science can be assessed in school.

How does the science assessment procedure work?

The GCSE science specifications place significant emphasis on the skills, knowledge and understanding of *How science works* and its application through given content. Assessment of this varies between the examination boards, either through examinations or through other means such as practical tasks or related coursework. The use of teacher assessment is fast appearing in all the Key Stages and is currently executed through Key Stage 4. The following example of assessment procedure applies to one examination board only; others are very different but the principles remain the same.

■ Practical skills assessments (PSAs) assess the pupil's ability to work in an organised and safe manner whilst working practically in the lab. They can be carried out at any time during the course.

■ Investigative skills assignments (ISAs) assess the pupil's ability to undertake a task and collect, process and evaluate data. They can be carried out at any time during the course. Pupils carry out a practical task set by the exam board under normal laboratory conditions; they then take a written test under controlled conditions. The test asks questions concerning the data collected during the practical task as well as that provided as part of the test. The test is then teacher marked using detailed marking guidance from the exam board.

Pupils may take several ISAs during the course and the ISA with the best mark is submitted for moderation by the exam board. The aim is that both the PSA and the ISA are seen as integral to the course and not an addition. Pupils are encouraged to practise ISAs and may use all or part of sample ones in this process. One of the most important uses is to allow pupils to become familiar with the terminology. They will need to identify the different types of variable used in an investigation, demonstrate that they can distinguish between reliability and validity, and precision and accuracy, whilst commenting on their effectiveness in the investigation. See Box 18.2 for an example.

Box 18.2 Example of an ISA taken from the Assessment and Qualifications Alliance (AQA) specifications (www.aqa.org.uk)

Biology 3 ISA 3.4 – Yoghurt

Teachers' notes
This ISA relates to AQA Unit B3: Biology (4411) Section 13.5.

Area of investigation
This work should be carried out during the teaching of the section relating to:

How are microorganisms used to make food and drink?

The practical work

Candidates should be given the opportunity to carry out an investigation concerning how temperature influences the production of yoghurt from milk.
　　Candidates can add a starter culture of suitable bacteria to a sample of milk. Candidates could then record:

- the change of pH with time at different temperatures
- the time taken to reach a certain pH at different temperatures
- the pH reached after a certain time at different temperatures.

If pH meters are available, these could be used. Alternatively, candidates could use indicator paper or indicator solution to record the pH change.
　　If measuring or observing the pH change proves difficult, candidates could instead record the consistency of yoghurt, for example by adding a small marble to the yoghurt and recording the time taken for it to disappear.

Key Stage 3

The Key Stage 3 curriculum is characterised by a series of yearly learning objectives targeting each year group from 7 to 9 (the documentation also includes learning objectives and other information for years 10 and 11; thereby indicating progression). As part of the Secondary National Strategy these learning objectives are made explicit and shared with the pupils. They are laid down within the Secondary Framework for Science in substrands of the major themes representing the relevant areas of study. For example, within the major theme of 'Energy transfer' is a substrand entitled 'Energy transfer and sound'. As the title implies, this is all about sound but within the context of energy transfer. Detail includes the target year group, their yearly learning objectives, and a section entitled 'amplification' which explains in more depth what pupils will be learning to do. There are strategies for progression and some rather interesting 'rich questions'; for example at year 9: 'Why can't we still hear the Battle of Hastings?', 'Is there noise pollution under water?', 'Can deaf people enjoy music?' and 'Should drums be nailed to a stage?' And at year 11: 'If you shout at something does it get hotter?'

To assess pieces of work, whether practical or written, peer and self-assessment are used on an informal basis, with immediate feedback being given. The aim is to encourage pupils to engage with their learning. Periodically pupils will be assessed within a structured approach referred to as Assessing Pupil Progress (APP). During this assessment the teacher will make judgements of attainment within National Curriculum levels. This ensures that pupil progress is tracked using diagnostic information about pupils' strengths and weaknesses to improve teaching, learning and the rate of pupils' progress. Assessing Pupil Progress describes a cyclical process:

- The teacher plans for progression for the National Strategy yearly learning objectives.

- They collect and feed back to pupils evidence of their progress during the day-to-day teaching and learning process.

- The teacher then reviews a range of evidence for periodic assessment (APP) and makes a level-related assessment using the APP criteria, which is then moderated.

- The teacher's planning, teaching and learning may then be adjusted to accommodate the emerging needs, within the framework of the Secondary National Strategy.

Various APP materials have been produced, all of which feature Assessment Focuses (AFs), as follows:

- AF1 – thinking scientifically

- AF2 – understanding the applications and implications of science

- AF3 – communicating and collaborating in science

- AF4 – using investigative approaches

- AF5 – working critically with evidence.

APP Science Assessment Guidance material is available from the QCDA website. This expands on each of these AFs, giving some suggestions for taking this forward. For example, Level 4 AF1 may be assessed by asking pupils to identify scientific evidence that is being used to support or refute ideas or arguments drawn from a range of contexts or practical situations. The same AF but at Level 8 asks the pupil to select and justify an appropriate approach, from a range of contexts or practical situations, to evaluating the relative importance of a number of different factors in explanations or arguments. Progression in learning and in application is therefore built into the process.

The pupil as scientist

Research scientists spend months or years developing ideas and methods and going up blind alleys. The results which actually achieve what they are after often come over the course of a few frenzied days. There is little time in school for this blind-alley, rather messy, pilot work. The more we leave pupils to devise and carry out their own investigations, the messier they get, so we resort to helping them by providing recipes of things that we know will work – and get GCSE marks. Partial investigations, through the ISAs, are therefore important as they allow pupils to plan (without having actually to do their experiments) and then to analyse (with 'clean' data provided by the teacher). This has been recognised as important and significant, not just to science education but to science as a whole, by the Science, Technology, Engineering and Mathematics (STEM) agenda (see Chapter 23). The agenda aims to:

- raise pupil motivation and achievement in the STEM subjects

- improve the teaching and learning of science and the other STEM subjects and their related skills, especially investigative and ICT skills

- increase the interaction between schools and the science and engineering community.

To achieve these aims the STEM organisations have developed curriculum activities and materials for use specifically in *How science works*. These have been well received by teachers and pupils alike, and can be accessed through the STEMNET website (www.stemnet.org.uk). We return to this theme in Chapter 23, p. 223.

Summary

In this chapter we have seen how pupils can assume the role of being a scientist within the constraints of the school laboratory. Much of the process involved, however, is not hands-on practical. As we saw in Chapter 6 (Figure 6.2), there is a need for the pupil to predict what will happen and then test these ideas and expectations. It is this testing that forms the practical aspect – and even then, unless pupils are blindly following a recipe, thought and preparation form a fundamental part of this.

For any of the above to be successful, *How science works*, and the investigations that invariably support it, need purpose – something that the pupil can relate to and have empathy with. *How science works* needs to be recognised as underpinning the activity of the wider scientific community, not just a way of getting marks at GCSE, however important that also has to be.

Box 18.3 Responses to the ideas/explanation questions on p. 167

- *Lemonade fizz.* This happens when any solid is added to a fizzy drink – the solid particles allow small stable bubbles to begin to form. The process is referred to as nucleation and is used in several processes, for example seeding clouds.
- *Pineapple jelly.* Superheating the pineapple denatures the enzyme pectinase, which breaks down pectin, a carbohydrate responsible for setting jellies and jams. The fresh, untreated pineapple contains pectinase so the jelly doesn't set.

One to try for yourself

When a can of diet cola and one of ordinary cola are immersed in a tank of water, the diet cola floats, but the ordinary cola sinks. Why do you think this is?

19

Managing Pupils in Science Lessons

Chapter overview

Managing pupils in a science lesson requires many specialised skills in addition to the usual classroom management. Although safety issues are considered in detail in Chapter 20, there are a number of other management points covered in this chapter that make the difference between a well-managed learning environment and chaos!

Starting the lesson

Entering the laboratory

You have planned the lesson and ordered your equipment and resources; you arrive in plenty of time, to find an unruly gaggle of pupils in the corridor outside the lab. Of course the door is locked to prevent unsupervised entry for safety reasons, and they are taking this opportunity to play 'tag', stamp on each other's feet, 'peanut' their ties and much more! It is important to assert your control immediately by using a firm and commanding voice (low pitch but not loud), wait for them to line up and calm down and then invite them into the room. If this is the first lesson with the class, you may choose to select your own seating plan: boy/girl/boy/girl is rather harsh on shy pupils and alphabetical order always seems to cause unfortunate pairings, but two boys/two girls seems to work well for Key Stage 3 classes.

Starting work quickly

All lessons need an engaging introduction which settles the pupils and focuses their attention on the topic for the lesson. Try displaying an interesting picture or demonstrating a short experiment; have some questions ready for pupils to discuss or answer in their books, or come draped in jewellery as in Chapter 1! For very lively classes it is useful to hand out this 'starter' work on a worksheet and demand silence while you call the register. As science teachers, we are very lucky to have such a wealth of stimulating ideas to use: anything from a picture of the 'toilet' bag used by early Apollo astronauts (in a 'Space' topic) to a demonstration of a toy hovercraft (in a 'Forces' topic)! Use the resulting discussion of these activities to introduce the learning outcomes for the lesson.

It is at this stage that the ground rules are set and the strategies developed to avoid potential dangers.

During the lesson pupils should be engaged in a wide variety of activities that take them closer towards achieving the learning outcomes. Ensure that pupils move promptly from one task to another and that they are clear about what they are learning ('*Tell each other* what you expect to see/have to do...'); this will create an atmosphere of pace in the lesson and prevent them from having enough freedom to 'mess around'. Sometimes it is useful to stand back and watch the learning happen. Allowing pupils the time to find their own answer is always more effective than diving in and providing the answer; pupils need time to accept new ideas and models. When they have to accept that their old ideas may be limited or incorrect they can display strange or unacceptable behaviour – for example, silence, aggressive behaviour and language, sulkiness, elation, tiredness, anguish. You will sometimes see pupils clutch their heads and moan, 'Sir/miss, you're doing my head in'. When this happens, you have really got them thinking!

There are also times in a lesson when you think you have introduced a topic well and the pupils are on task and working enthusiastically, then someone drops a bombshell, displaying a misconception that shows a complete lack of understanding of the topic covered in the lesson. It is important to identify these 'critical moments' and to respond appropriately. One response may be to abandon the planned lesson and attack the misconceptions; another is to acknowledge the confusion, check that it is not a problem with the rest of the class ('*Tell each other* what you think' and take some responses), and promise to discuss it with the pupil at a quieter moment in the lesson.

Crisis points and critical moments

It is when the unexpected happens that you are put to the test. Pupils will be watching to see how each incident is dealt with: are you in control, are you confident? Children can sense weakness and they expect a higher standard from you than they do from themselves or their parents. There are crisis points when drastic action is needed to maintain the integrity of the lesson and critical points when the focus of the lesson and the learning outcomes need to change. The incidents in Box 19.1 will occur from time to time. For each of them think how you would react. Would it depend on the class at the time, or are there universal answers? How many of these would not happen were your preparation better? As we work our way through this chapter, we use these incidents to illustrate some basic principles of classroom management.

Box 19.1 Critical incidents to consider

1. It starts snowing and they all stare through the window.
2. You hear breaking glass from across the lab.
3. Someone burns their hand on a hot tripod.
4. Someone trips over a bag.
5. Someone offers you a match to light the Bunsen burner.
6. A pupil asks, 'Did I see you working in the supermarket last summer?'
7. When the class has left, you find one of the hand lenses is missing.
8. A 'rugby scrum' forms round the front bench as pupils try to get their apparatus.
9. Someone carries on chatting as you try to address the class.
10. Someone carries on with their work whilst you are talking to the class.

It starts snowing: no. 1 in the list

This is beyond your control. Do not fight it, as it may provide a better focus for your lesson and a good vehicle for learning. If it is just a distraction then a 3-minute diversion may be what is needed to satisfy curiosity. Make a virtue out of necessity and use some science concepts with them (change of state, friction, light and colour, the atmosphere...).

Burnt hands and breaking glass: nos 2 and 3

The more quickly you can reach an incident, such as no. 2 (broken glass) or no. 3 (burnt hand), the more easily you can make a judgement as to whether you need to stop the whole class for a safety warning, or to keep calm and deal with the incident locally (send for the dustpan, or get the pupil to put their hand under the tap). By agreeing on the standard procedures at the start, you can prevent a lot of these minor accidents. Teachers must develop 'scanning eyes' that see everything in the lab at the same time; it is sometimes useful to stand at the side of the room so that the pupils' attention is not focused onto you but they know you are watching them.

A tripped-over bag – only one rule: no. 4

'Behave appropriately' should be the laboratory rule. We deal with safety precautions more fully in the next chapter, but incident no. 4 (tripping over a bag) is a case in point. Bags are put under the benches not because it is a rule of the teacher, but because it is dangerous to leave them in the aisles. It is appropriate behaviour to put them somewhere safe. Rather than tripping over a bag, suppose a pupil gets something in their eye because they refused to wear goggles. This is an unnecessary and avoidable injury all because you failed to notice their inappropriate behaviour (lack of eye protection). For this behaviour you need to have some alternative writing work for them to do in a safe corner of the laboratory – they are not allowed to continue with the practical work. Hopefully this happens before they have actually damaged their eyes. Emphasise calmly that you *must* be in control in the lab as there is only one of you but 30 pupils. They are there to understand science not to get injured!

Where are your matches? Pretend to be angry: no. 5

There are times when teachers have to be 'angry'. It can be an effective strategy to manage behaviour, provided that you are not *actually* angry (once you do get angry then you will have lost). You are on stage and you can 'act' but do remember to be angry at the behaviour, not the child. If you are offered a match (no. 5) you must be 'angry': it is against school rules for pupils to be carrying matches or lighters around. Don't get drawn into an argument with the pupil but adopt the 'broken record technique' of repeating your statement over and over again: 'Lighters are not allowed in school – sit there and do that work while we wait for [senior member of staff] to arrive'. Meanwhile, drive the lesson forward for the rest of the pupils – and remember to bring your own lighter to the lesson next time! With good planning and preparation many of these incidents should never be allowed to occur.

The supermarket – use humour: no. 6

Use humour to defuse or deflect possible problem situations and to stir up interest in the topic. You have to judge this carefully if you do not wish to lose control or trivialise the subject. If someone asks you if they saw you in the supermarket in the summer (no. 6) do not get sniffy: laugh it off but show that personal comments are inappropriate in lesson time. Above all, don't be tempted into believing that you have to be friendly with the pupils in order to be liked; they will like you more if they can *respect* and *trust* you as an adult teacher, not as their friend.

The missing hand lens – delegation of tasks: no. 7

Delegating tasks as part of a recognition/reward system can be very effective. Pupils (especially younger ones) love handing out books and collecting apparatus, tasks involving status and trust. Problems such as no. 7 (hand lens missing) are avoided by adopting clear systems for handing out and counting back apparatus so that the pupils know that it will be checked. You may not have time to count everything, but chosen pupils will do it diligently for you. Most schools provide small and desirable items of apparatus in trays with slots (see Figure 19.1), so it becomes easy to see if there is any apparatus missing at the end of the lesson. Be aware of larger desirable items (e.g. top-pan balances, sadly) and make sure that you check them well before the end of the lesson; once the pupils have left the lab, trying to get the item back is always time-consuming, stressful for all and seldom successful.

The rugby scrum – moving round the lab: no. 8

You need to manage the distribution of apparatus carefully to reduce the potential for fights in the scrum that could form (no. 8). Several techniques make things easier: distribute the trays of apparatus around the lab and ask one pupil from each group to collect various bits; have pupils take trays of apparatus around, giving each group their 'bit'; only allow collection to take place once the group has drawn a blank table for results, so they don't all come together.

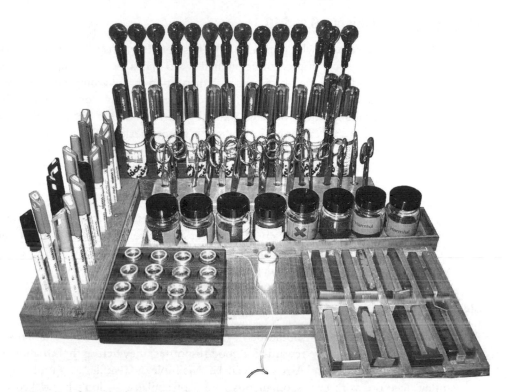

FIGURE 19.1 Apparatus in containers for ease of counting back

When bringing pupils round to see a video or demonstration, or just to have them close so that you can discuss better, you need to teach them where to go so that it becomes routine: 'Front row stay where you are, second row bring your stools to the side, third row…'.

Disruptive pupils or disruptive behaviour?

Dealing with disruptive pupils is usually the issue that is foremost in a new teacher's mind, and taxes some teachers well into their careers. It helps to know if there are any pupils in your group that most teachers in the school find hard to deal with – you will need to find support for these from the school management system. However, most pupils behave well for most teachers, and they will respond to a firm but fair approach, especially if you make the lessons interesting and useful. Remember to criticise the behaviour, not the pupil, and take an opportunity to praise the pupil as soon as possible after the incident for behaving appropriately. It is important for them to realise that they can earn back any punishments and this will encourage improved behaviour and concentration (there are exceptions to this; for example, swearing directly *at* you cannot be 'earned back' and must be dealt with by a senior member of staff). The key, as always, is to know each pupil by name (see later in this chapter, pp. 179–80).

Not paying attention: nos 9 and 10

There are many reasons why pupils disrupt lessons. They may be bored, or your lesson may lack structure or pace, or be pitched at too high a level for them to achieve. You will learn to identify the major causes of disruption in the groups you are teaching and take the appropriate action. Disruption begins quietly: for example, when pupils continue talking when you have asked for silence (no. 9 in our list). You need to take action, because it can only get worse if it is not checked. The action may be a simple pause and a quiet 'Please...'. If someone carries on working (no. 10), are they really a distraction? This time you can be gentler, but still insist that everyone is listening: if you (or a pupil) address the whole class you should expect that everyone is listening to you or them.

If there are persistent talkers or disturbers, you can use different seating plans to reduce disruption. Move an influential disturber to the front and away from the side wall; they will feel uncomfortable here, will become quieter and may be prepared to cooperate in order to win the privilege of returning.

Merits and sanctions

Rewards and punishments should be in the ratio 20:1. If you give punishments for poor behaviour always give rewards for good responses; they defuse the situation and help to modify behaviour. A reward can be as simple as a smile, a 'thumbs-up', a 'smiley' face on work or a spontaneous round of applause – don't be tricked into handing out material rewards too often as the cost will rise in line with the expectations. Rewards systems (e.g. merits) *must* be used but be more careful with sanctions. You need to be careful that you are consistent, and that the one pupil who is getting punished deserves it more than others who were excused. If you have had to reprimand a pupil in the lesson then you should praise them at the first sign of good behaviour. You may then be able to say, 'I am pleased with what you are doing now and if you continue to work like this you can earn back the punishment'. Never punish the whole class for the bad behaviour of the few: this alienates everyone.

Positive reinforcement

It is easy to forget or ignore those pupils who are getting on with their work and, instead, wrestle with the attention-seekers. You need to praise the quiet ones and the workers as well. A real plus is when a 'naughty' pupil gets something right; managed carefully this could be a turning point in behaviour. Instead of saying 'George, don't do that...', say 'George, will you help by giving out the books, please?' Then you have the opportunity to 'catch him being good' and praise his contribution. Other phrases to use are 'It is nice to see you settling quickly' and 'Thank you for listening'.

Active learning and some danger points

You can 'lose' the pupils in many ways: by talking above their heads, by not involving them in the learning or by becoming too involved with one small group in the class, to name just three. There are practical hurdles to overcome as well. Be aware of faulty equipment that is set out for you (check it as the technician brings it in if you can), or of circuit boards with flat batteries (ask the technician to supply a box of replacements). There are many hiccups that are harder to solve but you can prepare for them: if the projector isn't recognising your laptop or the wireless network is down, have a set of worksheets or books in reserve.

Providing a purposeful, challenging and useful set of learning activities (with clearly identified learning outcomes that the pupils understand) is the best answer for a happy and well-behaved classroom. This is about you and the well-structured lesson – being prepared. You have made an impact, you have elicited the pupils' ideas and you have taught the new material through a demonstration, a simulation on the internet or presentation. It is now the pupils' turn to be active in their learning. They need to make sense of the new information that they have seen and heard. Your role is to give them the time and the structure to do this *reformulation* effectively. Keep them busy, focused and challenged, and they will have little time to be disruptive.

Ending the lesson

The last 15 minutes of the lesson are probably more important than the 30 minutes in the middle. Many a good lesson is spoiled or the main aim is lost because of bad timing, especially when practical work overruns. To consolidate a good lesson you need to allow time for reviewing the aims of the lesson: the pupils and the teacher need to know to what extent they have met the initial learning outcomes. This can be achieved with a short quiz, a set of true/false questions, a mind map to show connecting ideas, making up questions to given answers and so on, or even a simple show of thumbs (up, down or horizontal) to represent their understanding of each learning outcome. Make sure that you plan for this time in addition to time for clearing up and setting homework. The really skilful teacher will set the homework as part of the plenary process as it will be a direct consequence of the learning outcomes.

Teacher intuition

This is a very personal section in which we discuss the 'higher-order' skills you will need to hone during the year to establish who you are, how you teach and what your personal and professional rules are. You need to establish rights, responsibilities and rules for yourself and others around you. We discuss those critical points that affect your inception into the school and the route to pupils accepting you as their 'teacher'.

Learning names

Pupils will warm to you when they feel that *you* know them. You may well know them, but they won't believe it unless you use their names regularly. In the lab it is also particularly important to be able to get an individual pupil's attention for safety reasons. You may be blessed with an outstanding memory; if not, here is a selection of useful strategies:

■ Pass round a blank seating plan for pupils to write their names in. Now you have an accurate plan and a copy of their handwriting.

■ Use school photos to make a named collage that matches the seating plan. Keep this in front of you during the lesson and use it to ask questions of named pupils.

■ After marking their books, put the books in a pile in the order that you will hand them back. At the beginning of the next lesson, you can walk around the room handing each book to the correct pupil; not only do they think you know who they are, but you have linked the face with the name.

■ Each lesson, ask say five pupils to tell you something about themselves; write a key word or phrase (dog; brother Jack; sprinter) in your markbook. Just writing down the association will help.

Pacing

It is not just in the lessons that you must get the pace right. You must pace yourself physically during the term too. The first year is a marathon, not a sprint. If you are tired or stressed, the pupils will quickly pick up on the fact. This will provoke them into pushing you further. You do not need to have every lesson as 'all singing and dancing'. *They* need to be working hard, not just you. Indeed they should be working *harder* than you.

The voice

This is a very powerful weapon in the 'body language' arsenal. The level and tone of your voice pass on huge signals to the pupils. The science lab is a large space, the pupils sit higher than in most classrooms *and* they come into the room expecting to move around. You need to modify the tone and level of your voice to suit the situation or even to create the desired environment. Shouting is not usually a good option: it means that you have lost control and it is hard to get it back with this method. It is a good idea to practise different tones and volumes in an empty lab to get the feel of the variation that you have.

Peer pressure

There is a culture that expresses the view that it is cool not to be 'clever'. The 'in crowd' may be a cool gang to be with, and swots or boffins need not apply. In this case the motivated pupil can be the focus of ridicule and the object of bullying. We need to address this by including all pupils in the lesson. It is not 'cool' to be seen to be too enthusiastic, and we may find that pupils do not interpret our requests as we would wish (see Table 19.1).

TABLE 19.1 Different expectations

TEACHER'S COMMAND	TEACHER'S EXPECTATION	PUPIL'S RESPONSE	PUPIL'S THOUGHTS
Hands up	Hands high	Indifferent	I'm not making a fool of myself
You at the back	All at back to stop	None	It's someone else in trouble
Come out and draw it on the board	Pupil comes out and draws it on the board	Terror; no movement	I'm gonna look a right idiot
Can anyone tell me...?	Three or more hands should go up	No response	I'm not gonna make myself look like a boffin

Family worries

You cannot know what the home situation is for any of the pupils. You must be sensitive to the realities but it is neither necessary nor desirable to know all of the problems and it is certainly *not* possible to sort them. A domestic upheaval during the night might explain *why* one pupil is shouting across the room, but it does not make this behaviour *acceptable*. You must explain that, whilst you can see she is upset, your expectations for behaviour have not changed. Tone of voice, not the words, is a key issue in this situation; you can offer her the chance to sit in a quiet corner and listen to music while she calms down. All pastoral care issues must be reported to a pupil's tutor or house/year head.

Frustration

Intelligent pupils who are not being challenged to think at a high level will react differently, and some will resort to disruption to show their disaffection. Less able pupils will indulge in any displacement activity when they are asked to do work that is too difficult, rather than fail and be seen to fail. Both groups of pupils may report that they are 'bored' – but in reality they are frustrated.

Attention-seekers

Develop a knack of ignoring low-level unacceptable behaviour and praising acceptable and desirable behaviour. In this way the pupils learn that they need to be *good* to attract attention. For example, the girl who arrives flamboyantly late for every lesson is probably choosing to do so for the attention she receives. Take the wind out of her sails by barely acknowledging her entrance, gesturing for her to sit down, and carrying on with the lesson *very* enthusiastically.

Setting and reading the mood

Pupils pick up your mood as soon as you and they enter the room. If you are tense and edgy, there will be an atmosphere. If you are comfortable and relaxed with yourself and the atmosphere is warm and conducive to work, there is less likelihood of disruptive behaviour. You may need to *act* this confidence at first, until you do actually begin to relax with a class. Learn how to make use of body language to appear calm, confident and relaxed: avoid standing symmetrically or clasping your arms around you, do smile and use frequent eye contact.

Summary

The key points to good management are ensuring that you plan and execute a well-prepared lesson that is aimed at the specific needs of all your pupils. To help you we have identified some areas where you need to be sensitive in order to keep the group motivated, and times when you need to question whether you stick rigidly to the lesson plan. We have also included strategies for managing pupils specifically in the science lab. At the end of the lesson, you need to reflect on what went well and learn from mistakes. Ask for advice: no one can resist a call for help. Your head of department and other colleagues can help you to become a better teacher, if you let them. Tell them about your successes as well as the failures. Talking is great therapy.

Health, Safety and Laboratory Management

Chapter overview

Although there are no national statistics on the types of accidents which occur to pupils in science laboratories the most recent suitable data suggest that school science is safe and, indeed, the science laboratory is one of the safest places in the school. Only 2.3 per cent of all reported incidents in school took place in the science lab (HSE 1997) and only 0.8 per cent of those resulted in significant injury. These early data are still corroborated by most education authority statistics. However, accidents do happen and legislation has been introduced to minimise them to protect staff and pupils and to maintain the high standard of safety that already exists. In this chapter we begin with general aspects of health and safety legislation and then consider particular problems arising from biohazards, electricity and very reactive chemicals.

The law and the science teacher

In 1974 the Health and Safety at Work Act (HASAWA) was introduced. This enabling legislation allowed Parliament to introduce new regulations imposing a duty on the employer to 'ensure as far as is reasonably practicable the health, safety, and welfare at work of all his employees'. There is also a duty of care on every teacher while at work for the health and safety of themselves and other people (technicians, teaching assistants, cleaners and pupils) who may be affected by their work (Borrows, in Wood-Robinson 2006, chapter 20).

Within the umbrella of HASAWA is a myriad of other legislation, but the greatest impact on schools comes from the 1989 COSHH (Control of Substances Hazardous to Health) regulations. These aim to protect employees and others from substances that might be hazardous to their health, ranging from microorganisms to all uses of chemicals classified as being harmful and corrosive. It also covers explosive, flammable, radioactive and oxidising agents. In order to assist in this procedure, documentation has been produced by a variety of bodies, including the Association for Science Education (ASE) and the Consortium of Local Education Authorities for the Provision of

Science Services (CLEAPSS). The latter, in association with the Scottish Schools Equipment Research Centre (SSERC), produces a series of *Hazcards* summarising relevant information about the range of chemicals used in school. Included are suggestions of alternative activities and chemicals that could be used to minimise risk.

Essentially, as a newly qualified teacher your legal responsibilities are twofold:

■ You must take reasonable, common-sense care for your own health and safety and that of others.

■ You must follow the health and safety arrangements of your school and education authority.

Issues of health and safety should therefore feature prominently in your lesson plans and you should be aware of training opportunities during the early years of teaching. The following two ASE publications are a good starting point:

■ Safeguards in the School Laboratory (ASE 2006a). This gives an overview of common problem areas, the potentially more serious ones, those where there has been a significant change of opinion in recent years, and areas of specific concern. It is intended to give a concise account of the best advice available.

■ Topics in Safety (ASE 2001). This gives some comprehensive examples of how you could control risks in basic Key Stage 3 science laboratory work, as well as illustrating how safety notes can be incorporated in a scheme of work.

At the very least you should familiarise yourself with both of these, but spending time with the laboratory technician, talking to other teaching staff, trying out the practicals for yourself and generally seeking advice on health and safety are also musts.

The Management of Health and Safety at Work Regulations (1999) outline explicit requirements placed on the employer in terms of managing health and safety issues. These relate to the following areas:

■ assessment and recording of risks

■ making arrangements for the effective control and monitoring of those risks

■ providing up-to-date and relevant information to all employees on matters to do with health and safety in the workplace

■ appointing appropriate health and safety officers responsible for their own department, usually the heads of department.

The science department safety policy

In many PGCE programmes trainee teachers are advised to spend a day with the laboratory technician early in their first school experience. This helps the trainees to become familiar with the workings of the department, where everything is and the importance of getting your preparation requirements in on time.

By law employers must have a safety policy and all science departments will have one. All science teachers, and trainee teachers, must be familiar with it. It defines procedures and areas of responsibility in order to promote safety within the department. The 'procedures' apply to the day-to-day running of the department, as well as to specific emergencies, listing where safety resources are and what to do in the event of an emergency. It identifies regular checks that need to be made and who is responsible for carrying them out. Such checks may include:

- fume cupboard

- portable electrical appliances

- autoclaves, pressure cookers and steam engines

- radioactive sources for possible leakage

- chemicals that are likely to deteriorate

- eye protection

- first aid boxes

- fire extinguishers and other safety equipment.

Although certain members of the department will be given specific responsibilities, it is important that you are familiar with the department's policy and know what to do if you notice anything untoward, or an accident occurs. So find out where the department's policy is, where the CLEAPSS *Hazcards* and the CLEAPSS *Laboratory Handbook* and *CD-ROM* are kept and familiarise yourself with the school's procedures for reporting and recording incidents during a science lesson. The following are general guidelines only.

The procedure for reporting and dealing with accidents

- All incidents of injury to a person or damage to clothing have to be logged in an incident logbook according to procedures in the school's safety policy.

- Designated, qualified members of staff, the names of whom will be in the staff handbook, deal with incidents requiring first aid.

- Any incident requiring treatment by the school nurse has to be reported to the head of department and logged in the 'main book' in the school office.

- All serious accidents are to be reported to a qualified first aider or the school nurse.

- If a child is not seriously injured, but is distressed, they can be sent (accompanied) to the school nurse.

Managing safety and risk assessments

Part of your legal responsibility is to anticipate problems that might arise; you can only do this effectively by the use of a 'risk assessment'. This is a procedure that all employers are obliged to carry out under COSHH 1989 regulations before hazardous substances are used or made. Owing to the enormity of the situation, your employers (the governing body or the local education authority) delegate responsibility for this to the teachers involved with the specific subject area. The head of department has to ensure that risk assessments are carried out on every activity involving potentially hazardous substances or equipment. Consider the following:

■ What is the difference between a hazard and a risk?

■ How can risks be eliminated?

A 'hazard' is anything with the potential to cause harm. This will include many chemicals, where the hazard is inherent within the material. In other instances it is associated with the use of that material, for example such activities as using a scalpel. On the other hand, a 'risk' is the probability that harm will actually be caused by the hazard. There are two elements to risk:

■ How likely is it that something will go wrong?

■ How serious is it if something does go wrong?

Risk can be reduced by good safety management: for example, strict adherence to wearing eye protection (e.g. when using acids) and good discipline when using scalpels (e.g. dissecting plants). If the outcome of an accident is likely to be serious it is better not to take the risk, however small, and to use a teacher demonstration or video instead. Although risk assessments generally apply to using hazardous materials or equipment, they are equally important in any aspect of science involving an unfamiliar environment, for example working outside the classroom (see Chapter 23).

General risk assessment

General risk assessments (GRAs) have been compiled by a variety of authoritative bodies, and are models against which activities can be compared. There are two main aspects of the GRA:

■ the thinking process

■ the informing process.

The first aspect involves answering a series of in-depth questions concerning the activity:

■ Is it educationally necessary?

■ Is there an alternative, less hazardous substance or procedure?

■ Is it a teacher demonstration, or pupil activity?

■ What are the age and experience of the pupils?

■ What personal protection or control measures are necessary?

■ How will residues be disposed of at the end?

The other aspect of a GRA involves recording and informing others of the outcomes of the assessment. It is not necessary for each teacher to conduct a detailed GRA on the same activity every time it is used. Risk assessment forms giving this general information can be attached to schemes of work, available to staff to make use of. Remember, it is not just the teaching staff who need this information: the technicians play a fundamental role in this, and their related work in the preparation room needs to be considered as well.

Before we consider how pupils are to be warned about hazards, we need to consider our own preparations.

Preparing to meet your class

Before even starting to teach we need to be fully prepared.

- We need to know where the gas taps, water taps and electrical switch-off points are for all labs. If the school policy is to turn off all the mains at the end of the day it is important to check that all bench taps are closed in the labs before the mains are turned back on and the pupils enter the room.

- We must never do an experiment for the first time in front of or with a class, however simple it may seem. If there is no chance to practise first, then it should be left out.

- No hazardous substance should be placed in front of pupils (or anywhere in the school) unless it is labelled. If you decant, say, propanone into a beaker, the beaker needs to have the same hazard warning as the original bottle.

Sharing good safety practice with the pupils

The Secondary National Strategy at both Key Stages 3 and 4 emphasises the importance of health and safety in science education and places an expectation on the teacher to ensure that pupils are fully aware of the hazards, and are able to assess risk and take actions to reduce risks to themselves and others. Traditionally pupils have been given a set of rules to abide by while they are in the science laboratory. Is it the set of safety rules or the sharing in the making of them that is important? Is it better to introduce them gradually as they are needed (and thereby seen to be relevant) or all at once at the beginning?

Telling children what to do, or how to be safe, is not the same as them knowing how to be safe: the 'tell-each-other' technique (see Chapter 8, pp. 71–2) is valuable here in allowing pupils to internalise what they are to do and how to be safe. For example, after agreeing the aim of an investigation, get the pupils to 'tell each other' about any potential hazards that they need to be aware of (15 seconds needed) and what precautions need to be taken. These can then be compiled as a list on the board. Some schools have a small 'safety board' alongside the white/blackboard especially for this.

Pupils should not have to wear eye protection all the time; at the very least it can alienate them from an experience and at the most, if severely scratched, goggles can be a hazard in their own right and therefore need replacing. They must, however, be worn whenever the risk assessment indicates a risk of damage to the eyes or face. Eye protection has to be taken seriously and when you ask for goggles to be worn you will need to keep reminding pupils of the requirements. Eye protection is for eyes, not for the upper forehead!

Too often safety is blamed for the decline in 'exciting' science. This need not be the case. Many of the practical activities that enthused and excited generations in the past can still be performed today, but in a safer, more controlled and perhaps more familiar environment. One problem of operating in a 'science' atmosphere is that links with 'reality' become less easy to make. We are not training future scientists, but giving the next generation a way of looking at and understanding their environment. In this respect, the laboratory setting can be alienating, and pupils may see 'science' as something that happens only in this room. We conclude this chapter by looking at some particularly hazardous aspects of science teaching: organising and managing class practicals, dealing with microbes and with radioactive and high-voltage sources, and working with very reactive chemicals.

Organising and managing class practicals

The importance of managing your pupils within the laboratory was discussed broadly in Chapter 19. From a safety perspective managing class practicals can be the most challenging aspect of a lesson. Careful consideration needs to be given to movement within the laboratory; how is equipment to be distributed, how will Bunsens be lit, how will the end products of the practical be disposed of and how will the equipment be collected in and tidied away at the end (including hot tripods)? On top of all this, do the pupils know exactly what they are doing and why, and are they all on target? Finally, can you stop them immediately if you need to?

All of this needs to be addressed during your planning stage, with consultation to existing, and if necessary your own, risk assessments and by ensuring the pupils are well informed on all aspects of the practical before they start. The following suggestions should be helpful, but also do observe and ask how other teachers address these issues:

- Ensure all the apparatus you need has been ordered in advance and is in working order (this is unfortunately not always the case).

- Ensure all coats, bags and chairs/stools are carefully stowed away.

- Have the equipment for collection available around the room in clearly labelled areas.

- Give your instructions about the practical and the equipment required very clearly, supported with a clear and concise written version for each group or pair. Ask the pupils to 'tell each other' what they have to do and check this back out loud from one or two groups. Reiterate any problem areas. This all takes time, but is important so build it into your plan.

- Reinforce and share safety issues.

- Ask one or possibly two pupils per group only to collect the equipment, depending upon the amount to be collected.

- Once the pupils move you must restrict your whole-class instruction to an absolute minimum. This prevents possible discipline problems and unnecessary waste of time. If you do have to stop them, make sure you use an effective strategy to gain their attention; a short sharp loud noise usually does the trick, then count down from 3. This 'wait-time' before you give instruction is important to allow the pupils to stop, ensure the apparatus is safe and then listen to you.

- Ensure there is enough time (a good 10–15 minutes before the end of the lesson) to clear away carefully and sensibly, with clear instruction for disposal. Any hot apparatus should be left safely until it is cool enough to handle; after the plenary perhaps.

- Try to minimise accidents by once again asking only one or two pupils per group to leave their station. The remainder can dismantle and make safe any remaining equipment or ensure a clear record of the results is available.

- Finally, remember that word work following practical experiences is essential if the pupils are to internalise and learn from what they have done (and experienced). Make plenty of time for your plenary discussions.

Biohazards: handling microbes and other biological hazards

The term 'microbe', or microorganism, covers a wide range of organisms that cannot be seen with the unaided eye, yet live all around and within us. With the aid of a hand lens, binocular microscope or laboratory optical microscopes, we can enter a world of mystery and intrigue. Members include protozoans, algae, lichens, slime moulds, viruses, bacteria, fungi and yeasts.

Are microbes safe to use in school?

If microorganisms other than the following are used, there is a risk of infection:

- brewer's and baker's yeast

- bacteria in yoghurt

- edible mushrooms.

As long as safety precautions are adhered to the risks can be kept to a minimum. The use of hay infused with liquid for the purpose of studying protozoa and animal life is a case in point. An infusion of this kind will provide nutrients for bacteria, which in turn are eaten by other bacteria and protozoans. Particular care has to be taken when sampling the medium and disposing of the culture, because unknown bacteria may be present. When preparing such an infusion, animal faecal matter must not be used to enrich the sample. Equally reliable and just as fascinating results can be obtained using leaf mould and bread mould, but we still need to take care.

Special risk assessments (ASE 2001 and SSERC 2003)

When using microbes in class, it is necessary to make sensible adaptations to the general risk assessment described earlier in this chapter. Suppose, for example, an unspecified culture of microbes, isolated from the school pond, was to be grown in jam jars of nutrient broth. These were to be opened by an unruly, unskilled year 9 group supervised by a newly qualified physics graduate teacher. This is a hazardous situation, accompanied by some risk. In general, there are certain factors the teacher would need to consider before deciding whether or not to continue:

- The nature of the organisms. Are they 'harmless', such as yeast used in baking, or fungi that are likely to release spores and cause allergies?

- The source of the organisms. Was it a pure culture purchased from a reliable supplier, or an unknown sample from the environment?

  Never use potentially dangerous sources such as the following: human mucus; pus from spots; faecal material; drains and toilets. All air, water and soil samples should be treated as containing potential pathogens and dealt with accordingly.

- Temperature of incubation. Material cultured at 37°C may possibly incubate human pathogens; incubation should be between 20 and 28°C (a week at laboratory temperature is usually sufficient).

- Culture medium. Media which selectively grow pathogens, for example blood agar, MacConkey agar and broth for studying coliform bacteria, should normally be avoided. Use nutrient agar for bacteria and malt agar for fungi. Successful results can be achieved by using bread as the culture medium, but the same safety procedures must apply. The plates must be sealed, must remain so and must be disposed of properly when finished with.

- Type of investigation and facilities available. Unless you are specially qualified and working with sixth-form students, all investigations should be with sealed containers. Inoculated plates should be taped with small pieces of sticky tape at intervals around the plate. This will allow access of air and help to prevent the growth of anaerobic organisms. If there is a risk of opening, the microbes should be killed before the plates are viewed, then sterilised.

- Correct treatment of all contaminated equipment. Whether for reuse or disposal, this is of fundamental importance and should be considered before the outset of the investigation. Items of contaminated equipment must be placed in sealable plastic bags and autoclaved to sterilise. They can then be disposed of in the normal way, wrapped in sealable plastic bags.

- Expertise of people involved. Never assume anything, check that the technician has had suitable training, consider your own level of training and the age, discipline and skills of the pupils.

Under the circumstances it would be unwise to proceed with the year 9 lesson mentioned earlier!

Levels of practical work with microbes

Topics in Safety (ASE 2001) identifies three levels of work with microbes:

- Level 1. Organisms used have little, if any, known risk and no specialist training or knowledge is required. Work may include investigations with baker's and brewer's yeasts, protozoans, algae and lichens.

- Level 2. Bacteria and fungi from recognised suppliers or organisms cultured from certain aspects of the environment can be grown on appropriate media. Incubated containers must be taped closed, labelled and not opened by pupils if they contain living cultures. They must be disposed of correctly after use.

- Level 3. The growth of known microorganisms from recognised sources and subsequent transfer of live samples from the incubated cultures, for example serial dilution techniques.

It is envisaged that only work at levels 1 and 2 will be carried out by pupils aged 11–16. For level 2 work the teacher should have experience in the basic techniques, precautions and disposal procedures. Level 3 work would normally be restricted to post-16 education, where facilities are appropriate. A more extensive knowledge of microbiology and sterile procedures is required for activities at this level. It would be inappropriate for such work to be supervised by non-specialist staff unless suitably qualified.

Using radioactive or high-voltage sources

There is a comprehensive summary of advice on both these sections in *Safeguards in the School Laboratory* (ASE 2006a) but it is worth reiterating a few points:

- When teaching about radioactivity in class, take the opportunity to review the pupils' perception of risk. The approved school radioactive sealed-sources are very safe if used and maintained appropriately (ASE 2006a). The radiation dose received is minimal compared with the dose we continually receive from natural background radiation.

- The use of high-voltage sources usually means a voltage of between 40 and 500 V. A teacher unfamiliar with demonstrations involving exposed mains connections must receive training before carrying them out.

- Power supply units that have both high-voltage and low-voltage outputs should only be used for demonstration purposes.

- Modern-day induction coils and van de Graaff generators available from school suppliers can only supply currents less than 5 mA and are considered within safety limits, but very old equipment or that not designed for school use may give an initial discharge which exceeds safe limits so the best advice is not to use them. This applies equally to electrophoresis investigations using do-it-yourself installations because of the possible proximity of a high voltage and a conducting solution.

Working with very reactive chemicals

Most of the materials we use around us are giant structures based on two elements from group 4 of the periodic table: *carbon* gives us living materials and plastics (life polymers), and *silicon* gives us rocks and soil. There are three other basic sorts of material (mentioned in Chapter 12, pp. 107–8): *metals* (elements from the left and bottom of the periodic table), *volatile materials* such as water, wax and oxygen (made of the non-metallic elements at the top and right of the periodic table) and *ionic* materials, formed when a metallic element combines with non-metallic elements. This simple classification system has been called the 'structure triangle' (Ross 1997, 2000a). The triangle is built up from all the possible combinations of pairs of elements from the periodic table. Although group 4 with carbon and silicon is the most significant group in the periodic table, containing the elements of both life and the rocks, it is helpful for pupils to experience the extremes of metallic and non-metallic reactivity (giving experience of the other three substance types: metal, volatile and ionic). This is provided by an exploration of the elements of groups 1 (the alkali metals) and 7 (the halogens).

Safety factors with elements of groups 1 and 7

On no account should Key Stage 3 or 4 children be allowed to handle these elements themselves. Do not attempt to react the metals in air by heating them. Only use sodium for the reaction with chlorine and bromine. All routes from the metals to the eyes must be blocked. Safety screens must be used in conjunction with eye protection in case metal explodes over the screen. A mobile fume cupboard is safer and gives a good view. A Petri dish on the overhead projector, covered by a large sheet of glass on a supporting ring, is also good, with pupils seeing a shadow on the screen of the reaction with water. Many schools now have flexible video cameras, so pupils can see the reaction on the television screen. Excellent video clips are also available of these reactions but it is good for the pupils to experience the real thing.

Reactions of the alkali metals

Most teachers will demonstrate the reaction of the metals with water and when left in air. The three demonstrations that follow provide additional experiences for the pupils, but must be tried out beforehand with the support of an experienced teacher or technician. What follows is only a guide, and you need to take all the normal COSHH precautions as provided by the *Hazcards*, your technician and colleagues.

Lithium has small atoms (hazardous: try out beforehand with your technician)

To show that the more reactive metals have larger atoms, cut pieces of lithium (Li), sodium (Na) and potassium (K) of equal size – a cube with side between 3 and 4 mm is perfect. Now ask which of these will contain more atoms? If you react these pieces with water which will produce the most hydrogen? Pupils may understand this better if you ask them to imagine three equal-sized boxes, one containing satsumas (Li), one of oranges (Na) and one of grapefruit (K). Now ask which box contains the largest (and smallest) number of pieces of fruit.

Lithium has the smallest atoms, so will have the most atoms in the cube we have cut and therefore we expect it to produce a greater volume of hydrogen than the others, even though it will be generated at a slower rate. To collect the hydrogen, hold, with one hand, an inverted boiling tube (Figure 20.1) full of water (no air bubbles) against the side of a pneumatic trough and just under the surface of the water. Now quickly introduce the cube of metal, held in tweezers, into the water and release it so that it rises up the tube. For sodium and potassium it is advisable to coat the cube of metal with its protective oil, so that it does not start reacting with the water for the fraction of a second when it first enters the water. This reaction is animated in Ross *et al.* (2002: CD – Matter). After collecting the three tubes of hydrogen (the least with potassium) you can expose them to a flame and listen to the hydrogen burn (and see the flame colours of the respective metals).

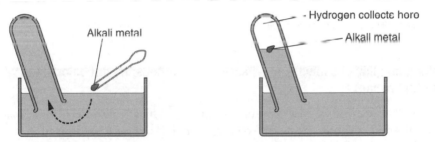

Alkali metal

Hydrogen collects here

Alkali metal

Hold the boiling tube, which needs to be competely filled with water, firmly against the side of the pneumatic trough with one hand and introduce the metal with tweezers using the other hand.

FIGURE 20.1 Collecting hydrogen from reaction of alkali metals with water

Making salt (hazardous: try out beforehand with your technician)

Have a Pyrex boiling tube full of chlorine ready before the lesson. Cut a cube of sodium (4–5 mm side) and immerse it in octane or a similar solvent to dissolve off its protective oil (which also reacts with chlorine). Now leave the cube of sodium on a filter paper for 30 seconds to allow the solvent to evaporate, then drop it to the bottom of the tube of chlorine, using tweezers, as you briefly remove the bung and exchange it for a Bunsen valve (Figure 20.2). It is now safe to heat the tube in the open laboratory, as long as you are all wearing eye protection. The demonstration is best done in as dark a room as possible. Hold the tube with a retort clamp and allow the hottest Bunsen flame to heat the tube exactly below the cube of sodium. Keep the hot flame firmly directed at the tiny piece of sodium. You may see a feeble yellow flame and soot if there is oil or solvent left, then suddenly the sodium catches fire with a brilliant orange (street-light) flame. Immediately remove it from the Bunsen flame and hold it up to watch it burn. Once the burning is over lighten up the lab and show the class the white smoke of solid salt (sodium chloride). (*Safety*: There may be unburnt sodium remaining in the tube, so wash it out with alcohol, not water. The black deposit on the tube where the sodium caught fire is silicon, from the sodium reacting with the glass.)

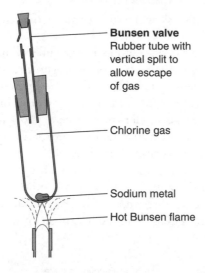

Bunsen valve
Rubber tube with
vertical split to
allow escape
of gas

Chlorine gas

Sodium metal

Hot Bunsen flame

FIGURE 20.2 Using a Bunsen safety valve for reactions with gases in a boiling tube

Making an alloy of sodium and potassium (hazardous: try out beforehand with your technician)

What will happen if we react two of these reactive metals together? Some may say they will react violently. However, sodium, a *metal*, is only reactive towards *non-metals* (such as the chlorine above). When two similar elements 'react' together they form a material remarkably similar to the original elements – thus sodium and potassium form an alloy that still behaves like an alkali metal, but with a melting point lower than either. Compare this with solder (an alloy of lead and tin). To make the alloy (*safety*: eye protection for everyone) place equal rice-grain sized pieces of sodium and potassium into a dry ignition tube and gently warm until the metals melt together. To the surprise of many there is no obvious reaction! Carefully place some of this alloy onto water (*safety*: eye protection for everyone), and it will burst into flame (like potassium) but burn yellow (like sodium).

Making a new halogen: the reaction between chlorine and iodine

The same principle of two similar elements reacting together to form a material remarkably similar to the original elements applies if you react the two very similar elements iodine and chlorine with each other. Drop a few iodine crystals into a tube of chlorine with a Bunsen valve (similar to Figure 20.2). A brown liquid (and vapour) of iodine chloride (ICl) forms, which looks and behaves like bromine, also from group 7. The yellow crystals are iodine trichloride, and decompose as you gently heat the tube. You can tell the difference between this brown halogen (ICl) and the real bromine (Br_2) by dropping a strip of tin foil (Sn) into the tube (replace the valve!). Bromine vapour will slowly attack the tin, forming tin bromide, with the colour fading, but the iodine chloride attacks the tin more rapidly, forming tin chloride and iodine vapour, so the brown colour turns *purple*. Dispose of these carefully, in a fume cupboard, because the tin bromide and chloride are corrosive and fume as they react with water vapour in the air. In contrast, when the two elements which react together are from opposite ends of the periodic table you get a compound that is completely different, as we saw when we reacted sodium and chlorine.

Summary

On the whole laboratories are safe places, and they become safer when pupils understand why they are asked to take various precautions, and when we undertake risk assessments for all our practical work and demonstrations. We have a duty, as teachers, to understand these precautions ourselves. The following documents make essential reading, and are collected here for ease of reference.

References and recommended reading

ASE (2001) *Topics in Safety*, 3rd edn. Hatfield: Association for Science Education.

ASE (2006a) *Safeguards in the School Laboratory*, 11th edn. Hatfield: Association for Science Education.

ASE (2006b) *Safety Reprints*. Hatfield: Association for Science Education.

CLEAPSS (1995 and later updates) *Hazcards*. Uxbridge: Consortium of Local Education Authorities for the Provision of Science Services (School Science Service).

CLEAPSS (1997, updated annually) *Laboratory Handbook*. Uxbridge: Consortium of Local Education Authorities for the Provision of Science Services (School Science Service).

DfEE (1996) *Safety in Science Education*. London: HMSO.

HSE (1997) *Health and Safety Executive 1996/7*. London: Health and Safety Executive.

SSERC (2002) *Hazardous Chemicals Manual CD2*. Edinburgh: Scottish Schools Equipment Research Centre. Available at: www.sserc.org.uk

SSERC (2003) *Microbiological Techniques CD1*. Edinburgh: Scottish Schools Equipment Research Centre. Available at: www.sserc.org.uk

Wood-Robinson, V. (ed.) (2006) *ASE Guide to Secondary Science*. Hatfield: Association for Science Education.

Teaching and Learning at 14–19

Chapter overview

In this chapter we emphasise the importance of active learning and the constructivist approach to learning at all levels of education. The government White Paper of 2005 on 14–19 Education and Skills aimed to transform secondary and post-compulsory education so that all young people could achieve and continue in learning until at least the age of 18. It took on board the idea that all students, with varying degrees of support, need to be self-researchers by the time they are 18. We look at the possible means of achieving this, including a new 14–19 initiative which introduces specialised diplomas running in parallel with GCSEs and A-levels.

Introduction

The standard approach at Key Stage 4 for many schools is to put everyone in for GCSEs with an aim of achieving the 70 per cent pass rate at grades A* to C. Retention rates post-16 and the dissatisfaction emanating from employers have raised questions about education provision at this level. Research has indicated that this is possibly not the best method of teaching and learning for all candidates (Twenty First Century Science Team 2003). There are two groups who are disadvantaged by this approach: those who do not perform well in tests and a small but significant group who are disaffected with the school system in general. It has been proposed that a vocational approach, in the form of a new suite of diplomas, may address their needs more effectively. The increased emphasis placed on responsibility and ownership of one's own learning not only marries well with the diploma approach, but also prepares sixth-form students for life and learning at university. As we have seen earlier (see Chapter 7) an active learning style suits the needs of all pupils. As pupils approach the end of Key Stage 4 they are presented with a choice of pathways: the conventional AS/A2 route, a diploma route and the option of taking up an apprenticeship. A recognition of the importance of achieving the functional skills in both English and maths underpins the new system, with a drive to increase the overall percentage of pupils gaining grades A* to C at GCSE in science and ICT.

Reform at post-16

Post-16 education has been under review for some years, with several attempts being made to reform the A-level. The narrow, specialist course of two to four subjects of study during a two-year period has been retained as a cornerstone of the new system. This was mainly due to the high academic standards claimed for A-levels and their use as the university entrance examination.

What are sixth-form students expected to do?

Following a conventional A-level pathway, post-16 students can expect to do the following:

- AS-levels (advanced subsidiary), worth half a traditional A-level, are studied in the first year sixth. Most pupils will take four AS-levels during this year.

- Students will normally drop one subject after the first year. During the second year of the sixth form, most will continue with three subjects to A-level (so-called A2s). Some will do a fifth AS-level; others may start three new AS-levels.

- Most students will study key skills as well: the application of number, communication and IT. This is a feature that started life in the GNVQ (see below). As a bonus, they will receive grades for their efforts in this area.

- In addition, the most able will be offered 'super A-levels', advanced extension papers retaining the high academic rigour of previous A-levels.

In a few subjects, there will be a free-standing AS (without an A2). A2s, however, are all full qualifications and must follow the AS route. Learning and assessment opportunities for some or all of the *key skills* will be signposted in the specifications of all AS and A2 qualifications.

This reform to the A-level system has been received with mixed feelings. The concern is that pressure is mounting on students and teachers. This is because it is becoming more difficult to choose the right course out of so many options and to ensure that the qualifications will be acceptable for the students to progress effectively. There is also the question of quality when we compare our system with those in the rest of Europe. It is important for all students to have a grasp of scientific issues, even if they are not following a science degree. The proposal in 2000 for an AS in 'science in context' (Hunt and Millar 2000) was an encouraging step in this direction. The aim was to give non-scientists a grasp of the big scientific ideas and their effect on society. Some schools, however, maintain a science presence by following the International Baccalaureate (IB) which ensures a broad curriculum post-16, of which science is a key feature.

Reforming vocational learning 14+

Running parallel to the A-level pathway is a new system of specialised diplomas. These are having a phased introduction: the first four (in information and communication technology; engineering; health and social care; and creative and media) have been available since 2008; a further eight will be available by 2010 and the remainder, including one in science, by 2013; the full national entitlement will be available by 2015. Working with employers, the aim is to offer more opportunities for young people to learn at work and outside school. At the same time, the apprenticeship system is being revised to improve the quality and number of employment-based training places; these too will be within the diploma framework. Diplomas aim to give students work-related skills, and a deeper knowledge of their main subject area. They aim to appeal to students who like practical subjects, problem-solving and applying what they learn to real situations. Diplomas involve a mix of classroom learning and hands-on experience, and will give students an insight into different careers within their chosen subject area, rather than merely training for a specific job.

There are three main types of diplomas:

■ *The Foundation Diploma.* This is equivalent to 5 GCSEs at grades D to G. It is a Level 1 qualification that recognises basic knowledge and skills and the ability to apply learning with guidance and supervision. Learning at this level is about activities that mostly relate to everyday situations and may be linked to a work-related environment.

■ *The Higher Diploma.* This is equivalent to 7 GCSEs at grades A* to C. It is a Level 2 qualification that recognises good knowledge and understanding of an area of work or a subject area, and the ability to perform varied tasks with some guidance or supervision. Learning at this level involves building knowledge and/ or skills in relation to an area of work or a subject area and is appropriate for many job roles.

■ *The Advanced Diploma.* This is equivalent to 3.5 A-levels. It is a Level 3 qualification that recognises the ability to gain and, where relevant, to apply a range of knowledge, skills and understanding. Learning at this level involves detailed knowledge and skills. It is intended for students who want to go to university, people working independently or, in some areas, those supervising and training others in their field of work.

Additionally, *Progression Diplomas* are equivalent to 2.5 A-levels and are Level 3 qualifications with the same demands as the Advanced Diploma but without the block of additional and specialist learning. At the time of writing suggestions are that from 2011 there will also be an *Extended Diploma* available at all three levels. It will contain more English and maths, as well as more additional and specialist learning.

Students who have completed a diploma can go on to pursue a variety of routes. They may:

■ take another diploma at a higher level, either in the same subject or a different one

■ take GCSEs, A-levels or another qualification

■ begin an apprenticeship

- enter employment

- begin studying for a degree at university.

Both Foundation and Higher Diplomas are targeted at 14–16-year-olds, while Advanced Diplomas are targeted at 16–19-year-olds. However, students do not need to have completed a Foundation or Higher Diploma in order to do an Advanced Diploma.

Teaching and learning 14+ and applied science

The 10-year *Science & innovation investment framework* presented in 2004 set out the government's strategy for sustaining a strong supply of scientists and engineers. As we shall see in Chapter 23, there is an increasing emphasis on the Science, Technology, Engineering and Mathematics, or STEM, agenda. In England this agenda is an attempt to co-ordinate the numerous initiatives in curriculum design of individual STEM subjects as well as to bring together STEM-related initiatives and implement them more effectively in every school and college. As well as the overarching economic aim, the agenda aims to develop STEM literacy within the general population. This runs hand-in-hand with other science-specific strategies put in place to help contribute to the realisation of the framework. These include:

- science remaining compulsory at Key Stage 4

- an expectation that at least 80 per cent of pupils will take, at a minimum, two science GCSEs

- the revised Key Stage 4 programme of study having a core which focuses on scientific literacy with options for further study

- introduction of a new suite of GCSEs including the applied sciences

- all changes to be supported through the Secondary National Strategy.

All the above were intended to raise attainment at 16 and increase the number of students going on to study science post-16. It is hoped that the Secondary National Strategy and the new GCSEs including applied science courses will address the concern that didactic-style 'teaching to the test' (done to ensure syllabus coverage) has increasingly switched pupils off continuing in science. The advantage of applied science is that the students have more involvement in how and what they learn. The emphasis is more on 'doing', 'finding out' and reformulation following teacher intervention than on 'learning through listening'. This is very well suited to active learning styles of lessons. It also ensures that there is more opportunity to improve key skills (a useful part of the National Curriculum).

Another advantage is that students know early on not only what GCSE grade their standard of work is likely to produce but also what they need to do to improve on this. A favourite question of pupils is, 'What do I need to do to get a C or B grade?' Both teacher and pupil can be realistic about the target grade and it may not be A* to C.

The course lends itself to industry links and this is encouraged, but it is not an absolute necessity. Each unit can be taken, or presented, twice. Most important is the emphasis of the course on how science is used or applied in the world of work and how it affects us as citizens.

Whatever the approach at Key Stage 4 – traditional syllabus or new diploma-style – the important point to remember is that we are aiming to help students improve the thinking skills they will need not only for their further education but also for life. To this end, students need to be able to:

- locate, sort and classify information

- process information, store it and retrieve it when required

- think creatively

- evaluate and make judgements

- plan, predict and pose relevant questions.

They can only do this at 14+ if they have been actively encouraged to do so from early on and we, their teachers, avoid the 'cramming' that can begin to feature as pupils move through an assessment-led Key Stage 3 and on to GCSEs.

Teaching and learning post-16

The optimists among the teaching profession often highlight the positive aspects of students as they enter post-16 courses:

- they are older

- they have chosen to be there

- they have chosen their subjects

- they are well motivated to work

- they have been successful and will continue to be so.

But the pessimists warn us that:

- they are only a vacation away from year 11

- they are entering the teenage rollercoaster of love and angst

- they regress in enthusiasm as the social scene offers far more attractions than academic achievement

- they are under additional pressure from part-time employment to pay for their social 'needs'.

Whatever the view, it is our job to help them to achieve their best. We are privileged as teachers to be involved with helping the development of these young adults; the time can be rewarding for both teacher and student.

Teaching post-16 is different from teaching further down the school and your approach will need to reflect this. The pupils are more mature, but we must still be the teachers and we must not ignore those active tasks that worked so well at Key Stages 3 and 4. We can and should try to recreate the 'awe and wonder' response in post-16 students as they are at the beginning of a journey that could lead to a life centred on your subject, rather than at the end of an exam trail. The need to create opportunities to encourage these students to take ownership and responsibility for their own learning is ever more important. Post-16 courses are for specialists now, but with the broadening of the number of post-16 exams that students take, we must also cater for those who are less confident and enthusiastic in science. Examples of some different approaches and strategies are given below and echo the active learning ideas from Chapters 7–11:

- Creation of *mind maps* for display (poster work). These serve to consolidate ideas and can help the students identify gaps in their learning.

- *Problem-solving activities* set within a topical and relevant context, that stretch and challenge the students either individually or in groups.

- *Teach the class*. Get the students to research a topic and 'teach it' using only outline notes. They could prepare a few Microsoft PowerPoint screens to assist themselves, and help to put over the message.

- *Mastermind/Millionaire quiz*. No one can resist the challenge of winning a quiz show (they can even phone a friend or ask the audience). This needs a good deal of preparation but can be used again with subsequent groups.

- *Hot-seating*. Like a talk show guest, the pupils must prepare to discuss issues with the interviewer and audience. They must also decide where they stand on issues like genetically modified food or the use of nuclear power stations, and support their position with research data.

- *Q card construction*. Each individual or pair takes one topic area and creates a miniature revision guide on A5 sheets. These are then edited by peer review to pick up misconceptions and omissions, and published on the school's intranet.

- *Pub quiz*. Once again we rely on the competitive spirit in the students. Set them homework to revise a topic and then split them into groups to answer sets of questions you have prepared; this is tough but rewarding. You can also get them to prepare a set of questions.

- *Use of IT*, set firmly within a science context.

Students at 16+ need the same learning cycle as everyone else. This involves using the same full range of teaching and learning strategies appropriate for Key Stage 4. It can also help you to cope with differentiation and different learning styles. Not all your pupils will achieve the top grades. Indeed, it can be argued that getting a weak pupil to a C or D grade is as valuable and rewarding as guiding the A-grade candidate through the course. However, teaching for understanding is vital, and the way to achieve good grades is to have students who are motivated by the subject. If they retain their misconceptions their only ploy is to learn by rote for examinations, an activity that is tedious, unrewarding and likely to lead to poor exam results and an inability to progress further.

Crossing the continuum

As a teacher you need to be aware that the teaching and learning styles needed at A-level are those to be practised at Key Stages 3 and 4. It may be quicker and easier to provide didactic teaching at Key Stage 4 to 'get through the curriculum', but in the long term the harder option of getting them to think for themselves will pay dividends. You need to adopt an active teaching/learning style to help you and your pupils have a seamless transition between Key Stages.

Summary

In this chapter we have recognised a continuum in the learning and teaching styles in science education. It is important for all pupils to challenge their own ideas and understanding, building a holistic picture of science and the various facets associated with it. We also need to ensure that, whatever the route they take post-14, the students are given the opportunity to effectively hone their thinking skills, with particular reference to:

- communication
- application of number
- ICT
- working with others
- improving their own performance
- problem-solving.

V

Professional Values and the Wider World

Introduction

The last part of this book covers some wider aspects of being a science teacher. Chapter 22 deals with issues of race, gender and special educational needs. In Chapter 23 we examine the importance of linking science to the everyday lives of our pupils. In particular we examine the educational value of working outside the classroom.

Our final chapter discusses a philosophy for science and the growing awareness of the need for the public to understand science. We re-examine the purpose of an education in science by considering the origins of science teaching in British schools.

We need to educate the next generation to understand the need for sustainable development on this planet: we attempt to show the role that science education can play in this.

Inclusion and Science for All: Every Child Matters

Chapter overview

The focus of this chapter is on the need for our science curriculum to cater for every one. Although this has been an aim for many years, the wider implications of the Every Child Matters (ECM) policy has brought this to the fore. We begin by explaining the philosophy behind ECM and exploring how this relates directly to the science teacher in the classroom/laboratory. We then focus on specific areas beginning with special educational needs (SEN). We recognise the unique benefit science has to offer SEN across the spectrum, and emphasise the importance of differentiation and equality of opportunity for all. The major role of assessment and recording as a means of informing planning is discussed. We then consider issues of race and gender. We conclude by considering the role an education in science has to play in promoting sustainable development on a global scale and recognise our role as teachers within this.

Science for all: Every Child Matters

It was the tragic death of Victoria Climbié in 2000 that first shook the nation into action, and exposed serious failings in the way services protected children. This, together with a series of government-initiated inquiries, led to the Children Act 2004, which underpins the Every Child Matters (ECM) policy. The policy relies on schools, health and social services, police and other agencies all working together to ensure the welfare of the nation's 11 million plus 0–19-year-olds through sharing information and providing services for families. Essentially it has freed teachers to concentrate on teaching and learning while referring the many problems pupils bring with them to the relevant experts. The long-term aim at the instigation of the ECM policy was that all children should be offered access to the extended services by 2010.

Figure 22.1 models how it should work: at the centre, the core represents the school, whose aims are to educate and raise standards of attainment and improve the life chances of the pupils. Its important constituents are the children, their parents, teachers and support staff. Factors outside the control of the school, however, might impede effective schooling taking place.

Under ECM, schools will be at the centre of a combination of services and supported by 'layers' of specific public and community workers. Each school manages its extended facilities, based on local needs. To demonstrate how this works we can use this model based on a cross-section of the Earth.

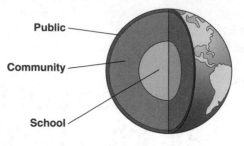

FIGURE 22.1 Every Child Matters (ECM) – how it works (adapted from DCFS (2008))

To support the school, a team of professional workers is assembled from a range of services forming the 'mantle' on the cross-sectional diagram. This will include representatives from the following:

- health (e.g. community support nurses or clinical psychologists)
- police
- social care
- education services (e.g. behaviour support)
- housing.

Their aim is to provide whole-family support by focusing on early intervention and prevention.

The outer layer or 'crust' on our model represents support from the wider community services. These may include liaison with local housing associations and neighbourhood watch schemes, for example. This wraparound childcare aims to free up parents to undergo training or work, with local authorities providing not only traditional adult education services but also information on issues such as drugs, health and self-awareness, whilst community action schemes might involve working closely with police and youth services in crime reduction.

> Pupils differ with respect to characteristics such as gender, ethnicity, class, the extent to which they have special needs, their preferred learning styles and other aspects of their personality and home culture. Not only do pupils differ in all sorts of ways, but you, their teacher, will have differing expectations of them from your previous knowledge of pupils. What is a science teacher to do with this diversity?
>
> (Reiss 1998, p. 34)

In the rest of this chapter we consider what the science teacher can do in relation to these three areas: special educational needs, race and gender.

Science for all: special educational needs

The 1988 Education Reform Act lays down that pupils, regardless of their differences, are entitled to receive a broad, balanced education and that teaching is differentiated according to their needs. Pupils have individual needs at different times during their schooling. The term special educational needs (SEN) refers to pupils who have been identified as requiring special support, which is initiated through a process called 'statementing'. Special educational needs covers the entire spectrum, from children with severe learning difficulties and those with physical and behavioural difficulties to the gifted and exceptionally able child. Within most schools there will be an SEN co-ordinator (SENCO) who would be your point of contact regarding special educational needs. Make sure you identify this person at an early stage.

The unique benefits proffered by science education

Science education, by its nature, includes a range of characteristics:

- a practical approach, nurturing first-hand experiences
- potential for group or collaborative work and peer support
- conceptual development in sequential steps affording opportunities for success
- development of understanding of the big ideas in science – that is, those broad conceptual areas that allow for internal differentiation and individual progression.

Nicholls and Turner (1998, p. 107) support this view and list the following perceived benefits of science that assist pupils with learning difficulties:

- the importance of first-hand experience
- the links between science and everyday experience
- knowledge and skills that can be acquired through practical activity
- many skills that are acquired in small steps, for example investigations include many subskills that can be taught separately and successfully
- activities and phenomena that capture the imagination of pupils, enhancing motivation.

As teachers, we need to recognise these benefits and incorporate them in our lesson plans.

Good practice for all

The Secondary National Strategy (DCSF 2009) recognises that good practice in relation to special educational needs is good practice for all. The keystone to this good practice, and indeed the effective learning that accompanies it, is 'differentiation', the process by which activities are matched to the competencies and context of the pupil. Associated with this is effective assessment, used to diagnose areas of difficulty and areas for progression.

Special needs can best be met when a general concern for individual differences is uppermost in teachers' thinking. This is all very well, but how can it be achieved with

9T, a large, mixed ability science set? The Secondary National Strategy recognises that although setting varies across schools, most organise year 9 pupils in ability sets for their science lessons and planning tends to be easier if the attainment spread in class is not too wide. The most fundamental approach to meeting the needs of all pupils within the class is to ensure that the learning environment is a safe, non-threatening place where pupils feel motivated, can concentrate and feel comfortable in contributing to the lesson. At times this is easier said than done. Expectation of all pupils should be high, but within their ability and accessibility range.

Effective differentiation

Differentiation is achieved by identifying the needs of individuals and developing opportunities to guide, encourage and support learning through whatever resources, processes and tactics are available. For this to be effective, the teacher must get to know their pupils and the knowledge, experiences and abilities they bring with them to their lessons. Good record keeping and regular marking of pupils' work achieve this. Pupils with specific learning difficulties may be referred to a well-defined procedure adopted by schools, termed the Code of Practice. The Code identifies the responsibilities of parents, teachers and the local authority in helping the pupil to progress. There are five stages the process could go through, depending upon the level of difficulty and the ability of the school to meet the pupil's needs (see Table 22.1).

Gifted and talented

Remember that special educational needs applies equally to the more able as it does to the less able. Within the Secondary National Strategy, considerable emphasis has been

TABLE 22.1 The five-stage process for reviewing pupils' special educational needs (after Parkinson 2005)

STAGE	PROCESS	WHO ORGANISES?
1	Teacher identifies that pupil has special educational needs. The SENCO is consulted. Advice is given to the teacher.	School
2	The SENCO co-ordinates the special provision for the pupil. An individual education plan (IEP) is drawn up.	School
3	Existing arrangements are reviewed and the IEP revised. The SENCO consults outside agencies (e.g. an educational psychologist).	School
4	The local authority (LA) considers if a statutory assessment should be made based on all the evidence from school and home.	School and local authority
5	Based on this assessment, the LA considers if a statement of special educational needs should be made. The existing arrangements are reviewed and new provision considered.	School and local authority

given to the more able group of pupils referred to as 'gifted and talented'; but how do you recognise them? It has been suggested (Parkinson 2005) that they can be recognised not just through their academic results but also by the characteristics they display in class:

- speed of information processing

- highly efficient memory

- ability to see patterns and make connections

- intellectual curiosity.

To find out more about 'gifted and talented' visit the website for the National Association for Able Children in Education (NACE) at www.nace.co.uk

Differentiation

So, armed with suitable information about the class they are teaching, the discerning teacher can fulfil the role of encouraging independent learning. This learning-centred approach follows the constructivist view of teaching and learning, building on or challenging pupils' everyday experiences and the conceptual models of understanding that develop from them. There can be a shift of emphasis from whole-class to individual-based learning, as pupils are encouraged to challenge and discuss their own models against the models presented by the teacher.

Once we know the range of ideas and capabilities of the pupils in our class it is the effective use of differentiation that will ensure that all pupils are working at their best and on the most appropriate activity for them. Begin the lesson with a starter activity that will involve and interest the whole class. This can be adapted (differentiated) to meet the ability range of the pupils and, with careful preparation, can be accessible to all pupils. This may be achieved through independent, group or whole-class working, using a range of differentiation strategies (see below). These can then be deployed in a similar way during the intervention section of the lesson (see Chapter 7).

Differentiation by task

Differentiated tasks, on a common theme, pitched at various levels of ability, are available around the room, with the pupils being directed to the relevant ones. This approach ensures that the pupils are working within their means.

Differentiation by outcome

Here the task will be the same, but we expect different pupils to achieve differently. Such tasks will have to be 'open-ended', such as creative writing or experimental design. Some will complete it fairly superficially, while others make a great deal of it.

Differentiation by support

If all the pupils have the same task, and are expected to complete the activity by the end of the lesson, some will need more support from the teacher than others. While we cannot spend our entire classroom time helping a minority of pupils, this approach is effective and the more able (or willing) pupils are happy to be given the independence and responsibility to get on by themselves.

Such support can lead to adjustments that make the task or the outcome different. Pupils' responses will provide important information about the suitability of the task, allowing us to adjust the task at that point, making it more challenging for some, and more accessible to others.

Some pupils with special needs will have support staff allocated to them: always ensure that they are involved in your planning and the production of any worksheets (see below, p. 212, for more on this).

Differentiation: summary

Naylor and Keogh (1998) suggest a full range of activities that can be employed to differentiate appropriately, including:

- adjust the level of scientific skills used

- introduce a range of learning styles such as using structured work cards

- designing an investigation to explore pupils' own ideas, using a computer simulation or textbook for research

- provide a range of suitable resources

- adjust the levels of oral and written skills required

- adjust the levels of mathematical skills required

- vary the amount and nature of teacher and assistant support

- vary the degree of pupil independence (investigations serve as a good vehicle for this)

- use suitable questions, prepared in advance

- vary the response required

- vary the pace and sequence of the lesson

- vary the method of recording and presentation.

These strategies could be employed at any stage in the lesson, as well as being incorporated in your planning.

Putting ideas into practice

The Secondary National Strategy online provides suitable resources for differentiation in whole-class oral and mental work, in written work and in homework for pupils who:

- are gifted and talented

- make less than expected progress

- need help with English, including English as an Additional Language (EAL) learners.

Lists such as those above only come to life with actual examples. What, for example, are *suitable resources*? Many SEN pupils find the written word the biggest barrier to learning. Anything we can do to provide additional clues for them will be useful for the rest of the class too. We focus here on two ideas: three-dimensional objects and models, and the use of colour clues for words.

Objects and models

It is simple to bring into your class a box of cornflakes, a bicycle pump, a banana, a coffee filter, or samples of building materials (plastic guttering, a brick, etc.). Holding something up as we talk about it is simple, and makes such a difference to pupils who are trying to make sense of what we are saying.

How often do we draw sectional diagrams on the board, or from the overhead projector, and expect our pupils to understand what they mean? The eye is usually drawn with the optic nerve (with the associated blind spot) coming off to one side: how many realise that this is a top view? If we show a model of the eye before the sectional diagram, everything becomes much clearer. This is true for most biological (and chemical) diagrams, which are drawn two-dimensionally, but many pupils never succeed in realising the three-dimensional shape these diagrams represent (see Box 22.1).

Box 22.1 Making three-dimensional models of cells

For plant and animal cells, why not get the pupils to make a three-dimensional model? For a plant we need a transparent rectangular plastic box, which we fill with jelly in which we suspend green bits (chloroplasts) and a round bit (nucleus). When the cell is cut through, children can interpret the two-dimensional diagrams much more easily. The animal cell needs to be cast in jelly and tipped out onto a plate – no chloroplasts this time.

The three-dimensional picture can also be brought to life through acting. We gave a few examples in Chapter 8 (pp. 75–6).

Colour

We mentioned the use of atomic models to replace word equations at Key Stage 3, especially in Chapter 12. If these model atoms are coloured (oxygen, red; hydrogen, white; carbon, black; nitrogen, blue), we can use the same colours to write the word and symbol equations. This gives pupils an enormously helpful clue: where words in black writing would be a blur of meaningless letters, the colours suddenly bring the whole thing to life. Diagrams can be labelled in colour too, so that the word and the part match. In their writing pupils can use the same colours in their text. This would be an example of a text-labelling DART (see Chapter 9).

Are all the pupils learning?

Well before the end of the lesson, a constructive plenary needs to be carried out. The purpose of this is twofold: to indicate the level of knowledge and understanding achieved by the pupils and to inform your planning for the next lesson. You will need to gain as much information as possible from the pupils. This could be achieved either orally (try the 'tell-each-other' strategy here – Chapter 8) or by group presentations.

Using the support teacher

Many pupils on statements will have support teachers or a teaching assistant assigned to them for some of their lessons, and this often happens in science. We need to plan carefully to make maximum use of them. It is a waste of their time if the lessons they come to are full of teacher-led intervention activities. If we know which lessons they are to attend we can plan to have the maximum amount of group work. When there is no support teacher we might want to mix up groups so that pupils can support each other, but when the support teacher is present it makes sense to put a group together so that all benefit from the additional personal adult attention. The activity can be made challenging, knowing that differentiation will be by support, full-time, for the whole lesson. Careful planning, and a meeting with the support teacher, are essential if we are to make full use of this valuable resource. It is unlikely that support teachers will have a strong science background, so we may have to provide them with brief background teacher notes, as well as explaining the activity we want them to do with their group. Although the support teacher will be assigned to one child or possibly to specific children in your class, it is wholly legitimate to include additional pupils who might benefit from the support – their presence may enhance the quality of the group discussions.

Science for all: race and gender issues

British society is a multicultural one, which is increasingly reflected in our schools. Pupils bring with them differences in cultural understanding relating to gender, class and ethnicity. We are all members of this multi-ethnic society, and pupils all have their own particular special needs but also bring with them unique experiences we can draw on in our teaching. Hoyle (1995) states: 'All aspects of the culture and ethnicity of pupils need to be recognised, valued and used if all our young people are truly to benefit from and have equality of access to education' (p. 227). When teaching we need to remember that racism remains a powerful force in our society, affecting pupils' attitudes and the way they learn. The National Curriculum 2000 reflected concern for this, encouraging teachers to draw on multicultural ideas, beliefs and successes when teaching science. It stated that pupils should be helped to:

> recognise how scientific discoveries and ideas have affected the way people think, feel, create, behave and live, and draw attention to how cultural differences can influence the extent to which scientific ideas are accepted, used and valued.
>
> (DfEE 1999, p. 8)

Its advice and recommendations are just as true today as they were then. All teachers should examine their own prejudices and ensure that they have high expectations of all children – lower expectations of children lead them to perform less well.

Pupil's views of how science works and is carried out affect both the way they learn science and their attitude to scientific knowledge. This being the case, it is important to elicit these views and images of what scientific work might be. Driver *et al.* (1996) worked with 11–14-year-olds exploring their ideas about how scientific knowledge is acquired. They identified a set of seven images of scientists, most embodying some notion of how scientists go about getting to know the world. These ranged from the stereotypical cartoon image of a 'white-coated, wispy-haired, bespectacled male doing something reckless with a giant chemistry set', via the 'vivisectionist', to the 'all-knowing' scientist as portrayed in television documentaries. They concluded that these ideas were a mixture of classroom experience and images gained from the wider community, but seldom from contact with a genuine scientist. The scientist as a *white male* dominated all these images. Although efforts have been made to move away from this, the image still persists in advertising and cartology.

Teaching and learning approaches

To ensure equality of access we need to recognise that, contrary to common belief, science is not objective and value-free (see Chapter 2), but shrouded in controversy and influenced by politics and economics. We need only to look to the debate on genetically modified foods for support of this view. We need to appreciate the influence of culture on science, to understand society's reluctance to accept scientific and technological advances. The story of Darwin and evolutionary theory reiterates this point. The context in which scientific development takes place is as important as the science itself. Once again this is reinforced by the Secondary National Strategy recognising that science provides the opportunity to promote social development, through helping pupils recognise how the formation of opinion and the justification of decisions can be informed by experimental evidence, and drawing attention to how different interpretations of scientific evidence can be used in discussing social issues.

Associated with this is the content through which the science is made available to the pupils. Hoyle (1995) cites a useful list of general principles for science education, promoting equal opportunities. We illustrate this list of what teachers could do with examples of ideas to use in school.

Incorporate a global perspective in teaching

Many people in the developing world live by subsistence farming, growing what they need and relying purely on (indirect) solar energy for their cooking (firewood), transport (animal muscle power) and ploughing (muscle power again). This is a sustainable way of life that we explore in Ross *et al.* (2002: CD – Energy). We are encouraging a move towards a more sustainable transport policy in the UK through greater use of human power (cycling and walking, for example, in the 'safer routes to schools' movement). We need to applaud all these solar technologies, not look at them as 'underdeveloped'. However, sustainable development means sharing the advantages of technological development with all of humanity. We need to build on sustainable practices from all over the world (see Chapter 3 for further discussion).

Understand issues relating to justice and equality

Much of the land in the developing world is used for cash crop agriculture, providing us with cheap coffee and tea, bananas and pineapples, beef and groundnuts. If these crops were produced in the UK we would not allow the workers to live in the conditions they do. The moral issue is more about the way we, the consumers, are being profligate with the world's resources than about the sustainable conditions under which these cash crop farmers live. We must not teach science in isolation from these issues.

Elaborate science in its social, political and economic context

This is clearly apparent in a discussion exercise comparing the use of chewing sticks and toothbrushes (Leicestershire LEA 1985). Chewing sticks are fully replenishable (unlike the plastic toothbrush and toothpaste). They are also equally effective in keeping teeth clean. Chewing sticks are readily available and are used here in Britain. We need to see them (and many other sustainable practices, such as cycling) as being beneficial to the world.

Make apparent the distribution of, and access to, power

Technological advances are very often linked to the multinationals. Many of these large companies are paying more than lip-service to the concept of sustainable development and to the welfare of their employees in the developing world. Many 'free' resources for science teachers are available from these companies. We need to ensure that we provide our pupils with a balanced world-view if we use such materials.

Incorporate a historical and global perspective

Two historical examples that support a global perspective include the story of Ibn al'Haitham, an Egyptian Islamic scholar (*c*.965–1038), who rejected the belief that light was emitted from the eye, taking the view that light was emitted from self-luminous sources and then entered the eye. The Islamic school was very active at this time in developing many scientific ideas, linked to experiments. The concept of an element as an indestructible part of material was grasped, as the extract in Box 22.2 suggests. Many of these Islamic ideas were translated into Greek or Latin and incorporated into the ideas of the Renaissance in Christian Europe, which looked back to the classical era for inspiration, but from which our modern understanding of science developed.

Box 22.2 Extract from the writings of Jabir Ibn Hayyan (738–813 CE) (from Butt 1991)

Mercury and sulphur unite to form one single product, but it is wrong to assume this product to be entirely new and that mercury and sulphur changed completely. The truth is that both kept their natural characteristics and that all that happened was that parts of the two materials interacted and mixed, in such a way that it became impossible to differentiate them with accuracy. If we were to separate ... the tiniest parts of the two categories by some special instrument, it would have been clear that each element kept its own theoretical characteristics. The result is that the chemical combination botwoon tho olomonto ooouro by permanent linking without change in their characteristics.

The second story is about the invention of blood banks. An Afro-American doctor, Charles Drew (1904–50), was responsible for the development and administration of the blood-bank programme used on battlefields during the Second World War. Drew was subject to racism all his life, and the cruel hand of fate wielded its final blow when he was seriously injured in a car accident. He was in need of a blood transfusion but (the story goes) the hospital he was admitted to would not treat him because he was black. He died before reaching a hospital that would treat him. Material developed by Leicestershire LEA (1985) includes three accounts of Drew's life, each providing about a third of the details. These accounts can be given to three pupils (in a group), who then have to compile the full details of his tragic life story by filling in a sheet, with the rule that pupils cannot show their story sheet to one another: they have to do it by talking.

These accounts hold a wealth of material for use in creative writing. Being highly controversial, they lend themselves to debate and discussion; but perhaps of more immediate value, they bring home to pupils the reality of life and the true nature of science.

Celebrate everyone involved in developments in science

Rosalind Franklin's role in elucidating the nature of DNA is a case in point. Francis Crick, James Watson and Maurice Wilkins received the Nobel Prize for their work in the project, but we tend to forget that many other people dedicated their lives to the cause, with little recognition. Issues of gender can often be addressed here, when we consider female scientists as well as male. Remember Marie Curie and her role in developing our understanding of nuclear processes. And Madame Lavoisier was an equal (if not greater) partner in her husband's work on the nature of air.

Start from and value the experiences and knowledge of pupils

Reiss (1998) explains the use of separating and purifying mixtures in terms of a pluralistic approach to teaching. He recounts seeing a very successful lesson in which much time was dedicated to exploring domestic devices for separating and purifying mixtures, brought in by a group of year 8 pupils. He explains how the exercise could be developed into a detailed discussion of why people need to separate substances: for example, 'Why do people want pure salt?', 'Where, in everyday life, do we use the idea that iron can be separated from aluminium through the action of magnets?' or 'When is it a nuisance that mixtures separate out?' (salad dressings, paints, etc.).

Use flexible teaching and learning strategies

Everything we have said about a constructivist approach to learning (Chapter 6), and the need to incorporate 'word work', applies here.

Integrate practical approaches as and when appropriate

The danger here, as always, is that we rely too much on the resources available in our school science laboratories. These are an essential part of our repertoire but should only be used to isolate and examine things that are too complex in pupils' everyday experiences. We must continue to point out the importance of using the everyday world of our pupils as our primary resource, such as the use of sieves and colanders in the year 8 lesson above.

Summary

In this chapter we began by introducing the overarching agenda behind inclusion: the Every Child Matters policy. We focused on the need to maximise pupils' independence in the learning environment, and in so doing involve them more directly in their own learning. With this in mind, differentiation becomes something that is not just for the less able, but also a means of challenging the most able. To achieve 'science for all' we need to know our pupils, and we need to recognise their special educational needs from whatever aspect they may arise. We need to be able to differentiate our teaching and their learning accordingly. This chapter has explored a range of strategies to ensure that this can be achieved, with effective teaching and learning as the outcome. These strategies can loosely be summarised as follows:

- including cross-curricular links in your teaching, especially to world cultures

- working closely with the SEN co-ordinator, and possibly team teaching with other specialist staff

- creating partnerships with home, the local community and other relevant organisations through the ECM agenda

- using global issues, including environmental and world development.

We need to make science relevant to everyday life and to enhance sustainable development in a peaceful world.

Learning Outside the Classroom

Chapter overview

This chapter re-examines the use of the outdoor classroom as a vehicle for enhancing teaching and learning in science. Embedding school trips across the curriculum has reached new heights in terms of the political agenda as government and educationalists recognise how they can enrich pupils' learning experience, boost academic achievement and make learning fun. All this has been known for some while but at last recognition within the curriculum has been given. This presents its own set of problems and professional issues, which we address in this chapter.

Learning outside the classroom

This idea in itself is nothing new; back in the 1980s the government introduced the Technical and Vocational Education Initiative (TVEI) which provided funding and guidelines enabling schools and industries to collaborate in a new and effective way, creating links and opportunities for pupils and their teachers to learn in an alternative setting. Mainly aimed at business and enterprise, the initiative soon sparked an interest in other settings for educational enhancement. Museums and non-government funded organisations such as the National Trust, the national park authorities and international organisations began to get involved. Educational events and visits were taking on a new image and meaning. Then, with the increasing emphasis on health and safety issues, potential risk of litigation, pressures of the curriculum and ever-increasing cost implications, these activities began to experience a sharp decline.

Recent changes to the secondary curriculum and the introduction of the new diplomas have given a new lease of life to 'learning outside the classroom'. It is now one of the seven components underpinning the secondary curriculum, with an entitlement for every child from the Early Years and Foundation Stage through to post-16 to learn in an 'alternative setting'. Fifty per cent of curriculum time during the Early Years should be dedicated to learning outside the classroom. This decreases to between 5 and 15 per cent for post-16 students but there is a strong commitment of 20 per cent for Key Stages 3 and 4.

What is the value of learning outside the classroom for science?

- Provides first-hand experience of processes such as focused observation and recording.

- Provides experience of the physical, industrial, social, environmental and ecological aspects of the real world.

- Provides opportunities for novel, unique and exciting learning experiences.

- Embeds science learning in a meaningful context.

- Provides practice in and application of skills developed and used within the classroom.

- Can expand the science curriculum and give it purpose.

- Builds closer relationships between pupils and pupils, pupils and teachers and pupils and other 'expert' adults.

- Provides stimulus and motivation.

- Gives opportunities to develop pupils' autonomy thereby encouraging independent learning and such attitudes as respect for others and for things.

- Helps develop a pupil's identity.

(Adapted from ASE 2006a)

Planning a school trip

Any form of off-site visit or activity necessitates thorough planning, with special attention paid to health and safety issues. This can be time-consuming but is vital to ensure that a safe, legal and educationally beneficial experience is obtained by all concerned. A general risk assessment will need to be carried out prior to the visit, with a more specific one being carried out once at the site. Companies will usually have their own generic one to help you. Often preparation for the visit begins a year in advance, when the initial booking is made with the organisation concerned. This will coincide with the preliminary visit by a member of the teaching staff. A couple of months before the visit a letter will need to be sent to parents to gain permission for the pupils to attend. If the visit is residential, details concerning special diets and any medical conditions must be identified. Money will be collected in at this time and you will need to be familiar with the 'voluntary contribution' system operated by most schools. A week or so before the visit a general meeting with the pupils will be necessary to inform them of final arrangements and any special clothing, and to reiterate aims and expectations. Most schools have a strategy informing parents about 'pick-up' arrangements if delays in travel occur. From your point of view, an up-to-date list of names and contact telephone numbers is vital – so too is a mobile phone. During the visit it is the responsibility of you and other members of staff to ensure the well-being of the pupils. Familiarise yourself with the legalities of this through the Department for Children, Schools and Families (DCSF) website and other organisations, such as the Youth Hostels Association and the Field Studies Council.

The planning and preparation required to ensure everything goes smoothly without any glitches is one of the key factors deterring teachers from organising trips. Since February 2009 this process has become easier. The government introduced a *quality badge* scheme as part of the Learning Outside the Classroom (LOtC) initiative launched two years earlier. The scheme provides quality assurance for working outside the classroom; this could mean within the school grounds or further afield. It sets a gold standard for those providers and locations around the UK wishing to attract school parties for a safe and educational trip. The scheme sets out a series of quality indicators to ensure the provider:

- has a process in place to assist users to plan the learning experience effectively linked to National Curriculum requirements

- provides accurate information about what it has to offer

- provides activities, experiences or resources which meet learner needs

- reviews the experience and acts upon feedback

- meets the needs of the users

- has safety management processes in place to manage risk effectively.

The above indicators (adapted from www.lotcqualitybadge.org.uk/home) are in tune with current curriculum stipulation and are implemented prior to, during and after the visit. The LOtC website offers support for the provider and continuing professional development (CPD) modules aimed at the teacher in all stages of their career.

Who are the providers involved with effective learning outside the classroom?

There exists a wealth of organisations across the UK providing experiences and activities for learning science. A good starting point is your regional Science Learning Centre. There is a network of nine centres across England, with the National Centre based in York. They all offer CPD opportunities for teachers and are linked to the regional Science, Technology, Engineering and Mathematics (STEM) network that specialises in initiatives linking industry and education. Other national centres offer related experiences such as the Science and Natural History museums in London, the Eden Project in Cornwall, Dynamic Earth in Edinburgh, Eureka! in Halifax and Techniquest in Cardiff. More locally, check out your city farm if there is one, local museum, art gallery, indeed any natural and built environments, as well as the major local tourist attractions. All are likely to have something to offer from an educational perspective; if they don't, but look promising, why not be proactive and initiate a link?

This type of liaison is most effective when it is part of a long-term partnership tailored to the respective partner needs and regularly reviewed. In the next section we explore how such partnerships can be established and maintained, citing industrial liaison as an example.

Establishing effective links and partnerships

What does industry want from education?

Part of any effective working relationship is the recognition that both partners have a role to play: both have their own expectations and needs. When asked what they felt school pupils would be expected to offer to industry, on applying for a job, our trainee teachers came up with the following list of attributes:

- an all-round education

- basic skills of literacy and numeracy

- communication and ICT skills

- social and academic skills

- commitment

- good time management

- good health.

This list illustrates something that all good education systems aim to achieve, but in reality, industry has found that the incoming workforce has often lacked even the basic literacy and communication skills and was weak in science and technology. The introduction of the Secondary National Strategy, changes at Key Stages 3 and 4, the STEM agenda, together with a revised apprenticeship scheme and the new suite of diplomas, go some way to responding to this. The increased emphasis on learning in alternative settings, and especially linking with industry, takes this response even further. It can help address many of these deficiencies, and at its best it is one of the most successful means of bringing reality into the classroom. If a pupil can see and understand the reasons for learning a particular subject then the learning process becomes more effective.

What does education want from industry?

Our trainee teachers were asked to summarise their views on what education could gain from industry. They said that it:

- enhances the curriculum

- contributes to economic and industrial understanding

- supports career awareness

- provides financial support and 'freebies'.

The ideas presented are self-evidently laudable. Presenting the curriculum through 'real-life' examples and experiences underpins the Secondary National Strategy. The industrial perspective has much to offer regarding the application of science and technology. This has influenced curriculum development over the years and continues to do so, bringing a more holistic view of the world beyond the classroom. This in turn raises awareness of social and environmental issues among tomorrow's decision-makers and consumers, with the long-term aim of encouraging a sustainable lifestyle.

All of the above are commendable and realistic benefits, but how can they be achieved?

Strategies for links

When trainee teachers were asked to list a range of initiatives they had either experienced themselves or heard of, the outcome was quite impressive:

- work experience and work shadowing
- talks at school by representatives from local firms
- sponsorship
- staff and curriculum development
- representatives on school governing bodies
- school visits to companies
- Young Enterprise Schemes
- STEM-related activities and events
- mini research projects for post-16
- industry days
- careers advice
- training
- resources and 'freebies'.

In the sections that follow we deal with two aspects from this list: resources and STEM-related initiatives.

Resources

A myriad of resources has been produced by industry, business and other organisations. The production of educational resources has had a chequered history; organisations learnt the hard way and, at times, wasted millions of pounds on a badly managed approach. They saturated schools with literature that was collected by enthusiastic staff or sent unsolicited by mail but later assumed the role of doorstop or 'shelf support'; other resources have disappeared into the depths of the staff room never to see the light of day again. The problem was that the resources were neither pitched at an appropriate level for the pupils nor related to the schools' curriculum. Although well presented, usually in a glossy format, they lacked the important hallmark of teacher input. Organisations began to rethink their approach. They recognised the need for effective, relevant resource material, produced by a suitable team of teachers. Several also appreciated the value of INSET sessions in terms of promoting and using the resource. Teachers were invited to attend a day or half-day session sponsored by the company concerned or possibly in association with the local STEM co-ordinator and Education Business Partnership. These organisations still exist and, being established to create effective links between both worlds, are often able to offer a contribution to travel costs and sometimes even supply cover. So look out for them!

Most curriculum materials are now produced with the involvement of a dedicated team of teachers whose role is to assist in producing a meaningful context for teaching and learning.

Coping with values and possible bias in resources

Despite the advances in resource writing, one has to expect a certain amount of company bias coming through. After all, they have probably put thousands of pounds into the production of the material and will expect some recognition and spin-off. By being vigilant and observing the following guidelines, the resource can be used effectively:

- Realise that nobody is completely free of bias. We all need to recognise our own bias.

- Identify the aspects of the material that you consider most credible.

- Ask yourself which information looks most suspect. How could you check it?

- Consider what important information has been left out.

- Debate the perspective of the person(s) who wrote the resource.

- If possible, obtain similar information from a complementary organisation.

SATIS and upd8 (update)

A section on industrial links would not be complete without mention of the Science and Technology in Society (SATIS) material published by the Association for Science Education (ASE) in the 1980s and reprinted in the late 1990s. The original series consisted of seven books, each containing 10 units. The units were designed to be used in conjunction with conventional science courses, especially at Key Stage 4. Each unit is self-contained and linked to the major science topics, as well as exploring important social and technological applications and issues. For example, SATIS 7 explores issues pertaining to electricity in the home, problems with gas supply, artificial limbs and biotechnology. Each unit has clearly defined aims, background information relating to the issues, suggested activities and guidance on further study. Although the series is becoming outdated, the approach used and much of the information given are still relevant and well worth including in your lessons. SATIS lives on as upd8 (see p. 72).

STEM initiatives

In July 2004 the government released its *Science & innovation investment framework 2004–2014*, which set out a long-term strategy to secure and sustain a supply of scientists, engineers, technologists and mathematicians (STEM) to support the science base. As part of this framework, the STEM Cross-Cutting Programme, jointly managed by the then Department for Education and Skills and the Department of Trade and Industry (DTI), was set up to examine the range of initiatives supporting this agenda and to look for ways to enhance the effectiveness of government funding in two areas:

- the flow of qualified people into the STEM workforce

- STEM literacy in the population.

> The Programme identified the need to improve the delivery of STEM initiatives particularly those which fall into the categories of professional development for staff and enhancement activities for learners so that the STEM system could be made more coherent; with better signposting and advice to learning providers; and giving every learning provider access to some STEM help.
>
> (DfES 2006b)

The recognised STEM learning providers form a network entitled STEMNET which is funded jointly by the DTI and the DCSF, with a collective vision to enable all young people to achieve their potential in STEM by:

- ensuring that all young people, regardless of background, are encouraged to understand the excitement and importance of science, technology, engineering and mathematics in their lives, and the career opportunities to which the STEM subjects can lead

- helping all schools and colleges across the UK understand the range of STEM Enhancement & Enrichment opportunities available to them and the benefits these can bring to everyone involved

- encouraging business, organisations and individuals wanting to support young people in STEM to target their efforts and resources in a way that will deliver the best results for them and young people.

They achieve this by bringing science, technology, engineering and mathematics to classrooms through activities and experiences that enhance and enrich the national STEM curriculum. They also apply a range of strategies to link organisations that employ STEM-related professionals with schools so that young people can gain a clearer perspective of the diverse range of careers available to them. To find out more about STEMNET visit their website at www.stemnet.org.uk

Taking the initiative and making it work

We have explored the history of learning outside the classroom and introduced the initiative that drives this forward nowadays, LOtC; this whole approach is central to all aspects of the curriculum and ever more so to the new diplomas. We must ensure, however, that the links we create are effective and productive. The quality badging scheme mentioned earlier is a tremendous asset but there are things that we can do ourselves before a trip takes place and links are established. The following pointers should be considered:

- identify your needs and those of the pupils

- establish initial contact with the organisation in plenty of time

- maintain one point of contact

- ensure mutual familiarity with both environments, which will necessitate a preliminary visit on the part of one or the other

- evaluate the exercise in terms of the original needs

- give feedback to both parties

- if the liaison worked, maintain a long-term link.

Important pivotal conferences for all aspects of learning outside the classroom are the national and regional meetings of the ASE and the Education Show. Organisations that have produced materials for use in schools exhibit at the ASE Annual Meeting held in January of each year at a British university and at the annual Education Show held in March at the National Exhibition Centre in Birmingham.

Summary

This chapter has re-emphasised the need to relate learning in science to everyday life. If we genuinely want our children to make sense of the environment they live in, they need to be in it; they need to know where the artefacts they use on a daily basis come from and how they were produced. They need to question the sustainability, in global terms, of the continuity of supply of our consumer goods and recognise the impact this is having locally and globally. Links with industry and learning in the outdoor classroom are therefore essential for the next generation to move towards a more sustainable future. If this is carried out in a safe and well-planned manner, it can make a significant contribution to the whole education of the pupil.

Useful web links

Learning Outside the Classroom: www.lotc.org.uk
Youth Hostels Association: www.yha.org.uk
Field Studies Council: www.field-studies-council.org
STEMNET: www.stemnet.org.uk

Becoming a Professional Science Teacher

Chapter overview

This chapter explores what we mean by being professional and becoming a professional teacher. It reflects on the changing face of teacher professionalism in the past decades and, drawing on recent research, sets modern-day professionalism back in the hands of the teacher. To achieve this a broader understanding of science education is required. So here we re-examine the nature of science and the picture children have of science and scientists. We review the historical events that allowed science to become a compulsory part of the National Curriculum. We look at the reasons why it should remain so by placing emphasis on the public understanding and social responsibility of science. We will see the important part science teachers have played over the past 150 years, either on their own or through what became the Association for Science Education, in enabling science to reach the place it has in the National Curriculum.

What do we mean by being a professional teacher?

The perceived role of a professional teacher has changed significantly over the past few decades, in parallel with educational policy, initiatives, strategies and directives, especially the Professional Attributes strand of the Training and Development Agency (TDA) Standards for Qualified Teacher Status (QTS) (TDA 2009). However, with the current changes in the secondary curriculum it is evident that the view of professionalism is going full circle. The professional qualities and attributes of a 1970s/early 1980s teacher emphasised developing and planning their own curriculum in tune with advances and developments in their own subject area and education generally (Lakin 2008). This is a far cry from the view of a professional class teacher as seen in the last 20 years. This is due largely to the implementation, since the mid-1980s, of centrally prescribed curriculum guidelines providing a framework for subject teachers to operate in, with curriculum control at a national rather than teacher level. This included the National Curriculum, GCSE and AS/A2 criteria and syllabuses, which had a set of approved knowledge and skills, and a static content led by assessment.

Together these curtailed the drive for updating curricula and creative thought. The quality of education was down to the teacher's interpretation and implementation of the curricula (Rawling 2003). This had significant implications as teachers 'delivered' rather than engaged in the process (Roberts 1995). Increases in administrative work put additional pressure on teachers and the focus for in-service opportunities shifted from being 'subject' related to one of methods of delivery, assessment and management. At the same time changes were afoot in teacher education as courses were restructured with limited subject-based training.

More recently there has been a shift from central government to hand curriculum planning back to the subject teacher, evident in the changes at Key Stage 3 and reduced content of the revised National Curriculum (DCSF 2007). These changes offer real potential to resurrect a level of autonomy within the profession. Already schemes of work are becoming more personalised and creative (see *Creativity: Find it, promote it* on the National Curriculum in Action website; QCDA 2007); the PGCE M-level *requires* trainees not simply to accept prescription but rather to analyse its effectiveness and adapt it to suit the individuals in their class and school (Lakin 2008).

Developing oneself professionally

From research into geography education Rawlings (2003) has identified five aspects of professionalism which will underpin on-going professional development:

1. Valuing yourself professionally.
2. Interacting with pupils.
3. Interacting with other teachers.
4. Interacting with the wider subject community.
5. Interacting with state and policy-making.

We will explore each of these in relation to science education and your continuing professional development.

Professionalism 1: Valuing yourself professionally

As you develop as a professional teacher you will recognise the importance and satisfaction of finding out about new developments in education, research and science specifically. This information will impact on the way you teach and how you look at your subject, your pupils and, indeed, your own role within the science education arena. We begin by asking one of the most fundamental questions relating to this...

What is science?

Our second chapter constructed a model of how science works (Figure 2.1) and made the important distinction between technology and science. It was possible for early humans to develop stone tools, wooden spears, clay pots and thatch that didn't leak, without understanding the science behind these technologies. However, ideas would be forming in their minds that enabled them to see the potential of stone, wood, clay and straw for their new purposes. These ideas would be strengthened through the successful use of the technology, and in turn provide inspiration regarding how to make improvements.

Thus, from humanity's earliest beginnings, the ideas of science and the products of technology have developed side by side. When we began to try to make sense of the heavenly bodies, to explain the cycle of the seasons and to tell stories of our origins, the *ideas* took on an independent existence. To be classified as scientific, however, the ideas must be able to be tested using our senses, and that distinguishes the creativity of science from that of art and of myth. We established that science does not progress by *induction* to find *laws*, as Francis Bacon in the sixteenth century and many scientists through to the twentieth century thought. Science deals not with the search for absolute truth but with the creation of testable models in our minds that attempt to make sense of our world.

Popper's conjectures and refutations

The *two conceptions* view of science by Karl Popper (1959) gives a more realistic picture. Stimulated by things we notice, we have an *idea* about what might be going on: Popper's *conjectures*. This must be followed by careful, controlled testing, where we check if the idea works, or attempt to prove ourselves wrong: Popper's *refutations*. This logical process of *falsification* was important to Popper, who wanted to distinguish science from the pseudo-science of political or economic ideas. For every scientific idea, there had to be a way in which it could be disproved or falsified. If it stood up to this test we would be able to use it more widely, and it would become part of our scientific understanding (though it might fail at any later time). Our current Science National Curriculum Sc1, *How science works*, features both these aspects of science: data collection and analysis form the logical side and the ideas that determine what is investigated form the creative side.

Kuhn's normal and revolutionary science

Scientists, however, do not spend their time falsifying their own hypotheses. On the contrary, they try to persuade others to believe in them and to use them to interpret and predict outcomes of their experiments. Thomas Kuhn's concepts of *normal* and *revolutionary* science are a more realistic view of what really happens (Kuhn 1970). *Normally* scientists work within a particular set of scientific ideas (which Kuhn called a *paradigm*). Over time anomalies build up, and questions remain unanswered – it takes more than one unexplained result (refutation) to make the scientists change their minds. For example, Newton remained an alchemist all his life, despite a number of important chemical results that were obtained by his seventeenth-century contemporaries that began to show that transmutation of elements was impossible. Eventually there has to be a *revolution*, and the new ideas displace the old.

Revolutions are difficult to effect

Chinn and Brewer (1998) studied learners' responses to anomalous data (i.e. data that conflict with their existing ideas). They asked students to read an account of one of two alternative theories for a particular phenomenon (e.g. why the dinosaurs died out). They then presented the students with data that conflicted with the original biased views. They found that the students were more likely to hold on to their original beliefs than to modify their ideas and adopt the alternative theory – it was *the theory they heard first* that they held on to. In science teaching, the naïve theory held by the pupil can be shown to be incorrect through presented evidence. Nevertheless, we must be wary of assuming that simple cognitive conflict is all that is required to effect conceptual change in students. Box 24.1 provides a modern example of how difficult it is to revolutionise our scientific beliefs.

Box 24.1 Modern-day paradigm shifts?

Read this commentary about whether fuels contain energy, then answer the questions below.

Everyone knows that we use fuels as a source of energy – for our bodies and for driving our technology. In Chapter 12 (pp. 109–15), however, we suggested that this energy is not *in* the food or fuels. We explained that those textbooks and cereal packets (just about all of them) that say food *contains* energy that is transferred when they are used are *wrong*. We argued, instead, that energy is stored in the *fuel–oxygen system*. Methane contains no energy, coal contains no energy and, except for the tiny anaerobic energy transfer when glucose rearranges its bonds during anaerobic respiration, there is no fuel-energy in glucose either.

Children who have not been exposed to the idea that energy from combustion is stored *in* the fuels find it easy to see the *fuel–oxygen system* as a store of energy. It makes understanding photosynthesis and trophic levels much more straightforward. It allows them to keep a separate account of *energy* (stored in stretched or broken bonds, released when strong bonds are remade) and of *matter* (atoms bond in different ways, but are never lost or made).

Science teachers and graduates, steeped in years of 'knowing' that fuels 'contain' energy, find it very hard to see systems in this (new) way. Many refuse to change their minds, preferring the old, comfortable, accepted paradigm.

This puts forward a 'revolutionary' view about 'energy in fuels/food'. Having now read and thought about an explanation involving fuel–oxygen systems:

- Do you reject our view?
- Do you accept it, but think it too difficult to use with your pupils?
- Or do you acknowledge a paradigm shift (or already accept this view) and intend to (or do) share it with your pupils?

Paradigm shifts are inconvenient: they turn your world over and they force you to rethink your world. Many science teachers are happy to take the middle way of Box 24.1: 'I've always said there is energy in food, and it makes it easier for my pupils'.

Professionalism 2: Interacting with pupils

As teachers we need to remember that the learner (the pupil) is central to the learning process. How they interact with and take ownership of the content we teach is vital. To understand this we need to know something about their perceptions of the world around them and, indeed, how children learn science.

Children's ideas about science and scientists

We may be happy to accept the view of how science works in the model in Chapter 2 and we may try to share this view with children. However, children come to our science lessons with their views about science and scientists already partially formed. Many have a vision of 'white men in white coats', often bearded and bespectacled (see also p. 213). These scientists, in the eyes of children, undertake experiments and observation, which then lead to the 'discovery' of theories. The idea that the scientists may already 'know' what (they hope) will happen does not make sense – why should they bother to do experiments if they already 'know' what is going to happen? Driver et al. (1996) show that it is not until the GCSE years that pupils begin to see science in ways other than this 'discovery' view. How can we, as science teachers, show children that the discovery comes *before* the experiment? You need a *guess* in order to set up the *check*.

Professionalism 3 and 4: Interacting with other teachers and the wider subject community

During your PGCE year you will be encouraged to discuss your classroom experiences with teaching colleagues and fellow trainees. These opportunities for peer discussion and support are fundamental to your own professional development. Continuing professional development (CPD) opportunities will be available to you in your Newly Qualified Teacher (NQT) year and beyond, but you need to be proactive in taking them and moving forward. The Association for Science Education (ASE) and the national network of Science Learning Centres are central to this process, offering opportunities for sharing, updating and innovation at all levels within the science curriculum. So having an interest in your subject, both in and beyond the classroom, together with its characteristics and relevance to society, are all important.

Professionalism 5: Interacting with state and policy-making

As you develop as a professional teacher you will find that your interests and influence stretch beyond your classroom, school and local community. Through networks such as the ASE and other subject associations, you become involved in the broader education arena. This provides opportunities to interact and influence policy-making both nationally and internationally. An awareness of how policy-making has taken place in the past is important, as too is the opportunity to look to the future.

A history of science education

In the sections that follow we trace the way in which the science education community has played its part in developing science as a core subject in the compulsory curriculum. Just as a sense of history helps us understand the way in which new scientific ideas were developed, so, as teachers, we should be aware of the path taken by education.

It would be hard to ask for science to be a compulsory part of our National Curriculum if it was only a collection of testable ideas, as we describe above. It would be justified only as a useful study for those making a career in science or technology and as having some cultural value for those with a love of learning. However, science, through technology, has a huge social impact, which has grown apace ever since the industrial, technological and digital revolutions. We have now reached a situation where our technology is causing global environmental change at an unsustainable rate; people need to understand science to enable them to play their part in democratic life. We return to this theme at the end of the chapter, but first, a bit of history.

How did science become a part of the National Curriculum?

By the start of the nineteenth century in England there were schools for the wealthy and universities at Oxford and Cambridge but little teaching of science. In Scotland there were universities at St Andrews, Glasgow, Aberdeen and Edinburgh. Developments in science itself since the Renaissance had taken place mainly through amateur efforts of the leisured classes. Cambridge only began awarding science degrees in the 1850s. The Victorian era saw the foundation of new universities in London, Durham and Manchester, and in Wales and Ireland. Elementary schools for the working classes were set up by the churches, with the government providing grant aid. It was then that two clergymen, Richard Dawes and John Henslow, inspired by scientific philosophy at Cambridge, started the teaching of science in their respective parish schools. In two rather different ways they laid the foundations for the appearance of science in our schools today.

Dawes' object lessons in elementary schools

Richard Dawes moved to his parish, near Winchester, in 1836, and built a model school (Layton 1973). Although the well-to-do paid more, once inside the school instruction took no account of social standing or fees paid. But the comprehensive ideal was not complete: girls had to do needlework, while the boys studied science. Science lessons were *object lessons*: pupils could observe for themselves the objects of common daily life to inspire them with an intelligent curiosity (see Figure 24.1).

Dawes' *Suggestive Hints towards Improved Secular Instruction*, published in 1847, provided teachers countrywide with a common-sense explanation of things used in everyday life. The newly formed government education department agreed to pay the cost of the apparatus list published in *Hints* for any school qualified to use it, so that by 1857 about 8 per cent of elementary schools (3500 total) had the apparatus sets and the newly formed teacher training colleges were including his ideas in their curriculum.

By 1861 it all came to an end when the grant stopped, science was taken out of the teacher training curriculum and the revised code – payment by results – meant that

The kettle: an object lesson

An old kettle, blackened at the bottom to absorb the radiation from the fire, and shiny on top to prevent radiation loss, has a metal body for good conduction of heat to the water and a handle made of poorly conducting wood to prevent you burning your hand.

FIGURE 24.1 An idea taken from *Victorians at School* (Ironbridge Gorge Museum Trust, undated)

schools and teachers were judged by their results in the three Rs. Schools resorted to rote learning and cramming pupils for the tests. Not unlike the effect of the league tables of today!

Science as process: Henslow's systematic botany

As a child, Henslow had a keen interest in natural history, which he pursued at Cambridge. His parish school in Hitcham opened in 1841 and there he developed his idea of using botany as a way of training the mind. His 'systematic botany' lessons involved the classification of plants on the basis of their structure. Pupils were trained in observation and rational thought. Henslow's approach to science education emphasised *how science worked* rather than the subject matter: the process rather than the content. Unlike Dawes, his ideas did not spread in elementary schools but were taken up instead by the public schools (fee-paying and 13–18 age range), where they were safe from the ravages of 'payment by results' (Layton 1973). A direct link can be made between Henslow's emphasis on scientific processes and the Nuffield Science revolution of the 1960s.

The rise of Nuffield Science

Apart from a few schools using Henslow's ideas, mainstream secondary science in the first half of the twentieth century became very content based, with lots of rote learning of laws and facts. Science teaching in school was geared to passing the university entrance examinations which developed into the School Certificate and then O- and A-levels.

The Nuffield Science movement in the 1960s was a direct challenge to this factual approach to science teaching, reviving Henslow's ideas from a century earlier. Pupils were to become 'scientists for a day', and the tedious learning of facts for exams was to be replaced by opportunities to do practical investigations and to think about the process of being scientific.

If the old method overemphasised facts, this 'new' approach overemphasised process. Research scientists may acquire a scientific understanding through their own inspiration, but we cannot expect children to have similar insights. Pupils' existing ideas remained unchallenged by these new process-based courses, and scientifically accepted ideas were not overtly being taught. Pupils were expected to 'discover' things for themselves by doing experiments. Few ever did, and teachers took to telling the pupils what they were supposed to have 'discovered'. We must not, however, lessen the importance of these early attempts to bring the nature of the scientific process into the school curriculum. The final section in this historical review brings us to the present, and to the teaching model we developed in Chapter 6: the constructivist approach.

An entitlement to science for all

We accept the double award science at GCSE, and its equivalent triple science, as the statutory right of almost all pupils in England and Wales, but it was not always so. Initiatives came mostly from science teachers themselves, through their professional association. The Association for Science Education (ASE) began life as the Association of Public School Science Masters in 1911. It was quickly joined by the women's association and they both took in teachers from the state schools to become the 'Association of Women Science Teachers' and the 'Science Masters' Association'. The ASE was formed in the 1960s when the men's and women's associations joined. The *School Science Review*, which began in 1919, was a joint publication almost from the start. Several policy statements for school science (1916, 1936, 1943, 1957 and 1961) were jointly published. The policy on general science (1936) was the first to campaign for broad balanced science. Originally Nuffield Science was to be integrated, but we had to wait for the Schools Council Integrated Science Project before broad balanced science for O-level pupils was available. Nuffield Combined Science (for ages 11–13) and Nuffield Secondary Science (for the CSE pupils who were now legally required to remain at school until aged 16) provided a broad approach for the rest.

The development of the National Curriculum (1987) was built on the results of the Assessment of Performance Unit (APU) project. The APU conducted tests nationally during the early 1980s, but only with a sample of pupils in a sample of schools, allowing them to look at how standards vary with type of school and location, and over time. This prevented the identification of individual schools or teachers, which might have upset the cooperation that existed between them. No teaching for tests needed here!

Brenda and Friends (West 1984; reviewed in Ross 1998) is a very exciting document, which though pre-dating the National Curriculum unfortunately had little impact on it: it sketched out a *minimum entitlement* in science for every child in the form of a series of stories. Each curriculum topic had a different child, 16 in all. See Box 24.2 for an extract from *Abdul* as he looks back on his school science experience of particles and the nature of science.

Box 24.2 Extract from *Brenda and Friends* (West 1984)

Abdul: particulate nature of matter

His new science teacher understood Abdul's problem with particles and to his amazement he discovered that she had had difficulty with particulate theory too. She explained that scientists couldn't see particles ... but accepted particulate explanations because of their usefulness, and because they are not disproved by any of their observations... Because Abdul's teacher appreciated his ideas she was able to set him a number of experiments to do to check out his thinking. He carefully observed two gases – one coloured – mixing together...

The government policy statement for science, *Science 5–16: a Statement of Policy*, in 1985, was the first in which science was recommended, as official government policy, to be a part of everyone's school experience. It also recommended that all branches of science be studied from 5 to 16. No longer were we to have physicists with no biology, and biologists with no physics.

Rosalind Driver (who died in 1997 shortly after becoming Professor of Science Education at King's College London – a great loss to the profession) directed one of the APU teams from Leeds. It was from her analysis of scientifically incorrect answers to the concept category questions that the Children's Learning in Science (CLIS) project was born, and we began to see how strongly held children's naïve ideas were.

Many of the questions we use today to probe children's ideas trace their origin to the APU questions (see, for example, the 'tub tree' question in Figure 14.1, p. 134). Projects researching children's ideas sprang up worldwide, led by work in New Zealand (Osborne and Freyberg 1985). Since then much work on primary pupils' concepts has been done, resulting in the Science Process and Concept Evaluation project (Watt and Russell 1990) and the Nuffield Primary Science materials (1993). The constructivist approach to learning, which we emphasise in this book, became influential as a result of this work.

The Science National Curriculum for England (and Wales)

On first publication in 1990 the National Curriculum had four dimensions (process, concepts, communication and context). *Process* became Attainment Target 1 (AT 1), with an emphasis on observation and systematic testing, *concepts* became ATs 2–16 (and now AT 2, 3 and 4), *communication* 'went across the curriculum' and *context* went originally into AT 17, which was called 'The nature of science'. The three *concept* attainment targets we now have (Sc2 biology, Sc3 chemistry and Sc4 physics) are similar to the original draft for the concepts, which were then deliberately split to provide a more topic-based integrated approach. In the current version (DCSF 2007) the nature of science (the old AT 17) has been brought into the programme of study *How science works*, enabling it to be assessed in AT 1. Hull (1995) provides a fascinating review of this turbulent early history of science in the National Curriculum.

The public understanding of science

Our science schemes of work tend to follow the sequence of ideas from a scientist's perspective. This suggests that to understand, for example, photosynthesis properly we must first introduce cells, gaseous diffusion, transpiration, the nature of carbon dioxide, chlorophyll and so on. This may not be the best way from a child's point of view. This book has argued that we need to start from the pupils' own ideas, thus we should begin by suggesting that plants grow by using materials not only from soil *but also from the air* and that this growth is fuelled by energy from sunlight. This overarching picture can be refined as necessary.

If we are to produce a public that understands science we need them first of all to be able to say 'green plants obtain carbon, their stuff of life, from the air'. Without this basic idea about how life works and how carbon is cycled, many environmental issues, such as carbon footprinting, make little sense. We need to ask what science will remain with our pupils once they leave school. Will everything be forgotten as they trade in their knowledge for a GCSE certificate (as we showed in Figure 7.2, p. 64)? Or will they, instead, retain usable knowledge of how the world works, enabling them to understand some of the pressures we are placing on ourselves and the environment? A National Curriculum composed of unrelated topics does provide a sort of checklist. However, when we build our schemes of work, the statements of minimum entitlement in *Brenda and Friends* (see Box 24.2) are far more useful in enabling us to relate the topics to the everyday lives of our pupils. The cross-curricular approach now required at Key Stage 3 promotes this topic-based integrated approach to learning.

Justification for the inclusion of science in the school curriculum

Some topics in our science curriculum owe their presence more to accidents of history than to anything else, though we could justify any part of our existing curriculum from a *cultural* point of view. If the ideas form part of our scientific heritage, humanity as a whole has a right to share this knowledge. We can justify including the cultural achievements of humanity from other disciplines of knowledge on the same basis: there is little distinction between studying the evolution of humans two million years ago (studied in science) and studying the rise of the Maya civilisation in Central America two thousand years ago (studied in history). Similarly, the second law of thermodynamics and atomic theory are just as much creations of human inspiration as the plays of Shakespeare and the music of Mozart, and children should be aware of these achievements.

There are, however, more immediate reasons to teach science, which 21st Century Science, mentioned below, has grasped (Twenty First Century Science Team 2003). Perhaps the most basic is that it has a *utility* value. If you understand the science behind everyday activities, you are more likely to undertake them safely. Once we understand the germ theory of disease, we are happy to follow basic hygiene rules, such as washing hands before eating, cleaning a cut, and storing cooked and raw meat separately. If they are followed only as rules, without the science, they are much less likely to be followed sensibly or at all.

Between these two extremes is what some have called the *democratic* justification for teaching science (Ratcliffe 1998). Some big ideas in science have no controllable effect on our lives. The idea of stars as element factories, for instance, is fascinating, and we are dominated by our nearest star, the sun, but there is nothing we can do about it, except to enjoy the knowledge – a cultural pursuit. However, there are some ideas that we need to understand if our lives on planet Earth are to be sustainable. Decisions are being made that affect our lives, and we need to understand the science to help to make choices ourselves.

At the Rio Earth Summit in 1992 a common agenda for the twenty-first century, 'Agenda 21', was agreed to by 179 governments (Lakin 2000). One commitment was to reduce carbon dioxide emissions. This could be achieved by burning less fossil fuel, meaning that less 'useful' energy will be available, or by finding ways of burying the carbon dioxide, an expensive option.

In a democratic state it is important that the public understands the reasons behind new legislation. We need to realise that the materials we use have to be (re-)cycled, just as materials are cycled in natural systems. We cannot continue to mine raw materials and dump them on land, in water and into the air, because the raw materials will become depleted, and the dumps will cause pollution. They also need to understand that this cycling needs to be fuelled. Natural systems rely mostly on sunlight, which drives both life and climate, but we have escaped from this reliance on solar power through our use of fossil fuels.

Many have said that the study of science is too difficult for this democratic justification to be valid. They claim that a little learning – for example, about genetic engineering or nuclear power – simply makes people frightened. A number of questions spring to mind:

- Since not even the scientists can ever understand fully, why do we bother at all with the general public?

- How can the public ever hope to understand 'enough' of these conceptual areas to help them to make democratic decisions?

- In any case, is such an understanding really necessary before any real action on environmental issues can be taken by a democratic society?

- Since the scientists cannot agree, why should the general public bother?

We must not fall into the trap that says that science is too difficult to understand, so the public has to rely on 'experts'. In this case the public has no choice but to build up emotional responses to issues. The science can be obscure, full of difficult words and complications, but it doesn't have to be that way.

Almost everyone can obtain a sufficient scientific understanding to make judgements on what the 'experts' say, as long as we teach science in the meaningful context of real issues, and begin from the ideas that the learners bring with them. A population ignorant of science will have a majority who don't care about the environment, and a minority whose only weapon is emotion, and who are dismissed by the majority as eco-freaks. A population that is ignorant about the nature of the scientific process will not appreciate the need for argument to continue among 'experts'. Science can only give us a 'best guess', and other considerations, for example moral philosophy, have their part to play – but we ignore the science at our peril. It is for this reason that the development of 21st Century Science is so exciting (see www.21stcenturyscience.org/home).

Summary

In this final chapter we have explored what it means to be professional and how we can aspire to this throughout our education career. We have examined the nature of science, how it has become a part of our curriculum and why it should stay there. From these insights comes the imperative to teach by starting with the learners' existing ideas, and setting the teaching in an everyday context. From this pupils should become motivated to take responsibility for their own learning and leave school with a scientific understanding of their world – a world which, through our teaching and their learning, can be given a sustainable future.

References

Note: All web links were tested and were accessible at the time of going to press.

ASE (2001) *Topics in Safety*, 3rd edn. Hatfield: Association for Science Education.

ASE (2006a) *Safeguards in the School Laboratory*, 11th edn. Hatfield: Association for Science Education.

ASE (2006b) *Safety Reprints*. Hatfield: Association for Science Education.

Assessment Reform Group (2002) *Assessment for Learning: 10 principles. Research-based principles to guide classroom practice*. Available at: www.qcda.gov.uk/libraryAssets/media/4031_afl_principles.pdf

Black, P. and Harrison, C. (2004) *Science inside the Black Box*. Bedford: National Foundation for Educational Research.

Blackwell, L. S., Trzesniewski, K. H. and Dweck, C. S. (2007) Implicit theories of intelligence predict achievement across an adolescent transition: a longitudinal study and an intervention. *Child Development*, 78, 246–63.

Bloom, B. S. (1956) *Taxonomy of Educational Objectives, Handbook I: The Cognitive Domain*. New York: David McKay Co. Inc.

Butt, N. (1991) *Science and Muslim Societies*. London: Grey Seal.

Chin, C. (2003) Students' approaches to learning science: responding to learners' needs. *School Science Review*, 85(310), 97–105.

Chinn, C. A. and Brewer, W. F. (1998) An empirical test of a taxonomy of responses to anomalous data in science. *Journal of Research in Science Teaching*, 35, 623–54.

CLEAPSS (1995 and later updates) *Hazcards*. Uxbridge: Consortium of Local Education Authorities for the Provision of Science Services (School Science Service).

CLEAPSS (1997, updated annually) *Laboratory Handbook*. Uxbridge: Consortium of Local Education Authorities for the Provision of Science Services (School Science Service).

Davies, F. and Greene, T. (1984) *Reading for Learning in the Sciences*. London: Oliver and Boyd.

DCSF (2007) *National Curriculum Programme of Study for Science*. London: Department for Children, Schools and Families. Available at: www.standards.dcsf.gov.uk/secondary/framework/science

DCSF (2008) *Every Child Matters, Change for Children: Making it Happen for Children, Young People and Families*. London: DCFC [ref: 00226–2008 BKT-EN]

DCSF (2009) *The National Strategies*. London: Department for Children, Schools and Families. Available at: http://nationalstrategies.standards.dcsf.gov.uk/secondary

DfEE (1996) *Safety in Science Education*. London: HMSO.

DfEE (1999) *The National Curriculum for England*. London: HMSO.

DfES (2006a) *Secondary National Strategy*. London: Department for Education and Skills.

DfES (2006b) *The Science, Technology, Engineering and Mathematics (STEM) Programme Report*. London: Department for Education and Skills.

DfES and QCDA (2006) *Programme of Study for Science, KS4*. London: Department for Education and Skills and Qualifications and Curriculum Authority.

Driver, R. (1975) The name of the game. *School Science Review*, 56(197), 800–5.

Driver, R. (1983) *The Pupil as a Scientist*. Milton Keynes: Open University Press.

Driver, R., Squires, A., Rushworth, P. and Wood-Robinson, V. (1994) *Making Sense of Secondary Science: Research into Children's Ideas*. London: Routledge.

Driver, R., Leach, J., Millar, R. and Scott, P. (1996) *Young People's Images of Science*. Buckingham: Open University Press.

Frost, R. (1999) *Data Logging in Practice*. London: IT in Science.

Gilbert, J. K., Watts, D. M. and Osborne, R. J. (1985) Eliciting student views using an interview-about instances technique. In: West, L. H. T. and Pines, A. L. (eds) *Cognitive Structure and Conceptual Change*. Orlando, FL: Academic Press.

Goldsworthy, A. and Feasey, R. (1999) *Making Sense of Primary Science Investigations*, 2nd edn. Hatfield: Association for Science Education.

Goldsworthy, A., Watson, R. and Wood-Robinson, V. (1999) *Getting to Grips with Graphs: From Bar Charts to Lines of Best Fit*. Hatfield: Association for Science Education.

Goldsworthy, A., Watson, R. and Wood-Robinson, V. (2000) *Developing Understanding in Scientific Enquiry*. Hatfield: Association for Science Education.

Guesne, E. (1985) Light. In: Driver, R., Guesne, E. and Tiberghien, A. (eds) *Children's Ideas in Science*. Milton Keynes: Open University Press.

Gunstone, R. and Watts, M. (1985) Force and motion. In: Driver, R., Guesne, E. and Tiberghien, A. (eds) *Children's Ideas in Science*. Milton Keynes: Open University Press.

Hay McBer (2000) *Report into Teacher Effectiveness*. Report to the DfEE. Available at: www.ttrb.ac.uk/viewarticle2.aspx?contentId=10346

Holding, B. (1987) *Investigation of schoolchildren's understanding of the process of dissolving with special reference to the conservation of matter and the development of atomistic ideas*. Unpublished PhD thesis, University of Leeds School of Education.

Hoyle, P. (1995) Race equality and science teaching. In: Hull, R. (ed.) *ASE Science Teachers' Handbook*. Cheltenham: Stanley Thornes.

HSE (1997) *Health and Safety Executive 1996/7*. London: Health and Safety Executive.

Hunt, A. and Millar, R. (2000) *AS Science for Public Understanding*. Oxford: Heinemann.

Hull, R. (ed.) (1995) *ASE Science Teachers' Handbook*. Cheltenham: Stanley Thornes.

Keogh, B. and Naylor, S. (2009) *Concept Cartoons™*. Available at: www.conceptcartoons.com

Kerr, D., Lines, A., Blenkinsop, S. and Schagen, I. (2001) *Citizenship and Education at Age 14: A Summary of the International Findings and Preliminary Results for England*. Windsor: National Foundation for Educational Research.

Kuhn, T. S. (1970) *The Structure of Scientific Revolutions*, 2nd edn. London: University of Chicago Press.

Lakin, E. (2000) Stardust, takeover bids and biodiversity. In: Littledyke, M., Ross, K. A. and Lakin, E. (eds) *Science Knowledge and the Environment*. London: David Fulton Publishers.

Lakin, E. (2008) What will the PGCE at M level do for me? In: Sewell, K. (ed.) *Doing your PGCE at M-Level*. London: Sage.

Layton, D. (1973) *Science for the People*. London: George Allen & Unwin.

Leicestershire LEA (1985) *Science Education for a Multicultural Society*. Leicester: Leicestershire Education Authority.

Littledyke, M. (1998) Constructivist ideas about learning. In: Littledyke, M. and Huxford, L. (eds) *Teaching the Primary Curriculum for Constructive Learning*. London: David Fulton Publishers.

McGrath, K. A. (1999) *World of Biology*. USA: Gale Group.

Medawar, P. B. (1969) Two conceptions of science. In: *The Art of the Soluble*. London: Penguin Books.

National Strategies (2009) *Energy Transfer and Electricity*. Available at: http://nationalstrategies.standards.dcsf.gov.uk/node/102643

National Strategy for Science (2009) *The National Strategies*. Available at: http://nationalstrategies.standards.dcsf.gov.uk

Naylor, S. and Keogh, B. (1998) Differentiation. In: Ratcliffe, M. (ed.) *ASE Guide to Secondary Science Education*. Cheltenham: Stanley Thornes.

Newell, A. and Ross, K. (1996) Children's conception of thermal conduction – or the story of a woollen hat. *School Science Review*, 78(282), 33–8.

Nicholls, J. and Turner, T. (1998) Differentiation and special educational needs. In: Turner, T. and DiMarco, W. (eds) *Learning to Teach Science in the Secondary School*. London: Routledge.

Nuffield Primary Science (1993) *Nuffield Primary Science: Science Processes and Concept Exploration (SPACE)*. London: Collins Educational.

Nussbaum, J. (1985) The Earth as a cosmic body. In: Driver, R., Guesne, E. and Tiberghien, A. (eds) *Children's Ideas in Science*. Milton Keynes: Open University Press.

Osborne, R. and Freyberg, P. (1985) *Learning in Science*. Oxford: Heinemann.

Parkinson, J. (2005) *Reflective Teaching of Science 11–18*. London: Continuum.

Piaget, J. (1929) *The Child's Conception of the World*. London: Routledge & Kegan Paul.

Popper, K. R. (1959) *The Logic of Scientific Discovery*. London: Hutchinson.

Postlethwaite, K. (1993) *Differentiated Science Teaching: Responding to Individual Differences and to Special Educational Needs*. Milton Keynes: Open University Press.

QCDA (2007) *National Curriculum*. London: Qualifications and Curriculum Development Authority. Available at: http://curriculum.qcda.gov.uk [*Creativity: Find it, promote it* was a story run from the TES on 13 August 2008 and can be found at: www.tes.co.uk/article.aspx?storycode=6000829]

Ratcliffe, M. (1998) The purposes of science education. In: Ratcliffe, M. (ed.) *ASE Guide to Secondary Science Education*. Cheltenham: Stanley Thornes.

Rawling, E. (2003) *Connecting Policy and Practice: Research in Geography Education*. Nottingham: British Educational Research Association.

Reiss, M. J. (1992) *Independent* 24 April 1992, p. 26.

Reiss, M. J. (1998) Science for all. In: Ratcliffe, M. (ed.) *ASE Guide to Secondary Science Education*. Cheltenham: Stanley Thornes.

Roberts, M. (1995) Interpretation of the geography national curriculum: a common curriculum for all? *Journal of Curriculum Studies*, 27(2), 187–205.

Ross, K. A. (1989) *A cross-cultural study of people's understanding of the functioning of fuels and burning*. Unpublished PhD thesis, University of Bristol.

Ross, K. A. (ed.) (1990) *Can children learn science?* Mimeo, Cheltenham and Gloucester College of Higher Education.

Ross, K. A. (1991) Burning: a constructive not a destructive process. *School Science Review*, 72(251), 45.

Ross, K. A. (1997) Many substances but only five structures. *School Science Review*, 78(284), 79–87.

Ross, K. A. (1998) Science: Brenda grapples with the properties of a mern. In: Littledyke, M. and Huxford, L. (eds) *Teaching the Primary Curriculum for Constructive Learning*. London: David Fulton Publishers.

Ross, K. A. (2000a) Matter and life – the cycling of materials. In: Littledyke, M., Ross, K. A. and Lakin, E. (eds) *Science Knowledge and the Environment*. London: David Fulton Publishers.

Ross, K. A. (2000b) Constructing a scientific understanding of our environment. In: Littledyke, M., Ross, K. A. and Lakin, E. (eds) *Science Knowledge and the Environment*. London: David Fulton Publishers.

Ross, K. A. (2000c) Energy and fuel. In: Littledyke, M., Ross, K. A. and Lakin, E. (eds) *Science Knowledge and the Environment*. London: David Fulton Publishers.

Ross, K. A. and Sutton, C. R. (1982) Concept profiles and the cultural context. *European Journal of Science Education*, 4(3), 311–23.

Ross, K. A., Lakin, E., Littledyke, M. and Burch, G. (2002) *Science Issues and the National Curriculum* (CD-ROM). Cheltenham: University of Gloucestershire (www.scienceissues.org.uk). [References to this CD-ROM are given as Ross *et al.* 2002: CD – [topic]' (one of the 10 topics on the CD) – see Preface, p. xii.]

SSERC (2002) *Hazardous Chemicals Manual CD2*. Edinburgh: Scottish Schools Equipment Research Centre. Available at: www.sserc.org.uk

SSERC (2003) *Microbiological Techniques CD1*. Edinburgh: Scottish Schools Equipment Research Centre. Available at: www.sserc.org.uk

Standards (2009) Available at: http://nationalstrategies.standards.dcsf.gov.uk/secondary/framework

Stannard, R. (1991) *Black Holes and Uncle Albert*. London: Faber and Faber.

Stavey, R. and Berkovitz, B. (1980) Cognitive conflict as the basis for teaching cognitive aspects of the concept of temperature. *Science Education*, 64(5), 679–92.

Sutton, C. (1992) *Words, Science and Learning*. Milton Keynes: Open University Press.

Taber, K. S. (2002) A core concept in teaching chemistry. *School Science Review*, 84(306), 105–10.

TDA (2009) *Professional Standards for Teachers: Qualified Teacher Status*. Available at: www.tda.gov.uk/teachers/professionalstandards/downloads.aspx

Twenty First Century Science Team (2003) 21st Century Science – a new flexible model for GCSE science. *School Science Review*, 85(310), 27.

Watt, D. and Russell, T. (1990) *Primary SPACE Reports*. Liverpool: Liverpool University Press.

West, R. (ed.) (1984) *Towards the Specification of Minimum Entitlement: Brenda and Friends*. London: Schools Council Publications.

Wood-Robinson, V. (ed.) (2006) *ASE Guide to Secondary Science*. Hatfield: Association for Science Education.

Useful websites

21st Century Science: http://www.21stcenturyscience.org

Association for Science Education: http://www.ase.org.uk

Concept Cartoons™: http://www.conceptcartoons.com

Data logging: http://www.rogerfrost.com

Earth Science Education Unit (Keele University): http://earthlearningidea.com and http://www.earthscienceeducation.com

Every Child Matters: http://www.everychildmatters.gov.uk

GCSE Examboards: http://www.educationalresources.co.uk/examboards.htm

Learning Outside the Classroom: http://www.lotc.org.uk

National Association for Able Children in Education: http://www.nace.co.uk

National Curriculum for England: http://curriculum.qcda.gov.uk

National Strategies site: http://nationalstrategies.standards.dcsf.gov.uk

Royal Society of Chemistry: http://www.rsc.org

Science Issues CDrom: http://www.scienceissues.org.uk

Science Update – ideas to link to everyday life: http://www.upd8.org.uk

Science, Technology, Engineering and Mathematics network: http://www.stemnet.org.uk

Scitutors: support for science teacher education: http://www.scitutors.org.uk

Size of the universe: http://www.powersof10.com

Teacher Training Resource Bank: http://www.ttrb.ac.uk

The Institute of Physics: http://www.iop.org

The Royal Society: http://royalsociety.org

The Society of Biology: http://www.societyofbiology.org

The Standards site: http://www.standards.dcsf.gov.uk

Training and Development Agency for Schools: http://www.tda.gov.uk

Index

Page numbers in **bold** denote figures, *italics* are tables.